School Inspection and Self-Evaluation

Around the world school inspection is subject to critical scrutiny. It is too cumbersome? Too expensive? Too disruptive to the normal flow of school life? Does it actually improve schools? And, what does the new relationship between inspection and self-evaluation mean for schools?

School Inspection and Self-Evaluation: Working with the New Relationship addresses these issues, and unpicks the legacy of an Ofsted regime widely criticised as invasive and disempowering to teachers. In this book, John MacBeath:

- examines in turn each aspect of the 'New Relationship', its potential strengths and some of its inherent weaknesses;
- debates issues that confront school leaders and classroom teachers, including Every Child Matters;
- offers advice on how schools can marry ongoing self-evaluation with Ofsted's expectations;
- describes how to deal with PLACS, PANDAS' and other beastly inventions';
- shows how to use web sources to best advantage;
- explains how to reconcile the tensions between accountability and improvement;
- provides a guide to a repertoire of tried-and-tested approaches to help teachers embed self-evaluation in day-to-day classroom practice.

The book also contains case studies from schools that have adopted innovative approaches to self-evaluation.

While of immediate practical interest for school leaders, managers and teachers in England, the book also speaks to an international audience, as the issues raised here have resonance in every country where quality assurance and standards are at the forefront of policy and practice.

John MacBeath is Professor of Educational Leadership at the University of Cambridge, UK.

School Inspection and Self-Evaluation
Working with the new relationship

John MacBeath

Routledge
Taylor & Francis Group

LONDON AND NEW YORK

First published 2006
by Routledge
2 Park Square, Milton Park, Abingdon, Oxon OX14 4RN

Simultaneously published in the USA and Canada
by Routledge
270 Madison Ave, New York, NY 10016

*Routledge is an imprint of the Taylor & Francis Group,
an informa business*

© 2006 John MacBeath

Typeset in Galliard by
Newgen Imaging Systems (P) Ltd, Chennai, India
Printed and bound in Great Britain by
The Cromwell Press, Trowbridge, Wiltshire

British Library Cataloguing in Publication Data
A catalogue record for this book is available
from the British Library

Library of Congress Cataloging in Publication Data
A catalog record for this book has been requested

ISBN10: 0–415–39970–X (hbk)
ISBN10: 0–415–39971–8 (pbk)
ISBN10: 0–203–96710–0 (ebk)

ISBN13: 978–0–415–39970–8 (hbk)
ISBN13: 978–0–415–39971–5 (pbk)
ISBN13: 978–0–203–96710–2 (ebk)

Contents

Figures

Tables

Acknowledgements

I would like to thank Janet Gibson for putting up with the constant revisions and search for missing page numbers and references, to my colleague, Sue Swaffield, for the eye of the critical friend, to HMCI David Bell for admitting me to inner sanctum of Ofsted where I was much less welcome in the past and to Anna Clarkson and Kerry Maciak of RoutledgeFalmer for their support and guidance.

1 New relationships for old

'She who has a hammer sees only a world of mails.'

This opening chapter sets the scene for the New Relationship with Schools, (NRwS), examining the perceived need for a new relationship in light of what had gone before. Each of the seven elements of the NRwS jigsaw are examined in turn, arguing that schools need to view these with a critical and enlightened eye.

There is a new relationship between government and schools. It is an implicit recognition that the old relationship had been damaged by a decade of tensions and antagonism between agencies of government and schools. The legacy of the Thatcher regime, which cast teachers and 'progressive educators' as the enemy within, was little attenuated under a Labour government which did not want to be seen as soft on teachers. The retention of Ofsted and its Chief Inspector were a signal to teachers, but primarily to a wider public, that this administration too could be tough. After nearly a decade in power it became increasingly apparent that the old relationship was no longer sustainable and that it was time for a new approach.

The concept of a new relationship was first spelled out by the Government Minister, David Miliband in a high-profile policy speech on 8 January 2004.

> There are three key aspects to a new relationship with schools. An accountability framework, which puts a premium on ensuring effective and ongoing self-evaluation in every school combined with more focussed external inspection, linked closely to the improvement cycle of the school. A simplified school improvement process, where every school uses robust self evaluation to drive improvement, informed by a single annual conversation with a school improvement partner to debate and advise on targets, priorities and support. And improved information and data management between schools, government bodies and parents with information 'collected once, used many times'.

The New Relationship, elaborated in subsequent documents, promised to allow schools greater freedom, to free them to define clearer priorities for themselves, get rid of bureaucratic clutter and build better links with parents. Advances in technology promised improved data collection and streamlined communication. A School Improvement Partner, described as a 'critical friend' would liaise with schools and support them in achieving greater autonomy, releasing local initiative and energy. The seven elements of the new relationship were portrayed as an interlocking set, framed by trust, support, networking and challenge (Figure 1.1).

It is not hard to imagine hours spent in offices of government, redrafting and refining images and terminology to achieve the right register and to convey a genuine conviction that things could be different. While it is important to welcome the apparent goodwill and the government's desire to build bridges, it is important to understand the political and economic context in which that relationship is set. On the economic front its main driver is the imperative to reduce public spending. Drastic reduction in the Ofsted budget, spelt out in the Gershon Report[1] specified the need for 'light touch inspection', as much a concomitant of reduced funding as an argument for 'grown up' quality assurance. The political driver, closely allied to economic policy and New Labour's embrace of the internal market[2], required funding to be pushed down to front line services, accompanied by consumer choice and institutional accountability.

The good ideas inherent in the New Relationship, symbolised in the interlocking pieces in the jig saw need therefore to be examined with a critical and enlightened eye.

Elements of the New Relationship with schools

Self-evaluation

Prior to the election of New Labour in 1997 the Conservative government and its Chief Inspector of Schools rejected self-evaluation as a soft option which, it was claimed, had done nothing in its previous incarnations to raise standards. The 1997 election of a Labour government was a watershed for self-evaluation as, over the following years, it moved gradually but progressively towards centre stage. With the coming of a new Chief Inspector, David Bell, it was given a new status at the very heart of the new relationship. The key difference in this reborn self-evaluation was its liberation from an Ofsted pre-determined template, schools now being encouraged to use their own approaches to self-evaluation with the self-evaluation form (the SEF) serving simply as an internal summary and basis for external inspection. That at least, is the theory.

In theory, there is no difference between theory and practice. In practice, there is.

In theory self-evaluation allows schools to speak for themselves, to determine what is important, what should be measured and how their story should be told. In theory self-evaluation is ongoing, embedded in the day-to-day work of classroom and school, formative in character, honest in its assessment of strengths and weakness, rigorous in its concern for evidence. The New

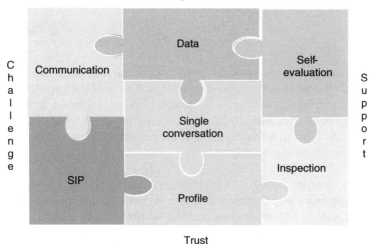

Figure 1.1 The seven elements of the new relationship.

Relationship explicitly accepts these tenets and advises schools to adopt and adapt their own approach.

In practice it is a different story. A recent study for the National College of School Leadership (NCSL)[3] asked schools to describe the framework or model currently used in their school. The predominant response was simply 'Ofsted', 'the SEF' or its predecessor the S4. Asked for reasons for their choice the following was fairly typical. 'We use Ofsted because we will be inspected and need to be prepared for that.'

While it was equally common for schools to say they used a combination of local authority guidelines and the Ofsted framework, the NCSL survey revealed that these are now closely matched to Ofsted protocols. Previous research by NFER[4] in 2001 surveying 16 schools in 9 LEAs reported that 10 were using a local authority model, 4 were using the Ofsted framework while others used a 'pick and mix' approach, in one case Ofsted, plus Investors in People plus *Schools Must Speak for Themselves*. Since then the convergence between local authority models and Ofsted has gown stronger and the earlier more creative models tend to have been marginalised.

However strong the disclaimer by HMCI that the Ofsted SEF is *not* self-evaluation it is clear that self-evaluation is seen by the large majority of schools as a top-down form of review closely aligned with the criteria and forms of reporting defined by the inspectorate. Faced with an array of consultant leaders, LA advisers, school improvement partners and governing bodies all urging conformity to the SEF, it is only a brave, and perhaps reckless, headteacher who would not play safe. The availability of on-line completion of the SEF is a further impetus to see self-evaluation as forms to be filled and an event to be undertaken rather than a continuing process of reflection and renewal.

Inspection

The new inspection process takes the SEF as its starting point, so allowing a shorter and sharper process, given that schools have laid the groundwork and provided the Ofsted team with a comprehensive, rounded and succinct picture of their quality and effectiveness, strengths and weaknesses, allegedly warts and all. The main features of the new inspections are described in NRwS in the following terms:

- shorter, sharper inspections that take no more than two days in a school and concentrate on closer interaction with senior managers in the school, taking self-evaluation evidence as the starting point;
- shorter notice of inspections to avoid schools carrying out unnecessary pre-inspection preparation and to reduce the levels of stress often associated with an inspection. Shorter notice should help inspectors to see schools as they really are;
- smaller inspection teams with a greater number of inspections led by one of HMI. Her Majesty's Chief Inspector will publish and be responsible for all reports;
- more frequent inspections, with the maximum period between inspections reduced from six years to three years, though occurring more frequently for schools causing concern;
- more emphasis placed on the school's own self-evaluation evidence as the starting point for inspection and for schools' internal planning, and as the route to securing regular input and feedback from users – pupils, their parents and the community – in the school's development. Schools are strongly encouraged to update their self-evaluation form on an annual basis;
- a common set of characteristics to inspection in schools and colleges of education from early childhood to the age of 19;
- a simplification of the categorisation of schools causing concern, retaining the current approach to schools that need special measures but removing the categorisations of 'serious weakness' and 'inadequate sixth form', replacing them with a new single category of 'Improvement Notice'.

'Shorter', 'sharper', 'smaller' are key downsizing elements of the new inspection. 'Shorter' applies to less notice so that schools may be seen 'as they really are', while a short stay in the school is premised on the school having 'hard' evidence of its practice, not preparing for inspection but always prepared. While it may easily be assumed from this that the purpose of the new inspection is to validate the school's own self-evaluation, Ofsted is quick to disabuse people of that notion. While self-evaluation is described as an integral element of the process, inspectors will continue to arrive at their own overall assessment of the effectiveness and efficiency of the school. They reserve their judgement on the capacity of the school to make improvements, *taking into account* its ability to assess accurately the quality of its own provision. 'Taking into account' is an important caveat as it signals clearly the nature of the relationship between the external and the internal team. There is no pretence that this is an equal partnership.

Every Child Matters

A key constituent of the new relationship takes account of the five outcomes for children and young people defined in the policy document *Every Child Matters*.[5] These are:

- staying healthy
- enjoying and achieving
- keeping safe
- contributing to the community
- social and economic well-being.

In judging leadership and management and the overall effectiveness of a school, inspectors examine the contribution made to all five outcomes. Claims made for validity and objectivity have, however, to be open to question given the breadth and ambition of the issues addressed. The highly subjective and sensitive nature of enjoyment, personal growth, parent and community links and equality belie any bold claims to objectivity and quantifiable 'outcomes'. While now deeply internalised in the linguistic canon of school improvement, outcomes in relation to these five areas of growth seems singularly inappropriate.

Undaunted by complexity and subtlety inspectors are required to quantify their judgements on the following four-point scale, while schools are enjoined to do likewise.

Grade 1   Outstanding
Grade 2   Good
Grade 3   Satisfactory
Grade 4   Inadequate

These rest on very broad and, to a large degree, impressionistic judgements. They are necessarily selective as to evidence that can be found and can be measured. It is open to question whether these labels enhance or diminish the nature of the judgements made. While their virtue is simplicity, their weakness is the gloss which undermines the nuance and complexity of what is being evaluated. As with summative assessment of pupils' work which is more likely to inhibit than motivate,[6] these categorical judgements do not of themselves provide the formative criteria which might qualify as evaluation for learning. While much thought and agonising within Ofsted has gone into these four descriptors they remain contentious, in particular the 'satisfactory' category which may be read either as a half full, or virtually empty glass.

A rush to judgement?

Inspection is judgement not description. In the New Relationship it is judgement rendered within the parameters of a two-day visit, and while there is a strong case to be made for a shorter more focused visit (see David Bell's rationale in Chapter 3) NRwS has in fact widened the scope of inspection to include *Every Child Matters*, so while not relinquishing its traditional commitment to rating the quality of school provision, as well as the robustness of its self-evaluation, inspectors are required also to make summative judgements including the five broad and often intangible ECM outcomes (Table 1.1).

These are the foci of inspection in the new relationship.

Overall effectiveness, including training, integrated care and extended services.

Achievement and standards, targets, qualifications, and progress relative to prior attainment and potential, workplace skills and positive contribution to the community.

Quality of provision, rigour of assessment, planning and monitoring learners' progress, provision for, additional learning needs and involvement of parents and carers.

Programmes and activities, matched to learners' aspirations and potential, responsiveness to local circumstances and contribution of extended services to learners' enjoyment and achievement.

Guidance and support, safeguarding welfare, promoting personal development, guidance on courses and career progression and provision which contributes to pupils' capacity to stay safe and healthy.

Leadership and management, performance monitoring, high-quality care, equality of opportunity and tackling of discrimination, links with other services, employers and other organisations and governors discharge of their responsibilities.

Provision causing concern

Inspectors must consider whether provision is failing to give learners an acceptable standard of education, in which case they must state this clearly in the report. There are two categories of schools causing concern:

- Schools which require special measures because they are failing to provide an acceptable standard of education and show insufficient capacity to improve.

Table 1.1 Some features of Ofsted's new approach to inspection

Previous inspection	NRwS inspection
6–10 weeks' notice before an inspection	Shortening the notice of an impending Ofsted visit. 2–5 days notice prior to inspection
Large inspection teams visiting for around a week	Small teams visiting for not more than 2 days
A maximum of 6-year interval between inspections	A maximum 3-year interval
Inspections cover: standards and quality of education; leadership/management; and spiritual, moral, social and cultural development	Inspection to cover standards and quality of education, leadership/-management; and spiritual, moral, social and cultural development
Self-evaluation not structured across all schools nor is it part of the inspection process	Self-evaluation as for all schools, the starting point of Ofsted inspection
Collection of a wealth of information – extensive use of lesson observation	Focus on core systems and key outcomes, informed by lesson observation and other indicators of pupils' progress
Detailed and lengthy (30 pages+) inspection reports produced.	Short, sharp reports (around 6 pages) focused on key outcomes with clearer recommendations for improvement
Reports produced within 40 days of the inspection event	Reports to be with the governing body, at least in draft, by the end of the week of the inspection
Schools required to prepare a separate post-inspection action plan	Schools feed their intended actions into the school development plan
Various categories of schools causing concern – special measures, serious weaknesses, underachieving and inadequate sixth forms	Rationalised system with two categories – special measures and improvement notice
Inspection usually conducted by registered inspectors	HMI leading many inspections and involved in all inspections

Source: Ofsted (2004) 'A new relationship with schools'.

• Schools which require significant improvement in one or more areas of activity, which should be served with an Improvement Notice.

A code of conduct

Inspectors work to a code of conduct[7] which stipulates that they uphold the highest professional standards in their work and ensure that school staff are treated fairly and that they benefit from inspection. They are required to evaluate objectively and have no connection with the school which could undermine their objectivity. They should report honestly, ensuring that judgements are fair and reliable, treating all those they meet with courtesy and sensitivity; minimising stress and acting in the best interests of those they inspect, engaging them in purposeful and productive dialogue. They should communicate judgements clearly and frankly, respecting the confidentiality of information and about individuals and their work. To this are added four demanding criteria:

- that the findings of the inspection are valid
- that findings of inspection contribute to improvement
- that the process of inspection promotes inclusion
- that inspection is carried out openly with those being inspected.

These are demanding principles and may, with shorter sharper inspections, be difficult to realise. It is, however, crucial for a school to be familiar with these principles as they offer a set of criteria which can be used by the school to evaluate inspectors and the process of inspection. The reciprocity of accountability in inspection's new clothes needs to be put to the test. Cast as friendly, collaborative and founded on a relationship of trust, schools, it is said, should feel safe enough to honestly disclose their weaknesses while inspectors listen sensitively to the school's own account. It is an ideal and idealistic scenario which appeals to the very best of collaborative quality assurance systems but nonetheless raises a number of prickly questions:

- How feasible is it for inspectors to render accurate and valid judgements across such a wide range of objectives?
- In what sense is the accountability agenda different under the NRwS?
- On what basis would schools be happy to be honest with Ofsted about their most serious weaknesses?
- To what degree is there a genuinely reciprocal relationship between a school staff and an inspection team?
- What is the nature of 'productive' dialogue?
- What does it mean for an inspection team to claim objectivity?
- What test may be applied to conform or contest inspectors' judgements as 'valid'?
- Is inspection under the new relationship any less 'high stakes' in its consequences than before?

The school improvement partner

For each of the schools that it maintains, the local authority appoints a school improvement partner from a pool of the people with current DfES (Department for Education and Skills) accreditation. The local authority is expected to consult with the school and to take account of objections for not accepting a particular individual but the final choice rests with the authority. The School Improvement Partner, in most cases should be someone with current or recent headship experience, is accountable to the authority which carries responsibility for his or her performance, carrying out functions previously performed by the External Adviser.

The SIP, is the 'conduit' between central government, the local authority and the school. It is a telling descriptor. A conduit suggests a flow in a given direction, and to a degree this is true of the SIP's relationship with the school. The direction of communication flow is from the government to the LEA to the school improvement partner and thence to the school, instrumental in the service of mandated target setting and establishing priorities in line with government policies.

As a school's governing body is responsible for the strategic direction of the school, the SIP also offers them 'advice' on the overall direction of the school as well as on the headteacher's conduct of performance management. In their monitoring role SIPs are also required to advise the local authority if they believe a school is causing concern. The authority may then use its statutory powers to intervene, and may want the SIP to take the lead in instigating action. So the SIP, described in the documentation[8] as a 'critical friend', may also make a 'friendly' intervention to move the school towards special measures. His or her accountability is to the local authority, which in turn accounts to government through the DfES's National Strategies contractor who, in partnership with NCSL, is responsible for the assessment, training and accreditation of SIPs. The renewal or ending of the SIP's contract is down to the National Strategies Contractor who also holds the local authority accountable for the performance management of SIPs in their bailiwick.

The SIP also has a relationship with Ofsted inspectors. It is spelt out[9] as follows:

- They may be inspectors of schools but must not inspect in schools where they have a connection or where they are SIPs.
- Their reports on schools are made available to inspection teams.
- They must not seek to secure information about a forthcoming inspection nor divulge it to schools if they become aware of it.

The SIP clearly has a complex relationship with the school, with the local authority, with Ofsted and with the DfES. It not only demands of SIPs that they tread a very fine line among their various accountabilities but their remit also casts a shadow on their relationship with their adoptive headteacher, raising some essential questions about that relationship.

- Where does the power lie within and outside the head–SIP relationship?
- What, in these circumstances, does it mean for the SIP to be a 'critical friend'?
- What is the nature of the SIP's accountability to the school?
- How should the success of the SIP's performance be judged? By the school? By the local authority? By government agencies?

- On what basis would a SIP report the school as causing concern?
- What is the latitude for autonomous self-improving schools to dispense with the services of their SIP?

These and other questions are explored further in Chapter 12.

The single conversation

> A single conversation with a wise man is better than ten years of study.
> (Chinese Proverb)

The single conversation is the occasion for the SIP and the headteacher to discuss how the school is performing and for the SIP to ensure that key policy priorities are being addressed. The rationale for this is to reduce the multiple accountabilities and need for schools to report to a variety of agencies, a slimming diet widely welcomed by schools.

The agenda for the single conversation is laid down rather than negotiated, with a clear focus on attainment data, variations in pupil performance, monitoring and planning for pupil progress and evidence as to achievement of outcomes identified in *Every Child Matters*. The nature of the school's self-evaluation is also on the agenda, framed primarily in terms of measurement of pupil progress and interpretation of attainment data. Under five key headings the nature of the 'conversation' is made clear.

- How is the school performing?
- What are the key factors?
- What are the priorities and targets for improvement?
- How will the school achieve them?
- How are the school's performance management systems contributing to raising attainment and achievement?

While it is acknowledged that the single conversation will vary from school to school, it 'will', have a common core as detailed in the guidance documents.[10] The single conversation, in common with other aspects of the New Relationship deserves closer interrogation.

- What is the nature of the 'conversation'?
- What latitude does it offer for the headteacher to set or negotiate an agenda tuned to the school's current and future needs?
- What latitude does it offer for the SIP to be responsive to the school's current and future needs?
- What is the essential difference between an accountability conversation and an improvement conversation?
- Where, how often and for how long should that 'single' conversation take place?

School profile

The government intention for the school is to reflect the breadth and depth of what the school does, but contained in a short accessible document. It is a document designed for parents, as well as for a wider readership, including the DfES, and should contain the following information:

- data on students' attainment and progress, set against benchmarks for schools in similar contexts;
- how the school serves all its students, not just the average student;
- the most recent assessment by Ofsted, set against the school's own self-assessment;
- what the school offers, in terms of the broader curriculum;
- how the head and governors see the priorities for future improvement;
- what the school offers the rest of the system.

This 'short, focused report', it was foreseen,[11] would be pre-populated by the DfES, containing standardised comparative performance data about a school and its students, derived from information held on the National Pupil Database, coupled with information provided by the school on its own view of its priorities and performance. It was described in Ministerial terms[12] as follows:

> To supplement the data contained in performance tables, parents also have a right to a broader and deeper understanding of what the school is doing. We think the answer lies in an annual school profile which would replace the annual statutory report to parents and increase flexibility around the statutory elements of the school prospectus. It will be light on bureaucracy, easy to access and powerful in impact. It will place new and challenging information in the public domain.

The school profile was envisaged as another conversation piece – 'We want to see the profile become an important part of educational discussion in the home and the school, as well as in Whitehall'.[13] It stretches the imagination to envisage the nature of the fireside chat that might take place in the home or the nature of the conversation that might transpire in the corridors of power. The tenor of the above Ministerial speech is worth a conversation analysis of its own:

- In what way will the school profile lead to 'a deeper understanding' among parents?
- What 'flexibility' will it allow?
- In what ways will it be 'light in bureaucracy'?
- What is meant by 'powerful in impact'?

- What will make it appealing enough to provide a conversation piece for parents? And what is likely to be the focus of such conversation?
- What from your own experience might encourage a rich conversation with parents?

Data

Data is the sixth piece of the seven piece jigsaw. It is in some respects the most significant as official documents and pronouncements insistently emphasise that data is the alpha and omega of school life in the new century and in the New Relationship. Data is in the driving seat. It is the centrepiece in the single conversation, the overriding concern of the school improvement partner, the focus of inspection and the litmus test of the school's self-evaluation. The Ministerial speech[14] describes data as the most valuable currency in school improvement.

> Data helps teachers, heads of department and the senior leadership team identify underperformance, and do something about it. In this sense it is the most valuable currency in school improvement. When data makes it evident that the same pupils are thriving in History but struggling in Geography, decisions about performance management and professional development suddenly become much clearer.

'Data collected once but used many times' has achieved the status of a mantra. While left open to wide interpretation it appears to imply that the annual sweeping up of performance data and its reproduction in multiple disaggregated forms provides enough riches to last a school until the next sweep.

'Schools are infuriated when different bits of government make their own data collections and waste valuable time and effort at school level', acknowledges the Minister. He makes reference to complaints from heads and governors at having to 'wade through mounds of paper and points to progress made in the last few years in reducing demand by 50 per cent. Life is being made simpler by the development of one simple set of what the Minister describes as 'binding protocols'[15] to ensure 'the full benefits of the national pupil level data that is now available through PLASC....to make a reality of the statement "collect once, use many times."'

It should, the DfES suggests,[16] boast the following elements:

- data that helps teachers develop themselves;
- data that helps school leaders promote high performance;
- data that helps parents support their children's progress;
- data that helps LEAs target resources;
- data that helps the DfES fine-tune its interventions to spread good practice and of critical importance;

- the combination of qualitative as well as quantitative data that is the foundation for any intelligent conversation about public service improvement.

What form this helpful data assumes is not made explicit but refers primarily to the plethora of statistics on student attainment, aggregated and disaggregated in relation to a cluster of variables on home background, prior attainment, gender, and ethnicity. These are, in Ministerial parlance, a core data set which 'drive the data demands of the education system'.[17] The implicit is made somewhat more explicit however in this Ministerial rhetorical flight – 'and we will really achieve take off when there is a maximum use of data and benchmarks by all those with an interest in pupils' progress'. A number of critical questions follow:

- What does the term 'data' mean to school staff and what is the emotional resonance of that term?
- What kind of benchmarking does this imply?
- Who is data for? To what extent are they for consumers or critical users?
- What are the potential disadvantages of a single simplified data system?
- In what ways may data be used many times?
- If data are described in terms of 'binding protocols' what flexibility is there for schools to be autonomous, to be creative and to speak for themselves?

Communications

Communication, the seventh interlocking piece of the jigsaw, is the necessary precondition of any relationship. The New Relationship promises a 'streamlined communications strategy'. It includes an on-line ordering service 'giving schools the freedom and choice to order what that they want, when they want'.[18] Documents and resources that would previously have been sent out, encumbering the headteacher's desk, and possibly waste bin, are now to be available on-line, easy to find and with detailed summaries of key policies. Schools are kept up-to-date with the latest additions to the on-line catalogue via a regular email notification – providing a direct web link to the latest information available online. Schools are able, therefore, to choose whether to download electronic versions or order paper-based copies of the information they need in the multiples required to be delivered to their school. Choosing to ignore them does not appear to be an option suggested. It is important to consider:

- What key elements would you want to see in a 'communications strategy'?
- What kind of documents are most, and least, helpful for school leadership?
- To what are teaching and other staff included in a communication strategy? And what is most, and least, helpful to them?

The four framing values

Easily overlooked in the NRwS jigsaw are the key words that frame the seven jig saw pieces. These words are *challenge* and *support, collaboration and networking* and *trust*. The implication is that a new relationship is founded on these and that it would be difficult to realise without these values being in place. But what do they mean?

The key word on which the others depend is trust. This could be interpreted in a number of different ways. For example:

- Teachers trust the goodwill of the government's intentions
- Teachers trust that Ofsted will be fair
- Teachers trust their own management to have their concerns and interests at heart
- The government trusts the professionalism and integrity of teachers
- Ofsted trusts the integrity and honesty of the school's own self-evaluation.

These are ambitious and probably unrealistic expectations because they imply some form of unconditional trust, whereas trust in an essentially politicised context is both conditional and calculative.[19] Trust, says Harvard's Richard Elmore[20] is a fragile commodity, hard to construct and easy to destroy. The very processes by which 'the connective tissue' of trust are created in schools are too easily reversible. At any point, for any reason, individuals may revoke their consent to have their interests encapsulated in others. Trust, says Elmore, is a compound of *respect*, listening to and valuing the views of others; *personal regard*, intimate and sustained personal relationships that undergird professional relationships; *competence*, the capacity to produce desired results in relationships with others; and *personal integrity*, truthfulness and honesty in relationships. He calls these 'discernments' exemplified as the way in which people make sense of one another's behaviour and intentions.

A measure of trust, however conditional, is a prerequisite of *support*, as support implies a relationship in which people experience a genuine intention to help on the part of the other without a hidden agenda, without a sense that this comes with caveats and some form of payback. At an individual level we experience support from friends and colleagues as an expression of genuine concern given unconditionally and without charge. The same principle applies at organisational level, yet in an accountability context it is hard to conceive of support which does not come with conditions and caveats attached.

Implicit in the New Relationship is that support is accompanied by *challenge*. These are uneasy bedfellows because they can only co-exist where the quality of support allows challenge to be heard and accepted. When people do not experience goodwill and genuine support they are very likely to respond badly to challenge. The combination of support and challenge is implicit in the role of a critical friend – friend first and critic second, but the critical hat is only donned once a mutuality of relationship has been established. Schools' experience of Ofsted has in the past typically been one of challenge – often fruitful and appreciated but not always accompanied by a sense of support, critical but not always friendly.

It is through the fourth of these framing words – *networking* – that support and challenge are most likely to be bear fruit. Networking implies a collegial relationship, founded on voluntarism and initiative. It is built on reciprocity and a measure of trust. The ties that bind are conditional not on authority but on mutual gain, give and take, learning and helping others learn.

Accountability drives everything

It is not accidental that the Miliband speech quoted at the beginning of this chapter justified self-evaluation in these terms: 'An accountability framework, which puts a premium on ensuring effective and ongoing self-evaluation in every school combined with more focussed external inspection, linked closely to the improvement cycle of the school.'

Accountability drives everything. 'Without accountability there is no legitimacy; without legitimacy there is no support; without support there are no resources; and without resources there are no services.' In this conception of accountability it is realised through data, attainment related, comparative and benchmarked.[21]

> The data upon which we base our accountability mechanisms must reflect our core educational purposes. It must be seen to be objective. And it must allow for clear and consistent comparison of performance between pupils and between institutions.

This, as government sees it, is 'intelligent accountability', a term attributed to John Dunford of the Secondary Heads' Association (SHA), demonstrating that government can at once be intelligent as well as tough and that it can listen to the voice of the profession. But what does intelligent accountability mean? Its origins are in the 2002 Reith lecture given by Baroness O'Neill in which she pleads for an alternative to 'perverse indicators' which erode trust, distort purpose and provide signposts which point people along diversionary paths.[22]

Elmore makes an important distinction between internal and external accountability.[23] The former describes the conditions that precede and shape the responses of schools to pressure originating in policies outside the organisation. Internal accountability is measured by the degree of convergence among what individuals say they are responsible for (responsibility), what people say the organisation is responsible for (expectations), and the internal norms and processes by which people literally account for their work (accountability structures). He concludes that with strong internal accountability schools are likely to be more responsive to external pressure for performance. Intelligent internal accountability suggests that schools will respond critically to external pressure, confident in the knowledge that they have a rich and unique story to tell, a story which rises above and goes beyond the mean statistics and pushes against prevailing orthodoxies of competitive attainment.

2 A view from the schools

The New Relationship has been given a cautious welcome by schools. This is because some of the seven elements of the NRwS jigsaw are seen as a positive step forward while others are viewed as potentially problematic. This chapter draws on recent studies which elicited teachers' views as to the perceived strengths and potential drawbacks.

What is the purpose of self-evaluation? What does it mean for schools? For heads? Teachers? Learning Support Assistants? Pupils? Or parents? Much of the rationale is taken as implicit rather than explicitly discussed and none of the suggestions for involvement of parents or any other group proposes a critical dialogue as to its essential purpose. The government's view of purpose appears to be uncontested, or uncontestable although within their public pronouncements we can identify a number of different purposes. These may be seen as incompatible, or complementary, depending on where you sit or stand.

Preparation for inspection

Self-evaluation may be introduced by a school as a prelude to inspection, and although this is a pragmatic response to external pressure it may then come to be seen as the primary rationale for engaging in it. In other words, its essential purpose is regarded as one of accountability to an external body rather than as something owned by teachers themselves. However, the SEF is *not* self-evaluation, insists HMCI David Bell, reiterating what is clearly articulated in the guidelines. It is simply a way of recording a school's own self-evaluation process which needs to be driven by a school improvement motive. Ofsted, for its part, encourages schools to use a variety of approaches.

Raising standards

For many, staff self-evaluation has as its key purpose to raise standards. This is in tune with what is widely seen as a key purpose of school education. 'Standards' may, however, assume either a broad or narrow meaning, and when interpreted narrowly, refers simply to the raising of pupil attainment scores. Interpreted more broadly, standards may apply to more effective learning and teaching in which attainment levels rise as a natural consequence of improved pedagogy. Where this is the case self-evaluation then serves a broader and deeper purpose.

Professional development

Self-evaluation may be seen as a handmaid of professional development. When this is its rationale the impetus is for teachers and other staff to use tools of self-evaluation to develop professionally, becoming more self-aware, more reflective and more self-critical by virtue of how they monitor their own performance and professional growth. When this happens, it is argued, pupil learning should logically follow in its wake.

Building capacity

If an essential purpose of school improvement is to build the school's capacity to respond to and manage change, such a goal cannot be achieved without a commitment to self-evaluation. This rationale sees self-evaluation as a multi-layered process, employing a diversity of approaches to measurement and evidence. Terms such as social capital or intellectual capital refer to the synergy within a school which has the knowledge and know-how to become more intelligent than its individual members.

Putting views to the test

How teachers and headteachers view the purposes of self-evaluation was one of the questions in a study for the National Union of Teachers in 2005.[1] Focus groups were conducted with 192 teachers, asking them first to complete questionnaires, following this up with discussion asking them to elaborate on their responses. The following is a summary of their views.

A question of purpose

Asked to choose among six possible purposes of school self-evaluation almost half of all teachers who completed the questionnaire identified *raising standards* as a fundamental purpose of self-evaluation in schools. Next to raising standards was *providing teachers with tools which help evaluate pupils' learning* (29.7 per cent). 10.4 per cent thought its primary purpose should be *the extension of the school's capacity to respond to, and implement change*. Few of them (6.3 per cent) identified the primary purpose as *helping staff to share ideas and practice more widely*, while even fewer (3.1 per cent) thought self-evaluation should *provide opportunities for the school to hear the views of pupils*. The smallest response, however, was the 2.1 per cent of teachers who thought that self-evaluation should be geared towards providing Ofsted with evidence on their schools' quality and effectiveness.

The priority given to different purposes was clarified during group discussion. Raising standards was put into a broader perspective. The purpose of looking at the school through the lens of self-evaluation was seen as making the school a better place for learning. 'That leads us to raising attainments.... We're in the business of raising our standards through learning,' argued one primary teacher, while a secondary colleague in another school made a similar point – 'Student learning is vital, if we can understand self-evaluation this way, we can make something of our teaching. It will enable schools to respond to and implement change.'

A consistent theme was that self-evaluation was for a school's and teacher's own improvement in learning and teaching and not for the benefit of Ofsted or other extrinsic purposes – 'Raising standards of learning isn't limited to what we do towards Ofsted inspection, we aren't talking about league tables,' said one primary teacher, while a secondary teacher argued 'Basically, what we want in self-evaluation is to help pupils learn and see them learn better.... It shouldn't therefore be a part of any external assessment standards.'

Although teachers used the language of raising standards their views typically went beyond examination results or performance measures to embrace the totality of the child's development: 'Standards in self-evaluation shouldn't be interpreted in a very narrow sense – exams. We're not just getting examination results...We're talking about the attainment of every individual capacity: academic, moral, spiritual etcetera' (Primary teacher).

Beneath the rhetoric of standards there emerged a learning-centred view in which pupil 'needs' were paramount.

> To me the priority area is meeting students' needs. Standards must be seen in this light. Hence I will put that at the top, after identifying their needs in terms of their views and opinions that would enable you to go ahead and implement the change that would meet their needs.
>
> (Primary teacher)

While only a handful of teachers had seen the purpose of self-evaluation as to hear pupil views, there was, in fact, the finest of lines between those who chose standards and those who chose pupil views.

> If the pupils know what they want it helps them. Pupils need to plan their learning and they also need to have some plan for them. It's got to be a dialogue. We can't always dictate to pupils...we are very aware now of the need to hear the student's voice.
>
> (Primary teacher)

A secondary teacher, explaining why he had not chosen the provision of tools, also brought the discussion back to issues of student needs.

I did not choose the provision of tools to help teachers to evaluate pupils' learning because if we have the pupils themselves evaluating their own needs … we are going to look more into motivation and that would influence their attitude towards learning etcetera leading to the attainment of standards.'

(Secondary teacher)

Those who chose *the capacity of the school to respond to change* could be seen as simply entering the standards issue by another door, arguing that the starting point for thinking about standards in self-evaluation should be 'the school's own culture, its systems and processes and their effects on students' holistic learning' (Secondary teacher).

What is perhaps surprising from the apparent disagreement among differing choices of purpose was the degree of consensus in how teachers appeared to be thinking about self-evaluation. Whatever their choice and wherever they placed their tick on the questionnaire, self-evaluation, was seen to serve one clear primary aim – to meet pupil needs and improve the quality of teaching directed to that end.

Providing Ofsted with evidence on their schools' quality and effectiveness was rejected by all but 2 per cent of the sample.

Who should be the audience for school self-evaluation?

Teachers were asked to rank audiences for self-evaluation from 1 to 5. In order to compare these, a mean score was calculated as a measure of the primacy given to different audiences (Figure 2.1). The school itself emerged as the first preferred audience with a mean of approximately 5.0. This was followed by parents, with a mean of 3.5. The LEA was ranked third with a

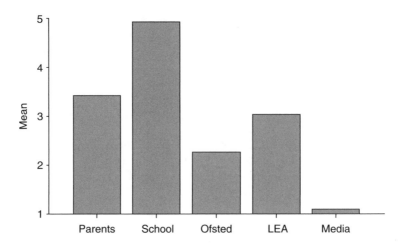

Figure 2.1 Teachers' preferred audience for school self-evaluation.

mean of around 3.2. Although Ofsted might have been seen as the obvious focus for a school's self-evaluation, teachers did not rank it highly, with a mean of 2.3, while the media was least preferred with the lowest mean – 1.0.

Asked to justify why Ofsted, the LEA, parents or media should not be the primary audience of self-evaluation there was a widely shared view that self-evaluation was a matter for the school and not for a wider public. As one primary teacher remarked, 'if we are talking about school self-evaluation, then it is the "self" – the school – which should use its outcome', while another argued, 'It should be the school itself because we're the workers. We need to internalise things that go on in our school and how we can change our school.' A similar point was made by a secondary teacher who maintained that 'self-evaluation is an internal affair...It is for internal guidance especially when it comes to the implementation of school initiated change'.

A secondary teacher using the business sector as an analogy, argued as follows:

> Our first and fundamental mission is to deliver a suitable and appropriate service to our primary client – our pupils...If you put it in the business context, you share views about the business internally before it goes externally to shareholders...Equally the school's staff/employees have a right to that information before it goes outside. I don't see why an Ofsted should have it before those within the school.

What should be the components of self-evaluation?

Bearing in mind Ofsted's third principle that 'effective self-evaluation should ask the most important questions about pupils' learning, achievements and development', teachers were asked what they saw as the most important components of self-evaluation. From a list of eight[2] they were asked to choose three which they considered to be the most important. The majority (34.4 per cent) chose *pupil motivation and interest* followed by *school conditions and factors that promote learning* (22.9 per cent). *Value-added or measures to ensure progress between key stages and/or exams* was a third choice with 20.3 per cent. The remaining five components assumed less importance. Few teachers (10.4 per cent) gave priority to *the quality of relationships between teachers and pupils* and few (6.3 per cent) opted for *KS4 and KS5 examination results* while only 2.6 per cent identified *pupils' attitudes to school* as most important. The least preferred components were *pupil performance on key stage tests* (1.6 per cent) and *pupils' performance in test and examinations in relation to school background* (1.5 per cent).

Reflecting on their choices during the group discussion, the interconnections among these varying purposes was highlighted. The consensus was that motivation of pupils, school conditions and value-added are both inseparable and indispensable in the school's pursuit of improvement. These are reflected in the following statement. 'The first should be school conditions and factors, which promote learning. There's a symbiotic relation between conditions and motivating pupils to learn. This will lead to value-added because we're trying to add value to children's learning' (Primary teacher).

Who defines criteria of quality?

Given the first Ofsted principle that 'intelligent accountability should be founded on the school's own views of how well it is serving its pupils and its priorities for improvement', teachers were asked where the criteria for self-evaluation should come from. A majority of teachers (55.2 per cent) were of the view that the criteria should be jointly developed by the school itself and a critical friend. 20.8 per cent thought that criteria should be customised by the school from a range of sources while 13.0 per cent opted for Ofsted. 8.9 per cent wanted the criteria to be developed solely by the school itself, while only a few (2.1 per cent) thought they should be provided by the LEA.

Probing the reasons for their choices it was generally argued that a critical friend would be more objective, more understanding and non-threatening in his/her approach to helping the school form its judgements. Many teachers said that they had benefited and continued to benefit from the support of a critical friend: 'a critical friend can help both pupils and teachers to understand themselves better...and help the school to make good use of self-evaluation' (Primary teacher).

A few teachers argued in favour of Ofsted. They were of the view that if self-evaluation was going to be used to inform external inspection then Ofsted should be the provider of its criteria. This, they argued, would ensure that all schools used a standardised set of criteria for evaluating themselves: 'I think if we're going to have a standard means of determining a successful school, then we need an external like body to provide the criteria' argued one primary teacher. Another stressed that the benefit of Ofsted would be objectivity and standardised criteria. 'From the scientific perspective, I will opt for OFSTED...we need a standard criteria from an external body to compare with...Critical friends will be okay but can they give schools a point of reference for comparison?' (Primary teacher)

What these comments reveal is a view of self-evaluation as a servant of inspection and set firmly in a comparative standardised perspective, in contrast with those who see it more as genuinely centre stage and within the school's ownership.

Factors that promote or inhibit the implementation of self-evaluation

Teachers attributed the success or failure in implementing self-evaluation to both external and internal factors. The most frequently mentioned factors that promote self-evaluation in schools included first and foremost a non-judgemental approach driven by trust, friendliness and support. This is reflected in statements such as 'approaching it in a positive way...knowledge that there will be a non-judgemental and supportive response'; 'friendly, non-confrontational or threatening approach'; and 'openness and honesty'. One teacher elaborated on this by stressing that individuals within the school would happily engage themselves in self-evaluation if they could be confident that it was being carried out in 'a non-judgemental manner and within a supportive atmosphere...where there is the knowledge that all individual contributions are valued'.

Second, a focus on professional development rather than accountability was emphasised. In the words of one teacher, 'self-evaluation can be promoted where league tables, SATS etc. are not the marks of how good a school is and when it is valued by external agencies as part of a process of development', while another remarked, 'when there's little obsession with paper evidence gathering and results used as professional guidance'. Agreeing with, this another teacher saw it as conditional on 'staff in the school seeing visible evidence of the outcomes of the process...and see them as beneficial to their development'.

Yet another teacher said 'when all staff (teaching and non-teaching) are agreed that it is a powerful tool for moving the school forward then self-evaluation will be fine'. For another, it was seen as possible 'when outcomes are used to advise staff on how best to improve and training courses are available as a result of highlighting areas for development'. 'An environment for self-reflection and dialogue' which allows staff to 'share ideas and practise across the school as a whole', also emerged as crucial for the success of school self-evaluation.

'Understanding of self-evaluation and its importance' and the 'willingness to take ownership and responsibility for the curriculum' were other factors identified as most likely to promote self-evaluation in schools. One secondary teacher suggested:

> If teachers have been trained to realise the time value of self-evaluation...have been helped to develop skills and attitude of being a reflective practitioner and have been part of self-evaluation, they may be more willing to accept and implement any changes that need to be made.

The absence of the aforementioned factors exemplifies some factors which inhibit the implementation of self-evaluation. Underpinning these is the issue of time constraints emerging from workload: 'lack of time to meet and discuss school issues' remarked one teacher. In the words of another:

> The demand, especially the paperwork is taking too much time...unnecessary amount of recording and processing...everything relating to assessments distract my focus from other things. Moreover there are after-school activities: putting extra time resources into planning extra dynamics for even more stimulating lessons.
>
> (Primary teacher)

Table 2.1 sums up the main favourable and frustrating factors seen by school staff as affecting implementation of self-evaluation in schools.

A change for the better?

In response to the statement 'Ofsted are currently moving in the right direction' 58.6 per cent of teachers agreed while 31.7 per cent disagreed. These figures include the *strongly agree* and *strongly disagree* categories which were hardly used, reflecting a more equivocal position in the face of an unknown quantity and a dubious prior history. The doubters worried that however new the regime, it would not get away from the top-down formulaic approach. 'The paperwork is still there ... Ofsted's self-evaluation processes merely involve working to someone else's formula ... it has some of form of accountability ... but it's the thinking process behind self-evaluation that's important – not just filling in pieces of paper.' (Secondary teacher)

Another statement reveals continuing doubt about its essential purpose as one of accountability: 'The paperwork process is very time consuming. It's purely an accountability process. Does what the school gets out of it warrant the time spent on it? I don't think so.' (Secondary teacher)

The optimists, however guarded, envisaged a kinder more supportive approach. It was likened by one teacher to the old more teacher-friendly HMI inspection: '(The new proposal) is like the old HMI approach to inspection ... HMI was very helpful to the teacher ... it offered criticisms but gave support ... it helped you find pathways forward. It was a very constructive process.' (Primary teacher)

Another teacher hoped that with a new relationship there would be greater room for dialogue, allowing the school to ask questions freely during inspections:

> The inspection process now isn't useful. ... Everyone is dreading the envelope arriving. Teachers don't do their best under this pressure – they play safe and are too frightened to do anything else. No one wants to let the side down by having an unsatisfactory lesson. ... This time we'll tell them what to focus on. The new system will give schools opportunity to build up their own portfolios and evidence of what they value.
>
> (Secondary teacher)

While telling inspections teams what to focus on may be more hopeful than realistic, there was a sense of optimism that a school's own values and priorities would be given more credence under the new dispensation.

A shorter sharper visit

Three quarters of teachers welcomed the new requirement for inspectors to spend a maximum of two days in a school. 63.2 per cent of teachers agreed

Table 2.1 Favouring and constraining factors for SSE

	Favourable conditions for SSE	Inhibiting conditions for SSE
External factors	• When self-evaluation results are exclusively used for development purposes • Opportunities for staff to engage in professional dialogue with inspectors • Open-minded inspection • Encouraging schools to take risks • Positive feedback • Respecting the professionalism of teachers • Friendly non-confrontational or non-threatening approach to inspection	• Inspector's excessive focus on accountability • Pressure from national exams • Imposition of self-evaluation criteria on schools • Disrespect from inspectors • Negative media publicity • Using results for performance-related pay • Inaccurate inspection reports • Paperwork • OFSTED over-scrutiny • Lack of genuine consultation with teachers on inspection policies • Perceived threat from outside audiences • Restriction to strict external criteria • When conducted against a background of school league tables/standards • Pressure from SATS
In-school factors	• Awareness of SSE purpose • The school's commitment to self-evaluation • Mutual trust and willingness to share knowledge and skills with colleagues • Teachers' access to SSE data • Availability of self-critical • Teachers confidence • When fitted directly into school improvement plan • Sharing good practice • Whole school ownership • Training/INSET on self-evaluation	• Time constraints and workload • Fear and ambiguity about the purpose of self-evaluation • Lack of non-contact hours for primary teachers to share ideas with colleagues • The fear of colleagues seeing weakness as failure • A blame culture • When SSE findings are not acted upon • Lack of support by school leadership • Staff reluctance to change

with the statement *a two-day sharper more focused Ofsted visit is welcomed* while 13.2 per cent strongly agreed with the statement. Nearly a quarter of them (23.7 per cent) however did not welcome the proposal. None, however, were prepared to *strongly* disagree.

Those who welcomed the two-day shorter visits were of the view that it would reduce the pressure that in past years has characterised their preparations for Ofsted: 'a shorter visit will give us the peace of mind to do the best that we can with what we have to do...we'll have time to concentrate on what we feel is important for our school' (primary teacher). Another argued that:

> The present system is flawed...the whole process of inspection does not favour the teacher...self-evaluation form filling, prolonged gearing up for Ofsted, the long inspection visit, recovering from the visit etc. tend to deflect the school from its real purpose... a two-day's visit will be better.
>
> (Primary teacher)

In contrast, those who did not welcome the short visit doubted whether it would make any tangible difference. This stemmed from a view that Ofsted could not be trusted because, over the years, as one primary teacher put it, 'the Ofsted inspection process has been used by government as a big stick. They've never been after improvements', she claimed, adding, 'and primary schools are a soft target'.

Notice of intent

The teachers' reaction to Ofsted inspection with shorter notice *(Ofsted should visit with short, or no, notice)* did not show the same positive response as to the proposal for a two-day's shorter visit. Opinion divided almost evenly between those in favour and those against, plus 8.2 per cent in the *strongly agree* category and 4.9 per cent in the *strongly disagree* category. Shorter notice was welcomed by those who saw it as lessening the long period of preparation, alleviating anxiety and helping an inspection team to get a more realistic view of the school. Some argued that arrival in schools with or without notice would be only useful if, as one primary teacher put it, 'it is going to help teachers become more reflective about their practice and help us improve children's attitudes to learning'. A common theme among those who agreed, as well as disagreed with shorter notice, was that Ofsted needed to overhaul its own attitude towards inspection by making inspection friendlier and more appreciative of a school's specific context and limitations. As an example, one secondary teacher suggested: 'They should be more constructive and committed to helping schools to improve...If the process continues to be judgemental then people put shutters down, shorter notice just won't help.'

Coming clearly through these views of school staff is a school-centred purpose for self-evaluation and a desire for it to be driven by teachers rather than by Ofsted. Yet in practice another chapter of the story is told when schools are asked what approaches they are currently using. As part of a study for NCSL[3] 200 questionnaires were sent out to schools asking them five questions, the first of which was to 'describe the framework of model used in your school'. Of the 68 returned 38 replied simply 'Ofsted' or 'the SEF' or its previous incarnation the S4. Twenty-two also mentioned the local authority framework in conjunction with the Ofsted model. This was either a customisation of the Ofsted model to the local authority context or an adaptation of the authority model to meet the requirements of the SEF. Other models receiving a few mentions each were EFQM (the European Excellence model), Investors in People, Capita, CEA, CSI, Target Tracker, How Good is Our School?[4] and one mention of Assessment for Learning. All of these were described as a complement to Ofsted.

The NFER study

In late 2004 the NFER reported on their evaluation of the NRwS pilot phase involving 93 schools in eight local authorities.[5] These schools already had experience of some key components of the New Relationship and were able to offer evidence of their experiences with the SEF, the SIP and the single conversation. The SEF was seen as 'more detailed', 'more rigorous', and 'more effective' than its predecessor the S4 but 'more onerous to complete' and posing an additional burden on school staff.

There was 'an overwhelmingly positive view' of their SIPs although with differing responses from primary and secondary heads. Secondary heads considered SIPs to be more challenging and more of a critical friend than previous LA link advisers, while primary heads were markedly less satisfied.

As a pilot none of these schools were, however, in a position where the SIP could present a threat or where confidentiality and accountability assumed a sharper critical edge. All were essentially responding to a new set of given procedures, in the main seen as preferable to what had gone before. While NFER reported a greater focus on self-evaluation, it could be put down to external pressure, while the importance given to SIPs as helping headteachers to prepare for an inspection underscores the extrinsic focus of 'self' evaluation.

What becomes abundantly clear from these various research sources is the gap between what teachers and headteachers say self-evaluation *ought* to be for and how it works in practice. Ofsted protocols are now so well embedded that counsel of the ideal appears to fall largely on deaf ears. Reading between the lines of the NFER pilot evaluation it is clear that the whole process is driven externally with schools responding to procedures, profiles, criteria, critical friends and reporting protocols rather than these arising organically from grounded and embedded work within the schools.

Having set the scene, established the parameters and made self-evaluation truly its own, it is now time for Ofsted to be as good as its word. It must now actively encourage schools to be creative in self-evaluation, to stand on their own two feet and to truly speak for themselves.

3   A view from the Bell tower

This chapter takes the form of a dialogue between the author and David Bell, at that time Her Majesty's Chief Inspector. It raises questions about the origins, strengths and weaknesses of the New Relationship and focuses in particular on the interface of self-evaluation and inspection. It starts with a comment on the headline of a leaflet proclaiming 'school inspection is changing'.

School inspection is changing. So says the headline of the Ofsted publicity leaflets in the foyer. So what is at the heart of that?

I think it is about maintaining the independence and rigour of school inspection but trying to learn the lessons of the last 12–13 years. In other words, I do not think we need to inspect in the all-encompassing way we have in the past. Some of the features of the New Relationship are a natural evolution of a system that has evolved over a period of time.

The leaflet says it was time for a rethink. How do you rethink? Do you sit down in a darkened room and think great thoughts? Where do your ideas come from?

It is very interesting when people ask you where your ideas come from. I suppose they are a culmination of my thinking over three years as to where I wanted to take school inspection, as well as a lot of thinking already going on within the organisation. So I found the ideas to be warmly received. But you also pick up other ideas around in the system don't you? You pick up from what schools and teachers are telling you. Some of it comes from parents, trying to get a picture of what inspection should look like. When it came to publication of the consultation document in 2004, while we did not know exactly what the words would be, we were fairly confident that we were going to get the mood right. Subsequent events suggest we were pushing at an open door.

What role does SICI[1] play in this? Are you a part of that group?

Yes, I and my colleagues attend SICI (Standing International Conferences of Inspectorates) meetings and we do pick up ideas from what other countries are doing. Our conversations with our Dutch colleagues have been particularly fruitful. In Holland there is a statutory responsibility for inspection to contribute to improvement, which has never been the case in England, despite the Ofsted strapline, 'Improvement through Inspection'. But it is likely that it will appear in legislation here.

Actually the evidence from a number of studies says that Ofsted does not lead to improvement. And this is something accepted by Ofsted itself. But isn't it a strange kind of a conclusion, to say that inspection does not do any harm but it does not actually benefit either?

I have always been cautious in saying that inspection causes improvement because, frankly, we do not. But it has to be an important part of our thinking about inspection. You do try to understand what contribution inspection can make to improvement and that is a statutory base of the organisation. It forces us to be more articulate and explicit about that. To say inspection causes improvement is fundamentally unprovable. I think there are examples of where you have greater evidence of improvement being brought about by inspection, but again it is still not quite the same as saying it causes it. For example, our monitoring of schools with special measures is not causing improvement but most headteachers say to us that the process of professional debate and discussion with HMI brings some real bite to the improvement process. I think it is a bit too simplistic to say that either Ofsted does cause improvement or Ofsted does not cause improvement.

If you get more sharply focused recommendations, again you are not bringing about the improvement but you are contributing more directly to the process by providing good clues to those in the school who are going to bring about improvement. I think this is a wee bit of a sterile debate now, and you might say that Ofsted got itself into it by having that strapline 'Improvement though Inspection'. We are conscious that it is the question most often asked of us, not least by our friends in the Select Committee. They have always pushed hard on that and I am trying to enter into that conversation in a mature and reflective manner rather than simply saying 'oh well, you know, of course Ofsted causes improvement'.

How confident are you then that you now have got it right?

It has been the most piloted inspection system that Ofsted has ever undertaken. Two hundred and eight pilot inspections were carried out and those were all carried out under normal examination conditions, if you can put it that way, because for the schools concerned this was their real inspection. So, I felt as we embarked on the New Relationship in September 2005 we had pretty much tested the system to destruction across a whole number of types of schools in different parts of the country.

Yet, just as you move in one direction other countries are moving in an opposite direction. For example as you move down from a seven to a four-point scale, Scotland is extending theirs to six.

That was a great irony actually because when we were proposing the move to the four point scale we wrote to our counterparts across the UK and I got the message back from Scotland saying actually we are going to stretch the grading scale. When asked about this I say you probably cannot quite get it absolutely right because there is always going to be a set of arguments one way or the other.

If you start to evaluate yourself and you end up calling yourself a 1 or 2 or 3 or a 4 do you not lose a lot of the nuance and complexity that a more qualitative profiling would give? The label becomes everything.

I think you want to try to get self-evaluation to capture the richness of a school's work. I do not think that means where you position yourself on a scale somehow loses all that. I mean clearly it is always going to be a best fit, isn't it. Part of our piloting was to use the self-evaluation scale to see whether it actually worked, given that we were going to place considerable store by it under the new system. Interestingly, that bit about capturing where you were using a grading was not an issue raised by very many schools. It does not seem to have caused concern, nor have schools argued that they have been forced into a corner by having to nail their colours to a mast by saying this a 1 or a 2 or a 3 or whatever.

But don't people not tend to opt for a middle grade rather seeming too presumptuous by giving themselves a 1 or too self-deprecating by giving themselves a failing 4?

It worked both ways actually during the pilot inspections where some schools probably graded themselves too harshly and we have put them up a grade. Equally there have been cases where schools have graded themselves in a wildly optimistic way without any evidence to back that up. In some ways all that you are doing is illustrating a fundamentally flawed process at school level where for one reason or another the school is failing to face reality. I think it is important that inspectors can feel the confidence to put a school up in the same way that they might say 'No I'm sorry that's far too generous'.

There is an irony there, if a school has graded themselves less well than you think, and you put it up you are giving a double message. You are actually saying that you are not very good at evaluating yourself. So why raise the grade?

It is an interesting point that. Maybe schools are going to be a bit cautious the first time round but I suspect as they get more confident with evaluation and as they gain greater confidence in the inspectors, they will be better prepared to have the debate and dialogue. The other thing to say is, some of these are finely graded judgements, which in some ways you might think reinforces your argument – how could actually possibly put a number against it? But to go from that so you cannot possibly judge whether a school is inadequate by putting a number against it, to a school which is outstanding, seems to me to be a long stretch. It is about the dialogue and the debate. One characteristic of this self-evaluation, and this moves away from just the form-capturing data, is the increasing engagement that we want to see between the inspectors and the headteacher and other colleagues in the school. So that the self-evaluation form becomes the beginning of the conversation between the headteacher and the school about the strengths, the weaknesses and what the school does. So whilst we have to grade the school according to national criteria, we want discussion and dialogue. Why do you think this? And does that evidence stack up against this? You have to have that kind of dialogue and debate.

With shorter, sharper, smaller, downsized inspection aren't you actually reducing the room for dialogue? Are you not losing something that was there when you saw teachers and teachers wanted to be seen and acknowledged by HMI?

There is a certain irony that I comment on a little jokingly – I did not realise that the old style inspection was so popular. But when you think about it, it is what people have got used to, but there is also a serious point of substance. In the past we would guarantee that every teacher would be seen and you would cover the whole curriculum and other aspects of the school. I have known from day one that there are always trade offs when you move to a new system and some things *are* lost but I believe that what we have now is more intelligent.

You have said earlier that the SEF was the beginning of the dialogue with the school, with the headteacher. Why is it not working in the opposite direction where what the school does is work together as a staff, and students, building towards the SEF?

Which it does, absolutely, I mean that is the whole point. We have said time and time again, that the self-evaluation form is not SSE. Now, there are questions about whether or not by having a form to fill you can constrain the process or lay certain tramlines. We would say that in the best schools what the form does is capture a process, usually a process that is continuing within the school, assessing how well it is doing and understanding its strengths and weaknesses, what is to be done and what is realistic. In a real sense, without being too clichéd about this, it is much more about a journey than a fixed destination. The SEF will always be, in a sense, capturing a moment in time, but if a school says about self-evaluation 'oh we've completed the SEF', that raises alarm bells about their understanding of what self-evaluation is all about.

But isn't it then counterproductive to introduce the standardised SEF which conveys the wrong message about what self-evaluation is?

If you look back over the last few annual reports, SSE has improved over time but it is actually been one of the weaker characteristics of school leadership and management. So, I do not think I would argue with the point that we are perhaps starting from a very mixed base in terms of SSE. Some people said 'well why did you start the school this way in September, why didn't you give schools time to develop self-evaluation?' Well actually SSE has been around for a number of years. Ofsted has increasingly given greater emphasis to SSE over, certainly over the last five years I would think it is true to say. I think, I hope, that this will act as a further fillip to SSE and not just, 'this is how you fill in your self-evaluation form'.

What worries me is that when I look at local authority sites they are all tailored to the SEF. When we sent out the survey, and we said 'what are you doing by way of self-evaluation?' what we got back was the SEF the SEF the SEF or the Ofsted model. One of the effects is, I think, to drive people towards a more uniform way of looking at it because it is so high stakes. So filling out the SEF becomes an all-consuming kind of thing. It seems to me your message hasn't got there yet.

We were consulting on the nature of school self-evaluation and we were relatively open-minded as to whether there should be a standardised SSE form. We got a lot of feedback, particularly from headteacher associations, that they preferred to have a standard form because they said that if you do not do that, you do not have a single data capture form, you are just going to add immeasurably to schools' work, because what they will all do is do their own thing, they will all be slightly different and there will be additional bureaucracy associated with that. I have got some sympathy with that line. Now the danger is precisely the one that you have identified, that it then constrains the thinking, but I felt most schools who do self-evaluation, want some means or other of capturing the outcomes of what they have done, because they have to report that so that they can hold themselves to account, discuss it with the governors, engage the staff. There are inevitably going to be different ways to capture the process but it is not an absolutely free-flowing, loose exercise.

When you put self-evaluation into Google you get an endless list of private companies selling their wares. We will help fill out the SEF for you. So there is commercialisation which encourages form filling, a tactical approach which offers short cuts and further jeopardises the vitality of self-evaluation. I think that in a mature system schools must do it themselves.

Once you have completed your SEF for the first time one of our jobs I think will be to say to schools 'Right how do you use the evidence to feed it into the next part of the process of school self-evaluation?' So, one can argue that the SEF constrains peoples thinking, but one could also argue that it acts as a fillip to school self-evaluation to be done in a more systematic way. I think we have to be careful that we do not see self-evaluation becoming an industry. It is interesting that the teacher and headteacher associations are a bit concerned that we are going to get all sorts of rather bureaucratic and heavy processes introduced at school level in the name of SSE and I think equally, local authorities have to be very careful that they do not fuel that by implying a school has to do a, b, c and d. Perhaps headteachers that have not thought particularly about it, just do as they are told and do not actually engage their staff in the process of self-evaluation.

I am not sure that every school would get to that point of maturity, to use your term, by itself. I think what you have described is what I have recognised in some of the best schools where actually the SEF is completely irrelevant and they have their own mechanisms because the SEF is not a legal requirement of course. They have their own data and process to feed back with. I suppose it is an interesting issue of inspection as a policy lever isn't it. The extent to which you use inspection to achieve desired outcomes by saying this is something that has to be done. Then maybe people start to think about things in a way that they previously would not have. It is a very interesting debate. Would self-evaluation, both in Scotland and England, have progressed so far if you had not had it incentivised through inspection because I think in quite different ways it was incentivised in Scotland and England and I think it is probably important to say that we are a long way ahead of where we used to be 10 or 15 years ago. I am absolutely sold on the mature model but maybe you have to go through this process to get there for yourself.

And yet the apprehension and dependency on Ofsted is still there.

One of the other interesting things about the change to the Ofsted system is that we are now saying quite overtly that external inspection of every subject of the curriculum and every aspect of your work is just not going to happen, I think, yes, to some extent we have encouraged a sense of complacency in school of 'oh well inspectors from outside will come and tell us what they think of history, geography and a hundred and one other things'. You could argue that we are upping the stakes in relation to SSE because we are saying that actually you have got much more data at school level, some of which is generated in a sense from outside, public examination, value-added data and so on. But actually the real story of how well your school is doing will be told from within. The overt decision to reduce the volume of inspection activity gives quite a clear message. If you believe that schools should be more self-evaluative then I think you have to reconfigure the inspection system accordingly.

Does that mean that you used to inspect subjects but with school self-evaluation in the New Relationship that will be lost?

Absolutely. Last year you had 4000 separate school inspection reports which gave you a picture of history in secondary schools or science in primary schools. I think though we were a little bit seduced by the tyranny of the big number. Just because we had 4000 separate reports we thought we had something that was qualitatively better than if we carried out far fewer subject-focused inspections. What we are doing is having a much reduced programme of subject inspections. We are saying 'No that's actually your business. It's not inspectors' business to do that and therefore part of our engagement with you when we do come to inspect is to assess the extent to which you know yourself and progress actually matches up with what you're telling us is going on in the classrooms.'

You said there is no legal requirements to use the SEF. So what happens when schools take you at your word?

It happened last week in the last week of inspection and I think it will continue to happen with some schools that actually have not completed it, and that is fine.

Said positively rather than negatively?

Absolutely. We were very clear in briefing inspectors, first of all this is not a statutory requirement, therefore it will be for you to find out what processes the school have undergone, what information/evidence that they have. Schools have said that actually there is something quite liberating about not completing the SEF but having other information available to inspectors that is fine, we are quite open to that. I am really more interested in some ways about capturing the data in an intelligent way. I do not want to see a 100 page SEF. You are far better to get a few snappy bullet points that are properly evaluative, that draw neatly upon the evidence you have about how well the school is doing, than an extended essay about every aspect of every detail about the school.

You use the word 'object' quite a lot and interestingly, given the Every Child Matters five 'outcomes', a terminology which I have a problem with. But how do you use those kind of criteria to start to begin to collect evidence that is 'objective' and appears summative?

What contribution does a school make to help children to stay healthy or stay safe? Well, I think the vast majority of schools I can think of have a very powerful story to tell, and we have said that, you know for God's sake do not go around now looking for new evidence. No, I think that the vast majority of schools, the work that they do is, in terms of achieving those outcomes for children, it is part of the day job for the majority of schools.

I totally agree on that. These are things that have been at the heart of what schools do anyway but I have a problem with these as outcome criteria, for example providing healthy meals in the cafeteria or putting in place procedures for making sure children feel safe. These are input criteria not outcomes although no less valuable for that.

Some of these you could say are output data. I am not sure whether 'measures' would be the right word but we know that some schools for example, some sports colleges are now actually getting data that demonstrates the fitness, health, activity levels of students when they come into school and tracking their progress as they go out, identifying what contribution the school makes. You can control for that actually. I think it is partly just about getting schools to think a bit more about being 'productive', helping youngsters make a productive contribution. Again one might say 'Well, there are different ways in which one could evidence what students are doing such as taking part in enterprise type activities, making a contribution to the local community and so forth. I think we are quite clear on this John. We are not saying there are a few things you tick in the box, and I think you are right about inputs/outputs. This is going to be a hard one but, you know, those are good aspirations and I think schools will want to tell us how they are meeting such aspirations.'

Let me ask about the school improvement partner who looks to me a bit like your critical inspector rather than friend. This person is described as the conduit to local authority, to government. That's not my understanding of a critical friend relationship.

I suppose the government has tried to separate that out by saying that the final decision about special measures rests with the inspectorate. So you can keep the SIP clean in the relationship. I do not think however, it is wrong to suggest that the school improvement partner, outside of the inspection process, will act as an important source of information to local authorities and, arguably, all the way up the line. It is conceivable that in some cases the SIP will be so concerned about the performance of the school that she may say this requires more immediate intervention. Well that may not be necessarily a bad thing if you can see that the education of youngsters is going down the Swannie and the school is either not recognising it or has got no capacity to do anything about it.

The problem is when the consequences are high, as in recent government pronouncement – 'you've got one year to turn around'. For a SIP to work within that agenda with that accountability role while being a supportive critical friend. That is a real tension.

I recognise the tension that you are describing but I think, to be fair, the way which the programme is designed has surfaced that tension. It has been quite open that there is a supportive element but there is quite a tough element in the SIP as well. I think perhaps what you are articulating is 'Can you quite pull that off? Can you square that?' And that is not just about personal characteristics. Some individuals will be better at it than others, but the question is inherently 'can you do it in the same role?'

Isn't it ultimately about unequal power, the lack of reciprocity in the relationship, the politicised, somewhat inspectorial role of the school improvement partner?

You talk about prodigal friendship, unequal power, SIPs as a conduit to government. One of the really interesting issues about inspection, I think is the extent to which the government, certainly since 1997 has used public sector inspection, not just in education, as something of a lever, one might even say a battering ram to bring about improvement. Inspection has been a very powerful tool that the government's used, particularly in England. But I am not naive about the power of inspection, because obviously inspection acts as a powerful incentive to do some things rather than other things. I do think though that we need to move away from that concept of inspection as the policy lever. There's something about schools, and about education, schools being persuaded that there are things that are right to do, consistent with their mission and not just because Ofsted are going to inspect them.

Thank you very much David for being so frank.

4 Inspection and self-evaluation

A brief history

Quis custodiet ipsos custodes?
Who will guard the guardians themselves?

The New Relationship with Schools has to be understood in its historical context, a process of evolution which has never satisfactorily resolved the tensions between the external view of schools and how schools see themselves. In this chapter the uneven progress to the present is described, drawing on successive research reports which highlighted the imperatives for change.

School inspection, the guardians of educational standards, have kept a watchful eye on British schools for 150 years. In 1833 when government made a grant to put in place public elementary schools they followed this with the appointment of the first two HMIs. Lawton and Gordon[1] suggest that the creation of school inspection was based on the precedent set by inspecting factories, following the Factory Acts earlier in the century. These pioneering HMI, writes Grubb,[2] worked under a 'connoisseurship' model. There were no criteria and guidelines for inspectors to follow. They simply judged schools' performance based on their experience and personal wisdom.

As inspection developed in the late nineteenth century its focus was to afford assistance and encouragement rather than as a means of prescription or control. Over the years inspection practice became progressively more structured as detailed frameworks for inspection were gradually developed. For most of the late nineteenth and twentieth century inspection was a relatively uncontroversial topic and the literature during that period is comparatively sparse. It is in the last two to three decades as inspection became more controversial and more politicised that inspection provided a growing seam of literature. Since the early 1990s the role and impact of inspection has never been far from the news.

The higher public profile and newsworthiness of inspection is largely owed to the institution of Ofsted, a politically inspired initiative of the Thatcher government. It effected a paradigm shift in the nature of inspection and its relationship with schools and local authorities. The 1988 Reform Act had given to local authorities the power to inspect, putting in place a parallel system to HMI, but by 1992 then Secretary of State John Patten, impatient with the slow progress of local authorities argued for a tougher role of HMI, envisioning a new regime of 'big cats prowling the educational landscape'.[3] A year later Chris Woodhead was appointed as HMCI to turn that vision into a reality.

The politics of the early 1990s was a critical watershed in the relationship between government and schools and has to be understood within the context of a Thatcherite zeal to clear the Augean stables of underperforming authorities, progressive schools, left-leaning teacher unions, wrong-minded colleges of education, agencies of egalitarianism, and HMI too soft and collusive with the educational establishment – the enemy within. Enlisting the support of media receptive to 'common sense' arguments helped to create a public mood receptive to a series of tough measures to restore schooling to the golden days of selection, standards and discipline.

The publication of HMI reports had been in place for ten years prior to new Conservatism, but with advent of Ofsted, 1993 saw the introduction of what came to be known as 'naming and shaming' of schools graded as 'failing' or with 'serious weaknesses'. This was to prove a highly controversial policy as its effects were most acute in areas of disadvantage.[4] Within a national school failure rate of 2–3 per cent two-thirds of those schools were in areas now known by the kinder name of 'in challenging circumstances'. There is a broad consensus among countries which had studied the inspection regime in England that spotlighting failing schools was both undesirable and dysfunctional.

In its original form, Ofsted's remit was to inspect each state-funded school in England and Wales, whether primary, secondary or special, at least once over each four-year cycle. Schools were to be given up to a year's notice prior to an Ofsted inspection which began with[5]:

> An extensive time-consuming process of preparation and paperwork. Inspections were undertaken by a team of external observers over a full week focusing on various aspects of school life including 'classroom teaching and pupil reaction, enrolments, pupil background, the range of classes offered, results of national exams and the results of interviews with parents and school governors'.

One of the first steps taken under New Labour was for the cycle of Ofsted visits to be extended to require inspection only once every six years from the 1997/8 school year. While providing more breathing space between inspections it left in place the essential ingredients of the process, primarily what was seen as its narrow focus on accountability.[6] The extent to which Ofsted's top-down approach to inspection was helping schools to improve was widely questioned. For example, Cullingford and Daniels' 1999 study[7] of the effects of inspections on school quality and standards reported an adverse effect on exam performance for a sample of schools, although dismissed by the then Chief Inspector of Schools[8] as 'deeply flawed, ineptly executed and poorly argued' Rosenthal's[9] study in the following year, however, also found 'a significant negative effect of Ofsted visits on school exam performance in the year of the inspection'.

> Ofsted visits seem to have adverse effects on the standards of exam performance achieved by schools in the year of the Ofsted inspection. Perhaps the efforts required by teaching staff in responding to the demands of the school inspection system are great enough to divert resources from teaching so as to affect pupil achievement in the year of the visit.

This performance drop may be explained in part by the diversion of a school's energy into preparing for inspection. Employment of inspection consultants and rehearsal for the forthcoming event became an increasingly common feature of school life. A report by the University of Brunel in 1999 referred to 'anticipatory dread' which impaired normal school development work and the effectiveness of teaching.

In Hertfordshire a group of secondary students conducted their own study of Ofsted[10] and reported a tenser relationship with their teachers, special lessons being rehearsed beforehand, having to be constantly 'on show' ever ready for the inspector's visit. 'Trouble students' were sent away to an outdoor pursuits centre to partake in a week-long alternative education programme. Students also wrote 'Teachers are too busy being stressed'; 'Some of them have no time to teach, they are so busy getting ready'; 'Everyone is telling us what to say and how to act. What is this dictatorship? Are we expecting Stalin or Hitler next week?'.

In another study students counselled the research team to be wary of using impressions of visitors as a source of evidence. With the school's experience of inspection they said they had become very well trained on how to show the school off to its best for outsiders and inspectors. One student described the school as 'a Jekyll and Hyde school' with two faces. 'It has one face for visitors and one for us.'[11]

The Parliamentary sub-committee which reported in 1999[12] acknowledged the stress on teachers and recommended a briefer notice of inspection, suggesting it to be reduced to four weeks. While broadly supportive of a continuing role for Ofsted it also recommended that the Chief Inspector 'should be concerned to improve morale and promote confidence in the teaching profession' and that inspectors should 'take account of self-evaluation procedures used by the school'.

Ouston and Davies' study[13] in 1998 found that schools who were most positive about the inspection experience were those that did not allow the process to intimidate them, had a high level of professional self-confidence, enough to challenge the Ofsted team's findings and were able to make their own professional judgements as to what was right for their school. In other words there was already in these schools an incipient, or well-developed, self-evaluation culture.

A place for self-evaluation

In parallel with inspection self-evaluation experienced an erratic development during the 1990s. Where it existed in any formal sense it was often a legacy left behind by earlier models such as GRIDS[14] which had been subject to criticism due to the lack of any evidence to demonstrate an impact. This then allowed HMCI Woodhead to dismiss self-evaluation as having been tried and found wanting.[15] Although self-evaluation had become embedded in government policy in Scotland from 1991 in England it was resisted up until the election of New Labour in 1997.

In spite of lack of endorsement by Ofsted, or perhaps because of it, the mid-1990s was a period of revisiting self-evaluation during which numerous models emerged from local authorities across the country. The local management of schools and the advent of school development planning brought with them an inherent self-evaluation logic. An NFER survey[16] in 2001 *Evaluating school self-evaluation* found that all sixteen schools in the nine LEAs visited were using an explicit self-evaluation model, in most cases a combination of Ofsted and local authority frameworks.

The role of the NUT

The role of the NUT in advancing the cause of self-evaluation during the second-half of the 1990s was highly significant. The study which they commissioned in 1995, published as *Schools Speak for Themselves*,[17] had a wide impact on individual schools and on authority policies, many of whom had been in search of school-friendly approach and many adopted this as their policy framework. Among the first authorities to embrace this was Newcastle under the directorship of David Bell who personally launched it a headteacher's conference in 1996. Three years later the assistant director Roger Edwardson wrote:

> *Schools Speak for Themselves* is utilised in all Newcastle schools, and they have actively used a range of tools within the document, often on training days, with governors and with pupils themselves. This was a very powerful approach to a policy to support school self-evaluation.[18]

At an NUT fringe meeting at the Labour Party Conference in 1996 where *Schools Speak for Themselves* was presented, then Labour M.P. Estelle Morris endorsed self-evaluation and promised that it would be integral to Labour Party policy when elected. The contrast with the Conservative fringe meeting could not have been more stark. Apologising to his Personal Private

Secretary for not delivering the carefully prepared speech, Junior Minister Eric Forth delivered a polemic against self-evaluation, arguing that 'rotten' schools and 'rotten' teachers needed the tough hand of an inspectorate to sort them out. This was warmly applauded by his audience, a number of whom rose to the occasion to roundly deride the idea that teachers could be trusted to evaluate themselves and that pupils had anything useful to say apart from the quality of dinner hall chips.

The idea of self-evaluation as encompassing a range of stakeholder views, an integral aspect of the New Relationship was apparently, a decade ago, an idea too far and too easily lampooned. However, with the election of New Labour in 1997 self-evaluation was embraced as integral to self-improving schools although rudimentary in form and closer to self-inspection than what is now being advocated nearly a decade later. HMCI Woodhead was persuaded, or required, to overcome his own antipathy to self-evaluation and, in 1998, the document *School Evaluation Matters* was published, prefaced ironically with a Woodhead foreword posing the question *How Good is Our School?* a maxim borrowed from the Scottish model which he had not long before deprecated and dismissed.[19]

Among the numerous bodies and local authorities with an interest in self-evaluation, the GTC in particular has kept a close watching brief on the developing relationship between what schools do and the role played by inspection. It has argued for schools to be given more responsibility for their own accountability, a greater role in steering and shaping their own improvement and an emphasis on professional accountability to replace the culture of compliance to external mandate.

> The current accountability framework has been dominated by Ofsted inspections of schools over the last ten years. Ofsted inspections have mostly been seen by the profession as a punitive, expensive and time-consuming system of 'policing' schools, resulting in snapshot views of school performance at a particular time, high stake judgements and the 'naming and shaming' culture.

The history of Ofsted post-1997 is one of slow and erratic progress towards a model which would try to reconcile internal and external inspection, which would attempt to resolve the tensions between accountability and improvement and which would both meet the needs of schools and satisfy agencies of government. The tensions between these two purposes, however, were to continue in uneasy juxtaposition. On the one side it was argued that improvement would follow on the heels of accountability, while the counter line of reasoning held that only with confident self-evaluation would schools improve and embrace accountability as an inherent by-product.

While not swerving from a commitment to improvement through accountability, Ofsted did respond to some of the criticism made against it. The revised framework for the inspection of schools, published in 1999, reduced the period of notice to 6–10 weeks and opened the way for differential inspections, short for schools deemed to be performing well (20–25 per cent of schools) and longer inspections for the rest. It included guidance on the use of the handbook for self-evaluation, with strong encouragement to use the Ofsted framework for the school's own internal evaluation. This clearly signalled a move from a parallel to a sequential model, in other words inspection and self-evaluation would no longer run side by side but in sequence. Self-evaluation, rather than having an independent existence would thereafter be complementary to inspection, prior to which schools would be required to complete an Form S4 with sixteen areas of performance, each to be rated on a seven-point scale.

This new sequential relationship does, however, fall short of what has been described as a co-operative model[20] in which there is reciprocity or partnership between internal and external evaluation. It fails to meet any of the nine criteria suggested by the Dutch academic Van Leeuw,[21] the most critical of these described as the 'me-to-you-too principle' on which collaboration rests.

The asymmetry of the 'old relationship' is made clear in the 1999 document in which the school's perceptions are set 'against those of impartial, external evaluators'[22] and 'using inspection to test the school's perception of itself gives an insight into how well it is managed'.[23] What these statements imply is some definitive and objective view of the school against which its own evaluation is a used as a measure of its effectiveness and leadership. The juxtaposition of 'perceptions' (school) and 'insight' (Ofsted) is revealing. It betrays a view deeply embedded in an inspectorate view of the world. The frequent use of the word 'objective' suggests that inspectors arrive with no preconceptions, no foreknowledge of headteachers or other members of staff, no selective focus on what they are to hear or see, no implicit theories about teaching, learning and management. Their classroom observation and judgement is, unlike any other visitor to a class, 'factual' rather than a matter of perception and subjective judgement.

Seven years into a Labour government and with a new Chief Inspector there has been a concerted policy to strengthen the sequential model and to move self-evaluation progressively to centre stage. This heralded a much needed 'new relationship' with schools yet some of the age-old myths linger on. Within that relationship there is still some way to go to ensure a transparency as to the nature and evidence base of inspectors' own work.

In the developmental history of inspection and self-evaluation we can perceive a number of interconnecting strands.

Ofsted leadership

Since 1992 there have been three HMCI each of which has brought a very different style and philosophy to the job. Chris Woodhead brought to the post a belief that schools, teachers and authorities need to be sorted out and throughout his tenure of office his style was adversarial, relishing confrontation and controversy. This was accomplished in part by vivid and hyperbolic language guaranteed to capture the headlines. He had greater interest in cultivating the media than the teaching profession, setting in opposition a Daily Mail view of schools and classrooms with those of researchers, academics and practitioners. This was the legacy left for Mike Tomlinson who acted for a brief period as a caretaker HMCI without enough to time or long-term investment to repair the ruins of his predecessor. As he has shown since leaving that office he has a much more sophisticated under-standing of education and is able to talk with, and listen to, the profession. David Bell brought with him recent experience of local authority leadership and a longstanding commitment to self-evaluation. He wanted to work with schools in collaboration rather than opposition but recognised that the development of a new relationship would take time and that his first duty was to establish continuity, moving cautiously and pragmatically away from the Ofsted of old. As an astute politician he was also keenly aware of the polit-ical parameters constraining the degree to which policy could move forward in more radical directions.

Political parties

Whether or not the New Relationship would have emerged had there been a Conservative party in power is simply hypothetical but it is highly unlikely given the party's opposition to self-evaluation up until the election and in light of its continuing love affair with ex-HMCI Woodhead since. The lati-tude given to HMCI, no matter how powerful that individual, has always to be located within party ideology and this was made apparent towards the end of the first Labour government as Woodhead became increasingly margin-alised. The various offices of government and those of non-, or quasi-, government agencies have co-existed in uneasy tension, much of which can be put down to the personalities of those who inhabit the offices of 'state'. Among secretaries of state and government ministers there have been marked differences over the years in their ability to work harmoniously with their peers or to listen to the voices of teachers. Estelle Morris was one of the most successful of ministers in this respect but her very facility to tune into teachers' voices made it more difficult for her to adopt a more ruthless ideo-logical stance that came so easily to some of her predecessors and successors.

Global policy movements

Party policy does not develop in splendid isolation but in conjunction with movements in other parts of the world. The four UK inspectorates are all members of the SICI, a body which exchanges views among participating countries and develops its own European policy. Its influence depends in part on the receptivity of country representative to the direction of SICI policy, and while its influence is marginal compared with political party ideology, it did presage a new relationship half a decade ago.[24] Nor should the influence of other English speaking and Commonwealth countries be overlooked. In New Zealand, Australian states and Canadian provinces progress has been watched and monitored. The policy traffic with the United States has long been a feature of thinking and practice, and developments in self-evaluation in Scotland at least were influenced significantly by HMI fact-finding missions to the States in the 1980s.

Research and educational literature

There is a whole library of literature on self-evaluation and inspection, both national and international. It is difficult to gauge how influential this has been on policy development as influence works in mysterious ways, infil-trating consciousness over time, setting a climate, and sometimes creating enough weight of evidence to move even the most reluctant policy-makers. For example, research into Assessment for Learning,[25] a close ally of self-evaluation, has been taken up enthusiastically by the government although, as in much of translation of research policy, made more prescriptive than warranted by the research. Government agencies do send emissaries to research conferences such as BERA, SERA, ECER and ICSEI[26] and some-times present papers of their own. A notable example is Judy Sebba, an ex-Cambridge academic (now Professor at Sussex University) who worked in the research unit of the DfES and was an effective conduit for the flow of intelligence between policy and researchers.

The DfES and Ofsted also commission research and evaluation on their own account which they may or may not publish, although the 2000 Freedom of Information Act gives people a general right of access to infor-mation held by or on behalf of public authorities.

Teacher associations and pressure groups

The influence of teachers associations has been highly significant over a decade and more. As already suggested, the NUT's promotion of self-evaluation from the mid-1990s onwards was highly influential, less perhaps with a direct impact on policy than through local authorities and schools and regular inputs into teacher conferences, in-service courses, newsletters and journals. John Bangs who has, for a decade, been a tireless campaigner for self-evaluation, is seen by political makers as the acceptable face of Teachers Unions. John Dunford of SHA was another Union leader listened to by the government. He has been a well-known face on the lecture circuit delivering a number of keynote speeches challenging of current policy while pursuing a pragmatic agenda in relation to the New Relationship. The NAHT has also championed self-evaluation and, like SHA and NUT, have published their own manifestos or guidelines.[27]

In the last three years the GTC has taken a major interest in self-evaluation, setting up working groups and running conferences with inputs from union leaders, teachers and headteachers and researchers from other countries as well as the United Kingdom.

The self-styled Office for Standards in Inspection (Ofstin) was set up in 2001 as a professional forum in response to Ofsted. Under the leadership of Professor Carol Fitz-Gibbon of Durham University it not only gathered together discontents and delivered some biting anti-Ofsted polemic but also conducted controlled research on pupil performance and school effects. In giving evidence to the Parliamentary Select Committee in 1999[28] members of Ofstin, described the Ofsted regime as 'a flawed system'. They said they had no opposition to external inspection but argued the need for fundamental change in its philosophy and modus operandi.

The voice of the profession

The voice of the profession is nebulous and multi-faceted in its expression. It works in part through research studies which help the voice of teachers to be heard. Teachers do also on occasion have direct access to policy-makers and politicians, through advisory groups, sub-committees and working parties. What many commentators find surprising,[29] however, is the degree of compliance of the professions with policies they patently do not agree with. While teachers have always been adept at subversion behind the doors of their own offices or classrooms, direct confrontation appears no longer to be on the agenda, rather a slow process of resignation in both senses of that word.

The lessons of history – and future history

Rather than denigrating the past we have to respect and learn from it, argues Andy Hargreaves.[30] Those who cannot learn the lessons of history are condemned to relive them. Peter Senge and his colleagues[31] propose that we need to learn from the future. 'Learning based on the past suffices when it is a good guide to the future. But it leaves us blind to profound shifts when whole new forces shaping change arise.'

They go on to argue that planning, monitoring, controlling are all that is needed when change is simply reacting to new circumstances, but when the future may be very different from the past a new process is required which is 'sensing and actualizing new priorities prior to their emerging'.

Perhaps we have not learned enough from the history of inspection and self-evaluation and have not looked enough to the possibilities of a very different future. As car manufacturers roll out their latest model, their design teams are already working on prototypes for the future, as much as three years ahead, anticipating rather than waiting for change. Ofsted may not be working on the next model as the New Relationship is rolled out but schools ought to be. That is, after all, what self-evaluation means.

5 Lies, damned lies and statistics

The ship of state sails on a sea of statistics (Sion Simon MP)[1]

Schools are now inundated with statistical data. New technologies have allowed schools a much closer look at pupil performance and the performance of the school as a whole. But how reliable, useful or relevant are those data to the day to day work of teachers? How may they mislead? And what is the political context in which they are presented and validated? This chapter examines those issues, with a health warning as to the potential of statistics to deceive and a plea for a more self confident critique by schools speaking for the themselves.

It is said that fish were the last to discover water. This is more than an amusing homily, reminding us that as higher beings, more intellectually endowed than fish, we should never take our environment for granted. It is only with continued critical awareness that we are able to detect the toxins that seep insidiously into our language and thinking.

This chapter is about only one source of toxins and, some might too easily assume, one of the least pernicious in its impact in school life – the policy context. However, the political and policy environment does not stand apart from the media or the social economic conditions which make schools the places they are. If we are to understand the viability and integrity of the New Relationship we have to grasp something of the politics in which that new relationship is situated.

Wrongly attributed to Disraeli by Mark Twain, the phrase 'lies, damned lies and statistics' was coined in the late nineteenth century by one J. A. Baines who was standing for election in New England in 1892. It was in fact a defence rather than an attack on statistics, as politicians have, for at least a century, been addicted to numbers, and in the twenty-first century use them pervasively, selectively and sometimes dishonestly to chart the progress of policy and practice.

In 1954 Darrell Huff wrote a best-selling book entitled *How to Lie with Statistics*. It alerted readers to the hundred and one ways in which data can deceive, whether by unscrupulous marketeers or in the hands of disingenuous politicians. Political lying with statistics is often a matter of spin and sleight of hand but there is also lying with a more deliberative and sinister purpose. The upbeat message with which Huff's book ended was the importance of 'talking back to a statistic'.

A more recent warning comes from the Levitt and Dubner book *Freakonomics,*[2] co-written by a leading American economist it is full of warning for the unwary about the deception of statistics ranging across government, estate agents, crime and education. A chapter on the Chicago school system examines in detail the range of ways in which teachers cheat on high stakes tests when the incentives, such as performance pay, are high. The need to cheat is to collude with, rather than challenge, the larger systemic corruption.

The need to be aware and talk back to statistics is made more acute by the American social commentator Eric Alterman,[3] who maintains that we are living in a 'post-truth political environment'. Drawing on evidence from the American context, Alterman illustrates how truth has been superseded by a new set of norms in which truth is pragmatically and politically determined and in which veracity has no intrinsic value. These themes find direct parallels in Peter Oborne's book *The Rise of Political Lying*[4] which charts an almost exponential rise in British politics of distortion which go beyond mere spin and half-truths to a process of systematic deception. 'It was almost as if there were a parallel world' writes Oborne, one inhabited by ministers, their spokesperson and spin doctors, with another world inhabited by everyone else. Rather than connecting these two worlds with the truth, Ministers 'make statements on what they would have liked to be the truth'.[5] 'Conventional wisdom', the term coined by the economist Kenneth Galbraith, meant in its original form, convenient truth.

Convenient 'truth' was no more vividly on display in the infamous statement by Chris Woodhead that there were 18,000 incompetent teachers in England, a claim which received high media attention. An Ofsted inspector describes its impact:

> Almost one in five it came out as, and all over the tabloids and quality press. As a profession inspectors were outraged as nobody working at that time had any experience of grading teachers a 4, as it was in the days of the five point scale. When eventually CW, rarely for him, was forced to backtrack he admitted that he had included in his data teachers who were graded a three which meant 'satisfactory'. It was an outrageous misuse of data and we lost what little respect we had for him.

In the parallel universe of school, not the 'real world' as we are so often reminded, there is a third world in which truth, and being truthful to the disciplines of knowledge, lies at the very heart of its educational mission. It is a place in which adherence to truth is the glue which holds social relationships together. Yet schools find themselves caught up in a statistical deceit not of their own making.

In the United States the famous 'Texas miracle' under the governorship of George W. Bush was shown to be a deception of a high order. An analysis by

Boston College's Walt Haney[6] concluded that the dramatic rise in pass rates for high-school students on the Texas Assessment of Academic Skills (TASS) and decrease in dropout rate was illusory, in part due to a doubling of the numbers 'in special education' and therefore excluded from Grade 10 tests, and a significant rise in grade retention (students held back for another year), including as many as 30 per cent of black and Hispanic students. In fact, rather than the reported 20 per cent increase, Haney's analysis shows a sharp decrease despite heavy coaching for the test.

Closer to home the miraculous rise of literacy and numeracy attainment under New Labour has been similarly weighed in the balances and found wanting. Peter Tymms'[7] meta analysis at the Curriculum Evaluation and Management Centre (CEMS) in Durham found government figures to be hugely overstated – their 2004 figures 84 per cent, and 74 per cent, respectively for KS2 English and Maths – his figures, 60 per cent and 66 per cent respectively.

Schools with less time and requisite expertise are in no position to conduct their own analysis of government claims, but it is critical for school staff to be aware of alternative sources of evidence, other voices, and to maintain a healthy scepticism as to politically inspired miracles. Failure to be alive to the politicised nature of data and the political context in which these are set, risks from the outset undermining the credibility of a New Relationship.

This is not to cast doubt on the integrity of civil servants or of those who work in other agencies of government but it is important to make the distinction between political parties in power on the one hand and policy-makers and advisors on the other. Not because they are not umbilically connected but because they operate in different moral arenas. Policy-makers and policy advisors both implement and shape policy, blind to whatever political party may be in power but nonetheless trying to act with honesty and impartiality, however strained that responsibility becomes. There was a time when Sir Humphreys of the Civil Service skilfully guided their ministers through the thickets of policy-making, but over the last decade that relationship has been fundamentally changing. Although government ministers still rely heavily on their departmental advisors, the balance of power has shifted. Educational decision-making is now much more politicised, much more driven from the highest seats of power, handed down from No. 10, from the Cabinet, from a small number of offices in Downing Street and a small group of people who shape policies that not only bypass permanent secretaries but even secretaries of state themselves.

The post-truth political environment in which ministers and others operate is not one they themselves have created but is a global phenomenon. In a globalised economy 'transparency', although much vaunted, is an illusion. Economic transactions are undermined by too much public disclosure. Add to this the threat of terror, civil disruption and the 'yob culture', all of which provide the pretext for secrecy and surveillance. However legitimate these may be at times, wholesale deception infects the context of thinking and behaviour in society and erodes the relationship between school and the agencies of government.

Schools for economic health

In a competitive world the burden falls heavily on the centrepiece of social and moral life – school education. However, schools are not simply to be held to account for the moral and social welfare of their charges, but are seen to be responsible too for the health and wealth of the economy. The link is most clearly seen in the growing influence of the Organisation for Economic and Social Development (the OECD). Successive PISA reports[8] comparing attainments of young people in participating OECD countries are taken extremely seriously by politicians. Together with other international comparative tables, these have contributed to what David Berliner and Bruce Biddle[9] term the 'manufactured crisis', claiming that the 'crisis' is unsupported by any evidence. The political spin is enough to convince the populace, as well as the profession, that only by holding schools and teachers to account for pupil attainment will we once again be able to revive a thriving and competitive economy. The link between what children study in school and the health of the economy has yet to be shown but the 'myth' is strong enough to put pressure on teachers to be more diligent and to work harder and longer hours.

Among the damned lies and statistics are those which present a correlation between earnings and educational qualifications. The sleight of hand is that the connecting factor is success in mastery of the school curriculum rather than the more plausible explanations of family influence or private tutoring, for example. In her well-argued critique of the specious links between schools and the economy Alison Wolf[10] writes: 'Our pre-occupation with education as an engine as growth not only narrows the way we think about social policy. It has also narrowed – abysmally and progressively – the vision we have of education itself.'

While, in fact, statistics do show strong and positive correlations between education and earnings it is a step too far to tribute this to the influence of schooling. As Wolf argues, much of this can be accounted for by natural ability, by the contribution made by the family, by peers and by other forms of out-of-school learning. It opens to serious examination therefore whether the huge and anxious investment in raising test scores and staying in school longer for more and more young people will actually be of benefit to national competitiveness in the global economy.

It is all too easy to accept the myth of education and economy, spoken with such authority and boosted by such compelling statistics. Who could argue with a brilliant chancellor or data presented by economists or prestigious organisations such as the OECD? Yet, without an examination of the counter evidence we are swept along on the assumption that more means better and that a D as opposed to an A-C grade is really significant for the nation's well-being.

If schools are to enter into a new relationship with the agencies of government it has to be with eyes wide open to some of the shaky foundations on which that relationship rests. A 'relationship' implies some form of equity or power sharing. Such a relationship is one entered into willingly, with foresight and with a measure of trust.

The magnificent myth

Hand in hand with the manufactured crisis is the perpetuation of magnificent myth. The myth, given birth during the Thatcher years, was that 'progressive' educators were destroying the country together with woolly minded teachers who cared nothing for standards and pedalled a pernicious child-centred ideology. In common with all myths it contained enough grains of truth to give it life and to convince succeeding Conservative and Labour governments to portray the 1970s as a black hole in English educational history. Famously, Michael Barber, recently of the Cabinet Office and close attendant on policy-making and politics, gave credence to the magnificent myth in his keynote lectures delivered nationally and internationally to a variety of audiences. A much used Powerpoint slide illustrates four quadrants, the upper right describing the 1970s as the era of 'uninformed professionalism', the upper left containing the inscription '1980s the era of uninformed prescription', the 1990s (lower left) characterised as 'informed prescription', with the 2000 (bottom right quadrant) as 'informed professionalism'. Denigration of the past in order to justify the present is integral to such myth making[11] but it carries within it an insult to dedicated teachers who, through the 1970s and 1980s, cared deeply for standards with a professionalism that was not prescribed but arose from the deep commitment to their craft.

How myths become internalised is illustrated in extracts from headteacher interviews conducted in the course of the ESRC Project *Learning How to Learn*.[12] Referring to the 1970s and 1980s a secondary headteacher claims 'a short period of time ago nobody was interested in achievement in schools'. A primary head makes a similar claim, referring to a previous time when 'teachers took no responsibility for children's learning at all. They had no expectation of them at all.'

There can be no new relationship unless there is a willingness to penetrate the rhetoric and unless it is approached on both sides of the relationship with honest, informed and critical professionalism. Henry Giroux,[13] the American scholar, alerts his readers to the 'omniscient narrator', the one, the agency or authority that tells the story on our behalf. There is no grand narrative that can speak for us all says Giroux. Teachers must take responsibility for the knowledge they organise, produce, mediate and translate into practice. If not there is a danger that they come to be seen as simply the technical intervening medium through which knowledge is transmitted to students, erasing themselves in an uncritical reproduction of received wisdom.

Rather than internalising the master narratives, argues Giroux, we need to examine how these become constructed, what they mean, how they regulate our social and moral experience and how they presuppose particular political views of the world, pre-empting debate as to what knowledge counts and what is worth learning. Why else the flurry of outrage at the publication of Bramall and White's book *Why Learn Maths?*[14] as if merely posing the question was as heretical as Galileo's enquiries as to the nature of the solar system.

Jerry Starrat[15] has been known to shock school leaders on both sides of the Atlantic with his uncompromising message. He makes the case that learning is a moral enterprise and that to devalue the integrity of the learner by teaching to the test is a 'ransacking' of the world of ideas, a betrayal of the educational mission.

There are echoes here of Postman and Weingartner's Teaching as a Subversive Activity,[16] a key text in an age in which subversion was still alive. If teaching is not essentially about questioning received wisdom and holding untruth to account, then they conclude, what is its value?

Three logics of self-evaluation

It is within this context that the promotion of self-evaluation by governments needs to be located. It has to be understood in the interplay of ideologies, politics, financial management and a cluster of beliefs as to what education is for and the place of schools in the social economy. While the case for self-evaluation has been argued by academics on primarily educational grounds, policy-makers argue on the basis of a more hard-headed economic logic, allied to accountability and founded in a value-for-money return on investment. In the self-evaluation literature we can identify three leading, and sometimes conflicting, logics.

The economic logic derives from a recognition that external quality assurance, whether through inspection or other means, does not offer value for money especially in a policy climate where finance and financial management is devolved to schools. In short, inspection is costly and with no commensurate guarantee of its effectiveness. School self-evaluation is a virtually cost-free alternative.

Accountability is a necessary complement to a value-for-money view. Management of finance entrusted to schools implies accountability for its use. The logical extension of the concept is accounting for the school's main purposes – the achievement and welfare of students. This implies schools keeping systematic, valid and reliable forms of evidence to make available to stakeholders including parents, wider public and government agencies.

The improvement logic sees it as axiomatic that self-evaluation drives improvement and contends that improvement is a misnomer without the means of knowing where one is as a school, where the school is going and how people will know when they have arrived.

There are clearly tensions among these three driving logics and it may be difficult to see how a new relationship can reconcile these. When driven by purely economic motives self-evaluation is resented by school staff and seen as an imposition on their time. When accountability is to the fore self-evaluation becomes ritualised. When improvement is the driving force, through that avenue a school staff may come to recognise the benefits of keeping a systematic account and telling their story to a wider audience. With heightened self-awareness the economy of provision may also begin to make more sense. Reconciliation among the three logics is, therefore possible, but reliant on visionary leadership, political nous and the self-confidence to be different.

As Henry Giroux argues[17], it is a sensitivity to uniqueness that distinguishes self-evaluation from the mechanistic pursuit of numbers and comparative benchmarks and helps to separate the important from the trivial.

> By its concern with what is unique, it can help us to appreciate the distinctive qualities of individual students, thus avoiding the anonymity that numbers invariably confer. By its concern for empathic knowing it can help us to know what it feels like to be in a particular classroom or school, and what it means to succeed or fail. By its concern for coherence it can offer us a narrative that helps us to make sense of what would otherwise be incoherent complexity. By being responsive to the subtle and significant, it reminds us that not everything can take the impress of the literal and measurable. Such contributions to our understanding of schools are far from trivial.

Within the New Relationship policy-makers are pursuing a diversity of provision as new forms of schooling emerge – extended schools, specialist schools, city academies – but however different their external features they are embedded in a common policy milieu. Schools, no matter how unique they may be, are expected to be self-managing, competitive as well as collaborative, bounded by tighter control from the centre but also extended in response to their local communities. There are five concurrent images of schools, which are difficult to reconcile.

Schools as self-managing

The trend to push down financial responsibility and decision-making power to the individual school is a world-wide phenomenon. It is driven by economic as well as political motives. The middle tier between government and schools has been widely seen as not only inefficient and, under both Conservative and New Labour, as counter-productive as well, mediating and often weakening decision-making at both school and government levels. School self-management carries it within it self-evaluation as a necessary and integral component.

Schools as competitive

The extension of a parental choice, the proliferation of information on performance, the increasing variety of school types and specialisations casts schools as competing in an educational market place. The popular reference to performance tables as 'league tables' illustrates the perception that in order to survive schools must be able to measure their quality and output. Self-promotion assumes a higher profile and makes self-knowledge a higher stakes imperative.

Schools as collaborative

The isolation of schools competing unsuccessfully with their neighbours, together with recognition of the adverse effects on some schools, has led to a greater emphasis on collaboration. The Beacon Schools Initiative, followed later by Leading Edge Schools, was designed to help schools provide mutual support and raise standards through collaborative enterprise. Clusters of schools working together has been further promoted by the National College's support for Network Learning Communities. In such Networks there is the potential for self-evaluation which goes beyond the individual school to encompass a collaborative view of quality and effectiveness.

Schools as extended

As schools extend their boundaries self-evaluation is required also to broaden its reach. It has to concern itself with an extended curriculum, out-of-hours learning, adult and community learning. Extended schools and 'full-service schools' work across professional boundaries with a child, family and community-centred focus. The implication is that self-evaluation must be attentive to the scope and efficacy of those relationships. The five key concerns outlined in *Every Child Matters* traverse the boundaries of school learning to include health and welfare and imply a more rounded role for self-evaluation.

Schools as bounded

In England schools also operate within the bounds of a National Curriculum, accompanied by key stage assessments and targets of attainment. These are powerful drivers of self-evaluation and other indicators of success count for little if the school is not able to demonstrate a trajectory of improvement, or at least a maintenance of performance, over time.

Living with contradiction, managing paradox

These five images of school illustrate the inherent tensions within the New Relationship. Each successive policy initiative adds another layer, impressing new growths on to sedimented strata, as if self-evaluation and school improvement could be carried through without some deep archaeological excavation.

In this disingenuous world of myth and contradiction the task of leadership is not to create a parallel world of its own, insulated from the 'real' world and the counterfeit world of political spin, but to confront deception and obfuscation with its own truth. Educational leadership is inherently a subversive activity as is the process of education itself.

6 Self-evaluation, review, audit, self-assessment and self-inspection

Caminante no hay camino, se hace camino al andar
Traveller, there is no path, you make the path as you walk

There is a plethora of terms for self-evaluation. Many describe the same things under a different name. However, often different terms refer to the same thing. This chapter teases out some of the important distinctions among common terminology, raising questions as to differing claims and outlines the seven key elements of self-evaluation.

Self-evaluation is a process of discovery rather than a tedious adherence to a well-trodden trail. Yet, as we have seen from surveys and research of what happens on the ground, the path is clearly marked out milestone by milestone for the weary traveller and is less a voyage of discovery than an impatient dash to the destination.

Self-evaluation has had a chequered history in British education. In the last half century it has been embraced, discarded and re-invented. It has, however, never gone away because it rests on an unassailable logic. As individuals, as groups, as organisations if we are blind to our faults and ignorant of our strengths we are unlikely to grow. There is a cartoon of an ugly duckling gazing at its own reflection in a pond and seeing an elegant swan. This may be the promise of things to come or it may simply be self-delusion. 'Know thyself', the counsel of the Oracle at Delphi was prescribed as the antidote to self-delusion and became the byword and underpinning philosophy of the Scottish approach to self-evaluation which has grown steadily from its first tentative piloting in 1989.

Previous incarnations of self-evaluation enjoyed a brief life because, as Brian Fidler comments in reference to a previous set of protocols known as GRIDS,[1] teachers were 'better at identifying improvement rather than bringing about improvement'. GRIDS and other forms of self-evaluation took a back seat as a new inspection regime in the early 1990s raised the profile of external evaluation. There was, within the government, an impatience with self-evaluation. It was seen as too soft, too complacent and too much in the hands of the profession. It needed the much firmer and more objective hand of an external inspectorate. It was to take a change of government in 1997 before self-evaluation was reborn and forced on a reluctant Chief Inspector.[2]

Because Ofsted occupied such a central place in the affections of both Conservative and Labour parties, in England self-evaluation took a different path from its more grass roots development in Scotland. It emerged from inspection, adopting an Ofsted logic, co-opting its criteria and many of its tools, taking on the guise of self-inspection. In the process this received model has tended to submerge other forms of self-evaluation developed by local authorities and by schools themselves. Figure 6.1 illustrates some of the essential differences between self-inspection and self-evaluation.

As an NFER study[3] in 2001 showed, numerous legacies from earlier periods remain and, as a consequence, self-evaluation appears in different forms and under different names. Its varying purposes are revealed by the diverse names often used interchangeably – terms such as self-assessment, self-review, audit and quality assurance.

A website search is bound to confuse as local authorities and schools use their own terminologies to describe the process. One of the most common variants in England is self-review, while in North America the term self-assessment is widely used. Although these various terms tend to refer to the same thing, it is important to make some conceptual distinctions as the New Relationship moves towards a more common lexicon of terms.

The following may be seen as lying on a spectrum from summative to formative in purpose:

Audit. The origins of audit are from a financial practice, designed to ensure the books were kept rigorously and ethically. It has also connotations of stock-taking and in a school context applies to obtaining an overview of the educational 'stock' or physical and human resource. Summative in nature.

Self-inspection	Self-evaluation
Top-down	Bottom-up
Is a one-off event	Is continuous and embedded in the nature ofteachers' and headteachers' work
Provides a snapshot	Is a moving picture
Is time-consuming	Is time-saving
Is more about accountability than improvement	Is more about improvement than accountability
Applies a common framework	Is flexible and spontaneous
Uses a set of predetermined criteria	Uses, adapts and creates relevant criteria
Tends to create resistance	Engages and involves people
Can detract from learning and teaching	Improves learning and teaching
Encourages playing safe	Takes risks
Requires consensus	Celebrates difference

Figure 6.1 Self-inspection and self-evaluation.

Quality assurance is a form of audit. The term denotes a systematic examination of quality, usually by an external body and, like audit, is essentially geared to accountability in return for the trust and responsibility invested in schools and teachers. Among the many web definitions you will find if you ask Google, one that speaks for the many, is 'All those planned or systematic actions necessary to provide adequate confidence that a product or service is of the type and quality needed and expected by the customer.' Summative.

Self-review tends to be used as synonymous with self-evaluation and is a term adopted by most local authorities. Some, such as Shropshire, make a distinction between the wider sweep of one-off review and ongoing self-evaluation. The term, 're-view' implies looking again, with a connotation of scanning as in 'scanning indicators', which take a comprehensive overview rather than an in-depth investigation of selected areas. Tends to be used summatively but may also be formative.

Self-assessment. Also used widely as synonymous with self-evaluation. The distinction between assessment and evaluation is, however, important. In the UK assessment refers to knowledge, skills and attitudes gained by pupils and is used both summatively (as in test performance) and formatively (as in assessment for learning). Evaluation, on the other hand, is concerned to critically examine the extent to which a process such as assessment is effective, bringing to it an evaluative judgement on the process or outcome. Both summative and formative.

Inquiry is a term with North American resonance, used to denote a more open-ended process, less tied down to pre-specified criteria. A form of this known as 'appreciative inquiry' sets out to understand the strengths of a school within its own frame of reference. It is essentially formative rather than summative.

Research is sometimes used as a synonym for inquiry and has much in common with self-evaluation in that it is a disinterested process aimed at uncovering the way things are or are seen to be. While much of student-led, teacher-led or school-based research looks very similar to self-evaluation and draws on similar tools, 'research' is a broader concept encompassing many schools of thought with application in multiple contexts. Can be both formative (action research) and summative ('pure' or fundamental research).

Self-evaluation as the term of use has a growing currency in European and Asia-Pacific countries and is now favoured by Ofsted which sets out its key constituents as follows:

1 Intelligent accountability should be founded on the school's own views of how well it is serving its pupils and its priorities for improvement.
2 Strong self-evaluation should be embedded in the school's day-to-day practice.
3 Effective self-evaluation should ask the most important questions about pupils' learning, achievements and development.

4   It should use a range of telling evidence to answer these questions.
5   It should benchmark the school's and pupil's performance against the best comparable schools.
6   It should involve staff, pupils, parents and governors at all levels.
7   It should be integral to the school's central systems for assessing and developing pupils and for managing and developing staff.
8   It should lead to action.

Some matters for discussion

These are far-reaching principles and need careful scrutiny and teasing out. As such they offer a useful starting point for dialogue within a staff as well as a set of criteria against which a school can begin to evaluate its own approach to self-evaluation. Each of these eight principles may be interrogated as follows:

What do we understand by 'intelligent accountability'? And what would unintelligent accountability look like?

The first principle suggests that intelligent accountability should be founded on the school's own views of how well it is serving its pupils and setting its own priorities for improvement. This provides considerable scope for a staff to think through, on its own terms and with its own goals, the criteria that will assess what it means to really serve pupils well. Such a discussion would immediately cast doubt on some conventional measures of success, and raise to the surface some of the constraints that impede an intelligent approach to the school telling its own story. It might expose some of the unintelligent accountability whereby teachers feel held to account for practices they do not believe in and to which they owe no allegiance.

What does it mean for 'strong' self-evaluation to be embedded in the school's day-to-day practice? And what would weak self-evaluation look like?

Strong self-evaluation may be taken to imply a concern for rigour and evidence as against intuition or subjective judgement. As such what form might it take in day-to-day practice? A reflective daily dairy? Systematic record keeping of pupil behaviour and achievements? End of lesson review? Pupil feedback forms? It may prove hard to justify formal systematic procedures on a daily basis and any single protocol such as pupil feedback or end of lesson review may become tedious and devalued, while a commitment to recording pupil achievement or daily diarying is likely to be onerous and demotivating for teachers. A more realistic counsel is for self-evaluation to be embedded in the nature of classroom practice, creating a learning/teaching climate in which reflection and critique are routine. Observations and reflections can be recorded on a more *ad hoc* basis, developing a portfolio of evidence which is available for sharing among colleagues and for scrutiny by inspectors or school improvement partners.

What does it mean for effective self-evaluation to ask the most important questions about pupils' learning, achievements and development and what are the least important questions?

The most important questions about learning are a matter for deep debate as is the question of where learning ends and 'achievement' and 'development' begin. Do the most important questions about learning refer to the process of learning or to the outcome? Is there a useful distinction to be made between learning as achievement and learning *how* to learn as process? Noel Entwistle's[4] distinction among surface, strategic and deep learning is apposite here as so much of measurement encourages surface learning and strategies designed to beat the examiner. Measuring deep learning is a much more taxing proposition and explains why it so routinely ignored. Authentic self-evaluation cannot afford to ignore it.

What does it mean to use a range of telling evidence to answer self-evaluation questions?

When can evidence be described as 'telling'? The language of evidence is, unfortunately, beset with dichotomies of 'hard' and 'soft', 'subjective' and 'objective'. Yet educational and school life is full of subjectivities. What worth can be placed, for example, on the subjective evidence of one child about bullying? 'By its concern with what is unique', writes Eisner,[5] 'it can help us to appreciate the distinctive qualities of individual students, thus avoiding the anonymity that numbers invariably confer'.

> By its concern for empathic knowing it can help us to know what it feels like to be in a particular classroom or school, and what it means to succeed or fail.... By being responsive to the subtle and significant, it reminds us that not everything can take the impress of the literal and measurable.

What does it mean to benchmark the school's and pupil's performance against the best comparable schools?

Benchmarking is concept borrowed from the corporate world. For example, the Xerox Corporation describe benchmarking as 'the continuous process of measuring products, services and practices against the toughest competitors or those companies recognised as industry leaders (best in class)'.[6] This definition does not sit very easily within an educational context where best in class is a much more contested notion. A more fluid and open definition is to think of benchmarking as learning from others through comparing specific aspects of their procedures or modus operandi.

Comparing pupil performance, as suggested in the above criterion is one aspect of this, a rather meaningless process unless accompanied by critical inquiry into how that level of performance may have been achieved.

What does it mean to involve staff, pupils, parents and governors at all levels?

Involvement at all levels may be seen as a ritual procedure of eliciting views through surveys and questionnaires. 'Involvement' however ought to carry a deeper meaning. It suggests something proactive rather than reactive, something integral to people's way of thinking rather than simply offering a view when prompted. A governing body may routinely reflect on its own efficacy and on the development trajectory of the school. It may suggest or initiate forms or tools for improved reflection. Parents' response, to their children's learning, sometimes emanating in complaint, is an implicit form of evaluation which is a valuable form of evidence that can be turned to a more proactive use. The energy inherent in pupils' day-to-day evaluation of teaching and of school life, as often negative as positive, can equally be turned to advantage by releasing and directing that energy to new and creative forms of self-evaluation.

What does it mean to make it integral to the school's central systems for assessing and developing pupils and for managing and developing staff?

Self-evaluation is integral to everything the school does. It is integral to planning. It is integral to professional development. It is integral to assessment and to pupil development. There is, however, more than a hint in this statement of something managed from the centre, planned, rational and top-down. There is a danger in arriving at what Bortoft[7] calls 'the counterfeit whole', a mechanistic summary, buried under the weight of numbers and rhetoric and devoid of the human side of the enterprise and the vitality which makes a school a school.

What does it mean to for it to lead to action?

Self-evaluation without action is a waste of time. Revealing evidence of success and excellence does not imply passivity and inaction, but rather an active commitment to maintain, or further improve and share with others. What appears to be implicit in this statement, however, is the self-evaluation as a summary event followed by action to put things right. Self-evaluation viewed as mini or micro cycles of reflection and action embed this principle deep in the nature of learning and teaching, of planning and review.

Some prior questions

Any discussion of the eight criteria suggested earlier immediately raises some prior questions about the nature and purpose of self-evaluation.

For example, why should schools engage in self-evaluation? What is its essential purpose and of what benefit to teachers and pupils? The case for self-evaluation may be argued on a number of different grounds – personal and professional, institutional, and with reference to national and international policy imperatives. The following are four kinds of arguments and applications.

- *As an essential human quality.* The counsel offered by the Oracle of Delphi to 'know thyself' refers to a deeply individual quality and may be seen as a fundamental tenet of what it means to be an educated person.
- *As a professional responsibility.* Self-knowledge assumes a greater sense of urgency when applied to teachers or other personnel who deal with children and are accountable to their colleagues, to parents and their employers.
- *As a policy imperative.* In a policy, or quality assurance context, 'self' is generally seen as applying to the school as an institution. Like the individual, a school is expected to know itself in all its complexity. Lack of insight into its own quality and effectiveness is to the detriment of its students and its staff and is apt to mislead parents.
- *As an economic indicator.* In an international climate in which nations are compared according to the performance of their students, politicians and policy-makers do not wish to be taken by surprise by external evaluations undertaken by OECD or by other influential external agencies. Self-knowledge, therefore, assumes great importance on an international stage.

The seven elements of self-evaluation

However embedded, spontaneous or intuitive self-evaluation may be, it is also systematic, evidence-based and with a clear sense of purpose and outcome. Table 6.1 suggests seven key elements and poses the question 'What happens if any one of these elements is missing?' What, for example is the likely outcome if all the elements are in place but there is no shared understanding of purpose? What if there is lack of clarity as to the audience to whom the story may be told? What if there is much ongoing activity but no coherent framework? How can self-evaluation be effective without criteria being thought through critically and matched to the needs of the school? How can self-evaluation operate well without the right, most appropriate, tools for the job? How is it implemented in order to vouchsafe the greatest engagement, ownership and promise of success? What is the final product one is aiming for and what kinds of differing forms might it take? In examining Table 6.1 the questions for schools are:

- Are all these elements in place?
- Have you considered the consequences of any missing element?

Table 6.1 The seven elements of self-evaluation

Purpose	Audience	Framework	Criteria	Tools	Process	Product
?	Audience	Framework	Criteria	Tools	Process	Product
Purpose	?	Framework	Criteria	Tools	Process	Product
Purpose	Audience	?	Criteria	Tools	Process	Product
Purpose	Audience	Framework	?	Tools	Process	Product
Purpose	Audience	Framework	Criteria	?	Process	Product
Purpose	Audience	Framework	Criteria	Tools	?	Product
Purpose	Audience	Framework	Criteria	Tools	Process	?

Purpose

Question: Why are we doing this?

The strategy through which to answer this question is to create a forum or forums for discussion, gathering differing views, examining the potential range of purposes and agreeing which one is pre-eminent for the school. There may not be one single purpose but a cluster of cognate purposes, brought together to provide one overarching visionary purpose, neither too vague nor grandiose but one that people feel represents their lived priorities. Where there is core purpose for a school as an entity it implies a sense of shared identity. As Limerick *et al.*[8] suggest, identity is never static or self-satisfied but constantly evolving ('growing up') in response to the challenges of a changing world.

> An environmental scanning exercise conducted every few years does not make much sense. The organization has to remain in a constant state of environmental scanning, so that it can revisit its identity in the face of discontinuous change.

Audience

Question: Who is this for?

It is difficult to discuss questions of purpose without considering the audience for self-evaluation. If the audience is seen as Ofsted, the purposes will necessarily be different from self-evaluation with an internal focus. When asked about audience teachers tend to see self-evaluation as for the school itself,[9] as informing planning and practice and putting the improvement of learning and teaching at its core. Reporting to an external audience such as Ofsted is then seen as subsidiary and the school's story becomes shaped by an improvement, rather than an accountability, purpose. Maintaining different documents for differing audiences betrays the tensions inherent in the improvement–accountability interface, a tension that can be resolved when there is a clarity as to the primary audience and the courage to follow that conviction.

Framework

Question: What is the best structure?

Self-evaluation is often a random unco-ordinated process, occurring in pockets within a school, in individual classrooms or departments. This is often a lively and valuable process in which self-evaluation takes root. In order to grow and infuse whole school policy however, disparate elements of practice do need a supporting structure of framework. There is such a plethora of these that schools often adopt the Ofsted framework because it is there and because it is on that basis that inspectors will judge the school. But if teachers, and pupils, are to feel any ownership, they should be encouraged to do one of the two things. Either adapt the Ofsted model to give it their own flavour or branding, or devise their own model and then cross reference it with the Ofsted framework.

Criteria and measures

Question: How are we to judge?

Self-evaluation has to be evidence-based. Many schemes pose the question 'How do we know?' We know because we have criteria against which to 'measure' success or progress. The most easily measurable criteria are attainment in tests or exams. These can be reported in scores, levels and percentages and for that reason have a compelling attraction. The danger is that these criteria override others because they are both easily measurable and carry high-stake consequences. Criteria which 'measure' the quality of learning or teaching, or school ethos and culture for example, are less easy to grasp and report on. These have most meaning when developed by teachers themselves with the help of pupils and if possible with the support of a critical friend. There are plenty of sources to draw on rather than having to re-invent the wheel, but engaging critically in the process of thinking these through for oneself will lend greater vitality and ownership to the process *'We must learn to measure what we value rather than valuing what we can easily measure.'* (Education Counts, Report to US Congress, 1991)

Process

Question: What do we do?

Self-evaluation often takes the form of an event. Groups of key 'stakeholders', including some or all of the following – senior leaders, middle leaders, teachers, support staff, pupils, parents – may go through the criteria and make a judgement on each, perhaps using a four-point scale such as the one adopted by many schemes including the new Ofsted reporting format.

This can be a time consuming process but if well handled can also produce a rich dialogue. It is also likely to throw up a very wide diversity of viewpoints and make it difficult to arrive at a consensus. That may be treated as a virtue rather than a problem, however, as it illustrates the complexity and diversity of what a school 'is' and what it means to different people.

The process is not always an event however. If self-evaluation is truly embedded in a school's way of thinking and being then the tools of self-evaluation (see Chapter 14) can be assembled to tell a continuing and evolving story.

Tools

Question: What are the tools for the job?

The tools of the trade come in a variety of shapes and sizes. Some of these are complex and cumbersome and people shy away from using them because they require time to read and digest. Tools that teachers, and pupils, are most likely to use are simple and accessible but at the same time powerful. They need to be amenable to use on an *ad hoc* basis, spontaneous and suited to the task in hand rather than as a ritual process at a given time. The most simple examples of such a tool are the thumbs up, thumbs down or traffic lights which a teacher can use to check out pupils' understanding or evaluation of teaching. Such a tool can then become part of the pupil repertoire and used by them rather than instigated by the teacher. As with all tools there are dangers of overuse. So selective use and variety is the touchstone here.

Product

Question: What does the final product look like?

The final product may take the form of a written report, a video, a power-point presentation, a set of photographs with commentary, a website or a combination of some or all of these. In a sense however, self-evaluation has no final product as it is ongoing and developmental. It may take the form of a sequence of reports or an open portfolio which goes on being added to and refined as understanding and insight grow. A website is a conducive medium for the progressive unfolding of the continuing story. The Ofsted self-evaluation form requires a set of grades on a 1–4 point scale. As a product these say little about the quality of a school, or aspects of it. When self-evaluation is discussed it is often in terms of different kinds of metaphors. Some draw from accountancy such as audit, balance sheet and stock-taking, some from the medical field such 'Sergiovanni's[10] listening to the heartbeat' or the 'health check'. The metaphors which we use may tell us something about how we understand what a school 'is' and what self-evaluation is for.

Metaphor 1: The health check

A health check-up taken by a doctor produces a set of key measures such as height, weight, good or bad cholesterol, heartbeat and blood pressure. These are fairly 'hard' numbers that together begin to tell a story of physical health. They might not only bear little relation to the subjective feeling of well-being but may also be misleading. For example, a doctor takes a blood pressure check in her surgery on a given day at a given hour, perhaps in a situation perceived by the patient as highly stressful, failing to take into account proceeding our successive events surrounding that visit – a rush through traffic, a violent domestic argument, or an anticipated financial transaction. The blood pressure reading reveals a high diastolic and systolic level and may look something like this: 165 over 102. The doctor counsels a return visit the following week to check blood pressure again, warning he might have to apply special measures if there is no tangible improvement. Against the doctor's advice the patient goes out and buys a do-it-yourself blood pressure kit and begins to take her own blood pressure at regular intervals over the course of 24 hours. Her reading looks something like the one shown in Figure 6.2, plotting rises and falls against events of the day and night. Peaks and troughs become understandable and, set in the context of his daily activities, the 'patient' is able to monitor her behaviour and can both avoid, and learn how to deal with, the stressors and increase the calming influences.

There is a close analogy here between external and inspection and self-evaluation. Measures taken at a given time provide a static picture, a set of

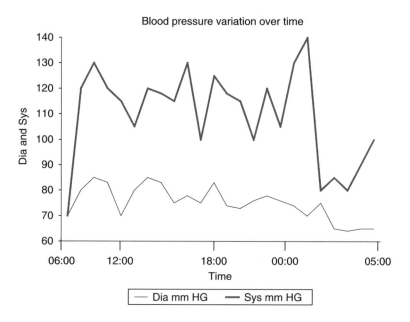

Figure 6.2 Blood pressure: reading over time.

data on the health of the school body which is potentially helpful but also potentially misleading. But they cannot chart the dynamic or capture the flow of activity that tells the school's own inner story.

The life of classrooms is not one of even flow but of highs and lows, peaks of interest and engagement, troughs of boredom and anxiety. As any teacher knows, time of day, place in the week of the term of the school year all have a bearing on the vitality or langour of lessons. All impact on anticipation and anxiety on and off task behaviour. The flow of classroom life may be depicted in similar ways to the blood pressure chart period by period in a secondary school or over the course of a day in a primary classroom (see page 147).

Metaphor 2: the wedding cake

The wedding cake model (Figure 6.3) comes from the University of Washington. It illustrates the upward and downward flow of learning through the three levels, implying that without professional and system-wide learning student learning is necessarily impoverished, and that student learning in turn informs and shapes professional and system learning. It is metaphor for organisational learning or, as some writers[11] prefer, a 'learning community'.

What lies behind the wedding cake model are outer layers which look beyond the institution of the school to the external environments. The first outer layer is described as 'Family and Community contexts', the second layer referring to the 'Larger policy and professional contexts'. This resonates with the broader focus of *Every Child Matters*. It implies an extension of self-evaluation to sites where learning and the relentless construction of reality

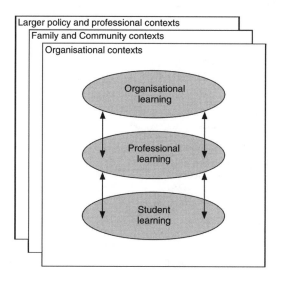

Figure 6.3 The weddingcake: pupil, professional and system learning.

take place in home and community, to the social agencies which support or conflict with a school's mission, and to the wider political environment which penetrates day by day the work of teachers and the learning of students.

Peter Senge and colleagues[12] write that 'the difference between a healthy and an unhealthy organisation is in members' awareness and ability to acknowledge their felt needs to conform'. The ability of a school staff or leadership to challenge ingrained habits of seeing and respond self-confidently to external pressures may be a reflection of a school's stage of development or it may simply stem from a conscious decision to pursue the path of least resistance. This is, however, ultimately self-defeating. Figure 6.4 illustrates some of the sources of pressure and support. Knowing the difference between these two is crucial as many of the apparently friendly sheep may in fact prove to be unfriendly wolves.

This diagram, or a version of it tailored to the context of the school, may be used as a focus for discussion, opening up to question the school's own response to these influences. Such a discussion might prompt a staff to ask where it would place itself on a continuum from conformity to self-determination. The greater the sense of self-determination the more the school may view some, or all, of these as sources of potential support rather than threat and come at the accountability question with greater insight.

The more decision-making power and financial independence has been pushed down to schools the greater had been the accountability required in return. The term 'accountability' is not one that immediately endears itself to teachers. Drawn from an accounting model it carries connotations of a bureaucratic and oppressive process. Yet accountability has always been implicit in the work of teachers and schools if not always observed in practice. With school self-governance and its immediate allies – self-evaluation and

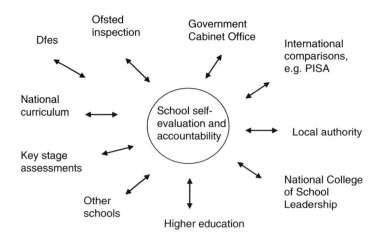

Figure 6.4 Sources of pressure and support.

in a form that strengthens the work of the teachers and of the school. The essential tenets of professional accountability are described by Eraut[13] as:

- a moral commitment to serve the interests of clients;
- a professional obligation to self-monitor and to periodically review the effectiveness of one's practice;
- a professional obligation to extend one's repertoire, to reflect on one's experience and to develop one's expertise;
- an obligation that is professional as well as contractual to contribute to the quality of one's organisation;
- an obligation to reflect on and contribute to discussion on the changing role of one's profession in a wider society.

These principles of professional accountability not only describe what good teachers do but also underpin a notion of self-evaluation which is integral to the teaching task, with a reach that extends beyond the classroom to parents and the wider community.

7 Hearing voices

The last few years have witnessed an enthusiastic embrace of student voice by government departments as well as by researchers and schools themselves. But schools are places in which many voices mingle and the ability to discriminate among them is a challenging but significant task for self-evaluation. Hearing the contribution of each of the various players – teachers, parents, pupils and school leaders is the subject of this chapter.

When we enter into a new relationship we become acutely sensitive to voice because it is only through that medium that we come to know and understand one another. Hearing voices with sensitivity and with accuracy is, however, a highly developed skill and one honoured most typically in the breach. Stephen Covey[1] captures something of the frustration of not being heard, arguing that listening for understanding is a high art.

> 'Seek first to understand' involves a very deep shift in paradigm. We typically seek first to be understood. Most people do not listen with the intent to understand; they listen with the intent to reply. They're either speaking or preparing to speak. They're filtering everything through their own paradigm, reading their autobiography into other peoples' lives. If they have a problem with someone – a son, a spouse, an employee – their attitude is 'That person just doesn't understand'.

In its simplest guise voice is elicited through the medium of a survey. A recent example[2] from Ofsted found that 90 per cent of primary pupils and 80 per cent of secondary students were 'very satisfied' with their schools. This is one version of 'voice', as embraced by government and, as in this example, exercised through the medium of a questionnaire. Other channels through which pupil voice is encouraged by Ofsted guidelines are through schools' councils and other formal avenues of consultation and communication. As widely perceived, 'voice' is seen as letting pupils have a say but within the strict parameters of school conventions. Within these boundaries, however, pupils quickly adapt to the rules of the game. They are highly sensitive to the grammar of different contexts and know how to talk to different audiences – inspectors, headteachers, counsellors, student teachers, teachers they know and teachers they are meeting the first time. They become adept at testing the limits of what can be said and heard.

In common with many other important movements, 'voice' risks becoming another add-on, like citizenship, assessment for learning, personal, social and health education, something else to which schools have to accommodate rather than embed in their thinking. As Ben Levin,[3] now in the Ontario Ministry has argued:

> The history of education reform is a history of doing things to other people, supposedly for their own good. Even though all the participants in education will say that schools exist for students, students are still treated almost entirely as objects of reform.

However, pupils merit no special privileged status as against the voices of teachers or parents or others who also have a right to be heard. Schools are places in which there are many voices which carry, and carry in differing bandwidths. There are voices which demand to be listened to by virtue of their status. Some voices have an inherent authority. Some are powerful because of their emotional resonance while others, reasoned and rational, fail to infect attitudes or practice. There are strident voices and voices which have been systematically silenced by rules and mores, or by the weight of historical inertia and frustration.

Pupil voice can only be understood and given its place when we grasp the complex dynamic of beliefs, relationships, conventions and structures that characterise the culture of a school and where, within that culture, authority and power lie, either hidden or are made highly visible. It is in the counter-weight and balance of the fluctuating acoustic of teachers', pupils' and parents' voices that a school culture either flourishes or flounders. A new relationship is one that is able to tune in to what Jennifer Nias and colleagues[4] described as 'the secret harmonies of the school' as well as discordant, less comforting and sometimes challenging voices.

Pupil voice is in fact something of a misnomer since it implies a form of homogeneity, whereas we know from thirty years or more of research[5] as well as immediate experience that young people speak in many and varied tongues. While schools draw clear lines of demarcation between pupils' and teachers' roles, the boundaries of their individual and collective powers of expression are less easily defined. Some pupils can be more articulate and persuasive than their teachers but it is at times of crisis that the weight of pupil and teacher voice is given its severest test, for example, when the testimony of a teacher has to be weighed against that of a pupil, the wisdom of Solomon and impartiality of judgement has to be demonstrated. While such adjudication at times of crisis crystallises issues of voice, it is in the day-to-day, moment-to-moment arbitration of voice that the true character of the school is exposed.

Voice is both an individual and collective phenomenon. It is verbal and non-verbal. It is neither constant nor without contradiction. It is highly responsive to context, politically sensitive and socially conscious. Celebration of pupil voice as if it were always naive, authentic and untrammelled by convention may lead to an equivocal place. What is expressed by a child or young adult may be spontaneous or may be a studied choice with an acute grasp of audience. The choice of appropriate linguistic and social register for different occasions is one of the principal lessons that schools try to teach but it is one learned more powerfully through the hidden than through the formal curriculum. The simple exhortation to pupils to have their say in the formal setting of the classroom or school council tends to neglect the powerful process by which voice is given shape in the less formal arenas of school life.

Expression of voice is not only bounded by precedent and protocol but assumes the presence of an appropriate metacognitive repertoire on the part of pupils. It is easier to admonish teachers to listen to their pupils than to help them acquire the management expertise and interpersonal skills to do so within the normal routines of classroom life. To hear the authentic voice requires the space, the calm and the patience to listen to what lies beneath the words and to offer a support sensitive enough to help young people expand their social and intellectual lexicon.

What is given expression by a child or young person reflects a prevailing internal voice which may be that of a parent, an older sibling, a teacher or a specific peer group, what the sociologist G. H. Mead[6] referred to as 'the internalised other'. What 'education' intends, whether by the agency of parents or teachers, is to help children unravel the disparate narratives that speak to them so to find their own voice and discover the confidence to express it.

Transactional analysis is a useful theoretical framework for explicating how different vocal registers work in the context of a school or classroom. In Berne's[7] model the individual is portrayed as expressing a view in one of three internalised voices – child, parent or adult. The pupil's conscious, or more commonly unconscious, choice of voice is shaped by the voice in which he or she is addressed. So a response 'in the child' is most likely to be evoked by an admonition from a teacher who is 'in the parent'. Helping pupils to express their views 'in the adult' is most likely to occur when teachers or others also adopt the mature 'adult' register. Characteristic of such adult–adult transactions is the ability to listen and, most crucially, to listen to views that differ from your own.

Voice grows from the roots up and only when allowed the space to grow. A school culture which wishes to achieve the acoustic balance among competing desires to be heard will consciously strive to maximise 'adult–adult' transactions. This implies a strategic approach on the part of leadership, neither achieved in the short-term nor by mandate, but through a process which models from the top-down and builds from the bottom-up.

It is an approach which recognises that teachers will not listen to pupils if they are not listened to by their managers or peers. It is an approach which understands that teachers are unlikely to tolerate divergent views from their pupils in a professional culture which can only live with sterile consensus.

The genesis of 'voice' is in the day-to-day business of the classroom where, no matter the subject of study, there is a respect for persons, a positive embrace of diversity, and an anticipation of surprise. A day without surprise is a teaching rather than a learning day. The learning day is one of continuing discovery of the talent and ingenuity that is uncovered in the dialogic classroom[8] and the dialogic school.[9] 'Dialogue' as a search for meaning embeds the singular notion of pupil voice in a wider more multi-layered discourse.

The end of consensus

'Organizations require a minimal degree of consensus but not so much as to stifle the discussion that is the lifeblood of innovation' write Evans and Genady.[10] These authors contend that it is the constant challenge of contrasting ideas that sustains and renews organisations. Schools that play safe, driven by external mandates and limiting conceptions of improvement set tight parameters around what can be said and what can be heard. As such they are antithetical to the notion of a learning organisation which, by definition, is always challenging its own premises and ways of being.

When we understand schools as marked by complexity and diversity we have to reach for an alternate paradigm to traditional measures of school effectiveness with their suites of key indicators. A learning school is open to dissent and paradox. There is freedom to break rules because the culture is resilient enough to learn from it.

In many of the self-evaluation schemata that you will find on the web (see Chapter 13) it is assumed that schools speak with a singular or limited voice. The Ofsted SEF, for example, is designed to eliminate paradox and provide a definitive statement of quality and effectiveness. On each of the given criteria or indicators a grade is agreed attended by definitive labels such as 'good' or 'outstanding'. In the final reporting what is concealed, however, is the very essence of self-inquiry – the contested views and appeals to evidence that lead to the eventual compromise. The real story to be told lies in the process by which knowledge is created and recreated, the beginning of insights to come rather than the extension of knowledge past.

Such a messy and conflicted story of a school's inner life is not amenable to the tidy requirement of external review, but for learning, developmental and improvement purposes it is indispensable. Managing the tension between self-evaluation for accountability on the one hand and for deepening self-knowledge on the other is a challenge familiar to schools in every administration in which quality assurance has been embraced. 'La qualita non e un punto da vista' (quality is not a point of view) was a subject for debate in a Spanish research[11] forum. It is a debatable proposition in many contexts where quality is the benchmark, but most significantly in the varied and heterogeneous mix of people, beliefs and values that is a school.

The vital process through which a school becomes a community of learners is what has come to be known as capacity-building. It is the means by which a school expands its intellectual and human potential. The term 'potential' as applied to individual pupils is a confining construct; when applied to a whole school community the inherent potential is similarly beyond realisation. Time, logistics, and external pressures conspire to limit what schools can do to liberate the inner resources of their pupils and staff, but tuning in to the range of voices through self-evaluation is the essential first step in transforming school life and learning.

Who tells the school's story?

Summative self-evaluation as represented by the Ofsted SEF is an attempt to bring together the most definitive version of the school's story, the best fit, the most adequate compromise of what the school 'is'. It is an unsatisfactory compromise among the many different stories that could be told. It is a point which Ofsted appears to concede when insisting on self-evaluation as ongoing and embedded, with the SEF as merely a shorthand summary. Built in as an integral aspect of the New Relationship is a requirement on schools to extend the franchise and involve a wider group of stakeholders.

Michael Fielding[12] asks schools to 'probe the rhetorics and realities of student voice', to consider:

- *Who* is allowed to speak?
- *To whom* are they allowed to speak?
- What language is encouraged/allowed?
- *Who* is listening?
- *Why* are they listening?
- *How* are they listening?

In 1998 Peter Coleman[13] conducted a study in Canada in which he brought together the voices of teachers, parents and pupils and examined the potential for schooling when these three voices were aligned. He described this latent potential as 'the power of three', alerting schools to a deeper form of listening, tuning in to the voices of those who matter most to school success. Rather than simply adopting a reflex position and sending out the annual questionnaire a staff might start with some key priori questions such as these.

- Who knows best about what happens in classrooms?
- Who is best placed to judge the quality and effectiveness of teaching?
- Who is best placed to judge the quality and effectiveness of learning?

Teachers?

The simple answer to all three of the above questions is likely to be 'well teachers, obviously'. Teachers are self-evaluators in their own classrooms. They employ a range of tools to determine the quality of learning and seek evidence on their own impact. They make intuitive and often explicit judgements on the quality of learning and on occasion ask pupils for feedback on their teaching. This is sometimes a teacher-initiated activity although it can too easily remain privatised within the bounds of their own classrooms. However, when the school climate is one that encourages teachers to share their insights there is a rich and powerful resource for telling the school's story.

Day by day, week by week and year on year teachers build a body of expertise that becomes a personal repository of ideas to draw on although in the past it has tended to be inaccessible to their colleagues. There is now a growing trend for teachers to observe one another and provide collegial feedback, learning opportunities for the observer as well as the observed. As such practice grows, observation becomes more systematic and less impressionistic. Teachers develop their own schedules or focus for what is to be observed and fed back which may start with lesson beginnings or endings, management of plenaries or questioning strategies, for example. These forms of inquiry and feedback are formative in nature but they also feed into the developing story of the school.

In evaluating the quality of a school the collective expertise of teachers, much greater than the sum of its individual parts, can all too easily be missed. Often teachers are involved at the periphery and what is offered to a visiting inspection team is the senior leaders' view, smoothing the wrinkles and ironing out the complexities of disparate voices. Exploiting the rich seam of teacher voice is a collective as well as individual activity. It is now increasingly common for a school to institute a cross-disciplinary group of staff such as a school improvement group, a teaching and learning group, or school evaluation group, entrusted with the task of evaluating, planning for and/or implementing change. A group of six to eight staff may include learning support assistants and other school staff such as caretakers or catering staff. Such a group, representing different experiences and viewpoints can serve as a reservoir of expertise and tools of evaluation and provide an important lever of school improvement.

A medium for expression of voice encompassing a whole staff is described in the following article:[14]

> At Barnwell School the challenge was to make practice visible on a large scale . . . . The strategic team constructed a mock-up of a brick wall on a notice board at the entrance to the staffroom . . . Whenever a teacher used a post-it to record an observation it would be posted on to the wall. Soon, posting observations took on a degree of competitiveness and it

was clear which departments were contributing most because of the colour of the post-its. As the wall grew, members of staff found that it was worthwhile to stop and read the post-its as they passed on their way into the staff room. These classrooms' observation therefore became the catalyst for cross-cutting conversation about teaching and learning.

Organisations are, says Chris Argyris,[15] generally less intelligent than their individual members. This is because they do not, as in the Barnwell example, find ways to bring to fruition the hidden capital of their staff.

The parents?

What do parents know about the inner life of classrooms? In fact, they often know a great deal but it is most typically through the medium of their own children. These tales out of school, brought home with vivid colour and emotion, offer a singular and selective lens through which to view learning and teaching but they can also give insights into learning to which a teacher is not privy. Parents will often ignore lurid stories, suspend disbelief, or, in some cases, react aggressively and demand to see a teacher. They are also likely to share anecdotes with other parents, at the school gate or through more formal channels such as the PTA or governing body. Parents have been viewed by teachers both as allies and as conspirators, sometimes accused of 'interfering' in their own children's education. Yet from a parental viewpoint there has been an investment in a child's learning for five critical years before a teacher even catches a glimpse of their child.

When parents and teachers meet in the context of parent evening, often held in the classroom, 'saturated with immaturity'[16], the teacher behind the desk and the parent perched on a low chair, there takes place an exchange of views about a child's behaviour, learning and persona. Exploring this *Essential Conversation*[17] in-depth Sara Lawrence Lightfoot describes the meeting as marked by decorum and politeness, wariness and defensive postures, both sides of the table 'wracked with anxiety'.

She describes these meetings as infused with histories on both sides of the table, occasions in which parents call up references to their own childhood experiences while teachers fall back on their adult experiences in the classroom.

> They sometimes lead to important breakthroughs and discoveries in the conversation, and at other times force an abrupt breakdown and impasse. But for the most part, these meta-messages remain hidden, inaudible, unarticulated. They are the raw, unvarnished subtext to the ritualized, polite, public text of the conversation.[18]

These interchanges are often an occasion for surprise that a child could be viewed so differently by a teacher, often more positively than expected. 'He is a different child at home' may often be said, and there is an almost literal truth to this as Judith Harris illustrates in her prize-winning book *The Nurture Assumption*.[19] Children become different people within their peer group, in the classroom, with their siblings and with their parents. She calls it the 'Cinderella syndrome'.

The involvement of parents tends to be restricted to surveys and questionnaires although group interviews or focus groups appear to be a growing trend. These formal mechanisms are not the only source by which a school can gain a parental perspective. Ongoing feedback through face-to-face conversation, telephone calls, letters to and from home, parent meetings and workshops all help to provide a parental perspective. The area in which parents have most to contribute is in relation to home learning, home study and homework. It is through their children's work in the home that parents can offer the most helpful insights to the school and the school can, in return, help parents to monitor or support their children's learning more effectively. A continually developing home–school dialogue is one of the most significant levers for enhancing learning and raising standards of achievement. For example, home learning logs in which pupils and parents jointly record their observations provides a bridge between school and home learning. In some special schools video recordings of children's learning in school is sent home and cameras provided for parents to record home learning which then travels back to school. These insights are not only valuable but essential if helping learning to travel from one context to another. As research has persistently demonstrated, it is only when there is traffic across that bridge that schools improve.

The GTC, which is the professional body for teaching, says parents are vital to supporting school improvement and argued for the government's New Relationship With Schools to include more consultation with both parents and pupils as part of school self-evaluation. GTC Chief Executive Carol Adams says:[20]

> With the New Relationship with Schools should come a new relationship with parents. Parents are vital to supporting the aims of schools and the work of teachers…We must find ways to better galvanize the valuable support that parents are able to offer, at the same time providing more satisfactory feedback to parents about pupils' potential and achievements.

The pupils?

When posed with the question 'Who knows best about what happens in classrooms?' heads and teachers will cite pupils as often as they cite teachers.[21] They are, after all, closest to the action, informed insiders with a close and detailed knowledge of the inner workings of school and classroom.

They are immersed every day and every period in its culture. While teachers, with a bird's eye view, are able to plane over a whole class and see patterns in classroom behaviour, pupils have a worm's eye view. They see the class and the teacher from where they habitually sit. They rarely get the overview which the teacher has but they see more of a hidden life of the classroom and above all, they are unique experts in their own feelings, frustrations and triumphs.

Pupils are the school's largest untapped knowledge source in a school, says SooHoo[22] 'the treasure in our very own backyard'. As he argues, a school which overlooks that intelligence source is inevitably poorer as a consequence. Much has been written[23] about pupil voice and about the role pupils can play as researchers into their own learning and as critical commentators on school life. Historically they have been the last to be consulted about school quality and effectiveness yet, as this developing literature attests, they may get closest to the heartbeat of the school and have the most compelling stories to tell. Those schools which do put pupils at the heart of the self-evaluation process have discovered just how rich pupils' insights can be and what can happen when that trapped energy is released. Teachers, almost unfailingly, testify to the honesty, fairness and acuity of pupils' views, giving them greater confidence in enlisting pupils in development planning and school improvement. Including their voice in self-evaluation can also be a risky business as they are usually fair but almost always honest critics. They challenge assumptions with counter evidence which may not always be immediately welcome. A Cambridgeshire teacher involved in the ESRC project on Consulting Pupils[24] about their learning describes six stages she went through with her class over a two to three-year period, a gradual maturing of their expertise so as to become collaborative commentators on learning and teaching. She described the process as evolving through six stages:

Stage 1. Delivering the curriculum. Fitting with the traditional role of the teacher as passing on curricular content from she who knows to those who do not know.

Stage 2. Beginning to discuss with pupils the purposes and objectives of what they were learning. What is the objective of your learning?

Stage 3. Involving pupils in considering and writing down indicators by which to measure their achievement. How will you know when you have learned something?

Stage 4. Involving pupils in assessing their own and others' work. How good is this piece of work? What criteria can be used to judge it?

Stage 5. Pupils become determiners of learning. They make decisions about when, how and what of classroom learning. What is the best way to organise learning in this classroom?

Stage 6. Collaborating with pupils as learning partners. What shall we do together to improve the conditions, processes and evaluation of our learning?

On what aspects of school and classroom life should students have a voice?

Jean Rudduck and Julia Flutter[25] suggest a continuum of voice which has at one end the 'comfort issues', toilets, lockers and school dinners, then moving through the discomfort issues of bullying, harassment and classroom disruption to the other end of continuum which reaches into the very heart and soul of school life – the quality of learning and teaching. They suggest that typically young people's voices are heard in descending order of frequency as one moves from the easy 'comfort' issues to the more contested issues of learning and teaching and staff selection. A decade ago it was brave schools that would involve children and young people in the process of selecting teaching staff. When experience of those leading edge schools showed just how insightful and fair those pupils could be, many schools followed suit, so that the heresy of 1996 is the orthodoxy of 2006.

Rudduck and Flutter suggest three key conditions for pupil voice to be heard together with two caveats:

Climate, marked by trust and openness, so that pupils are not anxious about reprisals if they comment critically on teaching, and will not be anxious if they acknowledge their difficulties in learning.

Positive perceptions of students and being able to see students differently and to believe that even their more difficult and disengaged pupils can be different.

Valuing of 'life' skills alongside academic achievement.

Equity. Hearing only the strident or articulate voices can make other students feel disenfranchised. One of the strengths of consultation is the opportunity to hear from the silent – or silenced – students and to understand why some disengage and what would help them get back on track.

Authenticity. Students are very quick to 'suss out' when consultation is tokenistic and will quickly tire of invitations to express a view on matters they consider to be unimportant or that are framed in a language they find alienating or patronising. Nor will they continue to express their views if doing so seldom results in actions that affect the quality of their school life.

What we have learned over the last decade is that pupils are not simply consumers of what schools and teachers put in front of them but share a responsibility in constructing their own learning and that of their peers, and can play a significant role in making their schools better places not just for themselves and their classmates but for their teachers too.

8 Learning in and out of school

Inspection and self-evaluation have traditionally confined their inquiries to school and classroom as if that was where the quality of pupil learning could be found and evaluated. The New Relationship and its embrace of Every Child Matters means that schools will now have to take a wider view of sites and contexts of learning. The advocacy of personalised learning raises the need to understand more about the nature of out of school learning, while learning in informal sites and through more formal provision in study support, is now at a premium. This chapter explores those issues and raises questions as to the compass of self-evaluation and the reach of inspection.

School as the site for learning

'My mother wanted me to have an education so she kept out of school', so said the anthropologist Margaret Mead, claiming, as did other luminaries such as Albert Einstein, that school had damaged their intellectual and emotional health. The Spanish author Gabriel Marquez who wrote 'I would give wings to a child but I'd let him learn to fly alone', was perhaps thinking of how much we underestimate the capacity of children to learn with minimal intervention or support. For some, perhaps many young people, learning to fly alone is a preferable alternative to the routinised approach to learning which they encounter in school. Mary Alice White captured this in her essay on 'doing school'.

> Imagine yourself on a ship sailing across an unknown sea, to an unknown destination. An adult would be desperate to know where he is going. But a child only knows he is going to school... The chart is neither available nor understandable to him... Very quickly, the daily life on board ship becomes all important... The daily chores, the demands, the inspections, become the reality, not the voyage, nor the destination.
> (Mary Alice White, 1971)

It is easy for children to become inured to the rituals of schooling, having lost the wide-eyed agility of their first encounter with that form of institutional life. It does not take long for that potentially rich and challenging world to become all too familiar and inevitable in its daily demands. The story is told of a 5-year-old returning home after the first day of school and being quizzed by his parents. 'How was it?' 'A bit funny but I suppose it was o.k.' 'That's reassuring', said his mother, 'You'll begin to like it the more you get used to it.' Surprised by his mother's reply the 5-year-old asks, 'What? I have to go back again tomorrow?'

Schooling may be a one-off event but it is one that lasts for ten or more years. It is a world of its own in which adults rule and children obey and questioning is restricted to a classroom routine in which pupils answer rather than ask questions and in which there are clear parameters around the kind of questions that it is legitimate to pose. What tends to remain beyond questioning are the very structures and cultural routines within which learning and teaching take place. The very essence of schooling has remained largely unchallenged by pupils since the invention of timetables, lessons, subjects, homework, tests, classroom layout, sanctions and rewards, hierarchies, permission to speak or act, restriction of language and behaviour and peer association and friendships, all of which come within the jurisdiction of authorised agents of the school.

'Agency' is the term used to denote a sense of authority to take the initiative, to think and act for yourself rather than at someone else's behest. The history of schooling has been one of fettering children and young people to the ritual demands of the institution, often blunting a sense of agency, personal authority and desire to learn.

Yet, schools matter. That was the triumphant message of school effectiveness studies in the late 1970s and 1980s.[1] It is at first sight a bizarre conclusion given the massive investment governments have made in school education over a century and an almost universal conviction that school is where you get an education. But it was a reassertion of the value of schooling, which had come under attack in the 1970s. In 1971 Ivan Illich published his blueprint for deschooling society, while Everett Reimer wrote an educational best seller *School is Dead* and Jonathan Kozol excoriated the Boston school system in his book *Death at an Early Age*. These often polemical tracts were written in a climate where doubt had been cast on the ability of schools to affect the predetermined patterns of success and failure which children brought with them from their homes and communities. 'Inequality',[2] a large and influential study by a Harvard team had concluded that school effects were marginal compared with the much more potent effects of family and community background, reinforcing an equally influential study five years earlier by James Coleman.[3]

While later studies of school effectiveness were able to demonstrate that some schools were significantly better than others in mitigating the influence of social class and family background[4], the effects proved to be marginal. Despite decades of school improvement initiatives and the range of government interventions, the gap in GCSE attainment levels by parental socio-economic group has changed little in the last ten years.[5] In 1992 the attainment gap (five or more GCSEs grade A* to C) between children with parents in managerial or professional occupations and those with parents in unskilled manual occupations was 44 percentage points. In 2002 it was

45 percentage points. In 2002, 77 per cent of young people in Year 11 in England and Wales with parents in higher professional occupations gained five or more A* to C grade GCSEs, nearly two and a half times the proportion for young people with parents in routine occupations (32 per cent).

The gap is explained not by differences in schooling but by social, economic, health and lifestyle factors, chronic illness, unemployment patterns, housing and amenities and mobility. Households in disadvantaged areas have less amenities, less space per person, higher incidence of dampness and associated ill health, susceptibility to break-in, proximity to street crime and high incidence of drug abuse. In 2001/02, 86 per cent of households in Great Britain in the highest income group had access to a home computer, almost six times as many as for households in the lowest income group. The gap was even wider for Internet connections.

There is a combination of factors whose impact is cumulative and powerful, transferred inter-generationally from parents to children. Behind the statistics lies something described as 'social capital', ultimately more telling than financial capital although clearly correlated. It is social capital that allows children from poor families to survive in their social milieu and achieve in the school context. Social capital has a number of key attributes – trust, social membership and access to networks, each of which are closely interrelated. Trust is measured by whether people have confidence in their neighbours, their peers or others who have an impact on their lives and well-being. Social membership is measured by the number of organisations, clubs, societies or social groups to which someone belongs and which decrease alienation and help to build a sense of trust. This is in turn linked to another central concept of social capital – networking. Formal and informal networks are accumulated when people interact with one another in local associations, in a range of informal and formal meeting places as well as in families, workplaces and their immediate neighbourhoods.

Social capital theorists[6] describe three forms of social capital – social bonding, bridging and linking capital. *Bonding social capital* is characterised by strong bonds, for example among family members or among members of the same ethnic group which help in 'getting by' in life. As peer bonds which young people develop can be anti-social and anti-educational, the more young people have opportunities to interact with adults the greater the likelihood of pro-social and pro-educational influences. *Bridging social capital* refers to more distant connections between people, characterised by weaker, more temporary links but in some ways more important than close strong links because they put people in touch with diversity of ideas, different ethnic groups, a broader range of models of thought and behaviour. *Linking social capital* is a process whereby connections are made with people in positions of power so that the ability to navigate through formal institutions such as school holds the key to survival and success.

As has been demonstrated by work within the National Youth Agency[7] 'doing school' successfully requires both young people and their parents to be able to engage successfully with hierarchies and authorities and to negotiate their path through school conventions. Young people from more privileged backgrounds owe much of their success to an ability to navigate the system with an understanding of the rules and with a safety cushion of home support. Grasping the complexity of this dynamic shows why it is futile to expect schools to compensate for society and unethical to pressurise teachers to compete as if there were an even playing field.[8]

The inherent weakness of school effectiveness research is that it has taken the traditional 'black box' school as a given and has not addressed the deeper and more vexed question of schooling as necessarily the best way for children to learn. The evidence[9] that schools can inhibit as well as promote learning has led to alternative forms of provision such as Steiner and Montessori schools and education in the home. The structure of conventional schools with their common curriculum and sequenced lockstep progress through a diet of subjects and assessments has been widely recognised[10] as inappropriate to the needs of many young people growing up in the twenty-first century. Yet the structure of schooling is bound tightly into a range of vested interests, powerful subject lobbies, teachers' organisations, government departments, quangos, private agencies who feed off the system, parental working patterns, the need for custodial care of young people whose presence in the community is a potential threat and much else besides. All of this leaves little room for manoeuvre let alone radical rethinking of educational provision. It is with this knowledge in mind that 'personalised learning',[11] the newest of the Emperor's clothes has to be situated and evaluated.

Personalised learning

Personalised learning is an important plank in the New Relationship. It is claimed[12] that rises in educational standards are attributable to individual learning styles, motivations, and needs coupled with rigorous use of pupil target setting, high quality assessment, well-paced and enjoyable lessons and support for pupils which extends well beyond the classroom. High-quality teaching, it is asserted, is based on a sound knowledge and understanding of each child's needs together with high expectations expressed in practical ways.

The New Relationship between the Department, local authorities and schools is seen as bringing a sharper focus to schools' endeavours and releasing greater local initiative and energy. Within that relationship personalised learning is designed to give schools more time 'to focus on what really matters'. As such 'it can only be developed school by school. It cannot be imposed from above.' Its three cardinal principles are to:

- nurture the unique talents of each pupil;
- achieve excellence and equity – the twin engines of progress;
- give every single child the chance to be the best they can be, whatever their talent or background.

It would be ungenerous to quibble with any of these aims or to argue with many of the key principles on which they rest. They are both highly ambitious and radical in implication. What, for example, might it mean to nurture the unique talents of each pupil? Can we take at face value the statement that schools should have time to 'focus on what really matters'? What evidence is there within mainstream schools to suggest that schools can cater to individual learning styles? Indeed is there any body of consensus as to what that means either in theory or in practice?

To turn these ambitious aims into reality five key processes are proposed:

1   Assessment for learning that feeds into lesson planning and teaching strategies, sets clear targets, and clearly identifies what pupils need to do to get there.
2   A wide range of teaching techniques to promote a broad range of learning strategies, facilitated by high-quality ICT that promotes individual and group learning as well as teaching.
3   Curriculum choice, particularly from the age of 14, and the development of subject specialism.
4   The organisation of the school, including the structure of the day and of lessons, using workforce reform to enhance teaching and learning and to ensure consistency.
5   Links to services beyond the classroom, involving the wider community and families, parents providing strong support; and the engagement of LEAs in the agenda set out in the Every Child Matters Green Paper.

These five principles, integral aspects of the New Relationship, have to be accommodated within the present conventions and the structures of the schooling which allow, only in a very limited sense, a genuine personalisation to the needs, proclivities or interests of the individual.

Construction sites

A collection of essays and research studies published under the title *Construction Sites*[13] illustrates some of the tensions between learning in the home and learning in the classroom. The site in which young people construct meaning from their experience is shown to be highly significant not only in the *what* and *how* of their learning but also in their very sense of identity. In one chapter Ward[14] describes how Marie's mother teaches her to survive in a racist society and school system. She teaches her children how to take a critical perspective, how to detect racial stereotypes, to understand how images shape perceptions and often distort the truth. Marie's mother instils in her daughter a desire to resist internalising other voices, those of the media or other stereotypical characterisations of African American people. Consistently through these accounts we see that what is learned in school fails to connect with lessons learned in the family. The evidence is that the academic self-esteem of black girls declines cumulatively through school and that for protection of self a school identity may be temporarily assumed. And boys too have their own struggles to overcome, as one Jewish student says[15]: 'You've got to leave some things at home to make it here. If you come to this school and bring the baggage of your home background, you'll likely meet with more failure than success.'

Our understanding of construction sites is taken further by accounts from a unique project known as the Learning School[16] in which we can perceive how far self-evaluation may extend its compass and impact.

The Learning School

The Learning School was the brainchild of, Stewart Hay, a teacher in a Shetland secondary school. The plan was to invite school students from a number of different countries to take a gap year from their studies to conduct a global self-evaluation project. The plan was for them as a group to spend four to six weeks in each of six different schools, in South Africa, Sweden, Scotland, Japan, Korea and the Czech Republic as visiting researchers, working alongside fellow students and with classroom teachers to research learning and teaching. In each location these young people would live with host families, in most contexts without a common first language and, in some cases, with no common linguistic ground at all. By travelling round the world on a single ticket and living off the hospitality and goodwill of host families project costs were projected to be minimal. Not only did the Learning School get off the ground as planned but building on the success of the first Learning School (LS1) six further cohorts followed in successive years.

Before embarking on their journey students spent an intensive two weeks familiarising themselves with research methods designed to ascertain the degree of students' engagement with learning in and out of school. As well as developing the tools of their research students were encouraged to keep weekly diaries, recording their personal reflections both on their work with schools and on their own developing thinking.

What these young people recorded in their diaries illustrated their view of the world, of other people and their sense of self as it became re-formed and redefined in the three primary contexts in which they lived over the course of nearly ten months. These were the schools in which they conducted their research, the host families they lived with for a period of four to six weeks and the peer group in whose close company they travelled, worked and spent their leisure time. As they described the impact of these new and unfamiliar contexts the impact on their learning was contrasted with their prior school experience. 'I have probably learnt as much in these 10 months as I did in 13 years of school. (Jolene)'[17]

A 16-year-old Korean student, described how for the first time he had found his own voice after ten years of school. Preoccupation with hard work, after hours cramming and swotting for exams, had left neither time nor incentive to think for himself nor to question received wisdom from his teachers.

For most of the students involved, the Learning School was their first extended disconnection from home. Many of them describe their sense of self as having been defined by parents, by school and by the peer group, all accidents of locality and propinquity. The greater the distance from the comfort zone of home the more the notion of 'home' gradually assumed new dimensions. A Swedish student, for whom home was hitherto the house in which she grew up in Malmö, now found an expanded and more ambivalent notion of home.

> This is my home, Malmö and the school is my home school and my home is my 'home-home' but now 'home' is something different. 'Home' was always where I lived with my mum and now home is also Logan's house because I stayed there, and Philippa's house, that's home as well. The Czech host sister and everything is the home, and the 'home' isn't clear now . . . .Home can be so many different things.[18]

With a broader perspective on self and with new insights into social values, home, community and national culture came to be seen through different eyes. Interviews reveal the extent to which students recognised the power of parental influence and how it had shaped and constrained their own views.

> When you have opinions and views, you realise your parents' influence. You do not notice usually how much your opinions are influenced by your parents. I did not think by myself and I used my parents. I should have my own picture.[19]

In this student's attribution of values to her mother's influence, there is also the implicit acknowledgement of room for dissent, a more hidden but perhaps equally powerful legacy. Interviews conducted by Learning School students with their international peers and parents document the power of parental expectation and reveal students' anxiety not to let their parents down, illustrating how powerful parental pressure can be in shaping ambitions for the future. These data also reveal the ways in which the weight of expectation not only shape identity in a positive sense but also through resistance and the resolve to be different from the older generation.

Parental voice is acknowledged by many of the young people as laying down a substratum of values with which they continue to struggle as they are exposed to the influence of different ways of being in other families and in the immediacy of the peer group with whom they spend a close and sometimes claustrophobic nine months. The study reveals individual lives lived in and through a kaleidoscope of sites, shifting daily from family to peer group to school classroom and back again, each new set of relationships requiring a different linguistic register and social protocol. In each situation self-concept is confronted by the novelty of the experience. Each new encounter required these young people to reframe their familiar self-conceptions and forced them to start a new form of negotiated identity. Having become comfortable with their new identities this proved to be simply a temporal respite, waiting for the next challenging situation to present itself.

It was in the context of South African townships that students faced the most profound culture shock and re-orientation of beliefs about self and society. Sophie's story as she told it to a Cambridge University audience was so moving in recollection that she struggled to distance herself from the experience. She had stayed with two host families, one in a 'coloured' community and the other in a 'black' township. The coloured family were poor and virulent in their dislike of black people in general. Knowing that after three weeks she would be staying with a black family it was hard to tread the line between respect for this kind family who had taken her in and tempering of racist views which she feared might prejudice her against the black family she would shortly live with.

> I remember that I was sitting in my room with my host sister and she asked me if I wanted to hear a joke, I said yes then she began to tell me a really racist joke and expected me to find it funny, how was I supposed to react to something like that? That was something that I found difficult to understand and cope with in South Africa.[20]

This experience was instrumental in helping Sophie reflect on her own prejudices, acknowledging her own ignorance as a root of bigotry and valuing such harsh experiences as an important 'lesson for life'.

For none of these young people had their school experience afforded them a meta perspective on their own learning or on the process of education. A predominant theme running through their accounts is the rediscovery of self, persistently returning to the evolution of individual and social identities. Their diaries, shared with researchers, reveal the continuing struggle to resolve the tensions between the 'I' of self, the 'us' of the peer group and the 'me' as defined by parents and teachers. It was their escape from the classroom that allowed them to stand back and reflect critically on their experience and to return to full-time education with new insights.

Perhaps not surprisingly many LS students had to deal with resistance from teachers on their return to school. They were now more challenging, less willing to passively accept what they were told, testing ideas more critically, less patient with oversimplification, more aware of the bigger picture. For some teachers the challenge to their own identity after twenty years or more of teaching had been a challenge too far.[21]

The most signal weakness of schooling has been its failure to understand what children and young people bring with them to schools and to consistently underestimate and undervalue the capacity of children to learn for themselves and with their peers. Sir David Winckley[22] tells the story from his days as a Birmingham head when he surprised himself by his own failure to acknowledge the unseen and unheralded gifts of his pupils. He describes coming into the assembly hall one morning to find a lad sitting at the piano playing classical music of a high technical order. Parodying his own reaction he describes the instant headmasterly response 'What do you think you're doing? Get to your class immediately', then catching himself to reflect on the wonderful hidden talent that had just become exposed, together with his own ignorance.

The hole in the wall

In 2001 researchers embedded a computer into a brick wall in an Indian village, connected it to the Internet and waited to see what would happen. They reported that within a few days most of the slum children were able to use the computer to browse, play games, create documents and paint pictures. This experiment, and others which followed in other Indian towns and villages were described by Mitra and Rana[23] as 'minimally invasive' because of lack of intervention by adults.

The success of children in using the computer led the researchers to conduct a controlled experiment, comparing children who had taken a computer course in grade 8 with students who had no instruction. The exam consisted of a practical, hands-on part with no instructional inputs plus an open book theory exam. Three groups of 12-year-olds took the exam, the experimental group who had no school instruction and two control groups, one with 20 hours formal teaching in class, the other with no formal teaching and no experience with computers at all. All the exams were conducted in Marathi, the language of instruction.

The experimental group did slightly better on the practical exam than their peers who had been systematically taught. Over 60 per cent of the untaught group were classified as 1st Class. When it came to the theory exam the experimental group fared less well than their tutored peers – 87 per cent as against 67 per cent – a creditable performance nonetheless given no previous exposure to theory or a computer vocabulary which they were meeting for the first time.

Minimally Invasive Education kiosks (MIE kiosks) were later set up in twenty-two rural and urban locations across India and similar results were reported. The researchers concluded:

> If given appropriate access, connectivity and content, groups of children can learn to operate and use computers and the Internet to achieve a specified set of the objectives of primary education, with none or minimal intervention from adults.

On the basis of these experiments they proposed that the curriculum could be divided into three bands:

1   A band that needs a human teacher who is conversant with the subject matter and teaching methodology.
2   A band that needs an assistant who is somewhat more knowledgeable than the learner.
3   A band that needs resources and a peer group alone.

Study support

These three themes play out in homework clubs, breakfast clubs, weekend schools, summer schools, the University of the First Age and other variants under the generic umbrella of 'study support', designed not only to complement classroom learning but to provide a different kind for children and young people to learn for themselves and with their peers.

Before 1990 the term 'study support' would have been unknown to all but a very small handful of schools. Although opportunities for young people to learn outside the classroom existed through extra-curricular provision and in the supplementary school movement within minority ethnic communities, the link with school learning was tenuous and the impact on school achievement had not been formally evaluated.

In 1996 The Prince's Trust, in partnership with Tower Hamlets and Sandwell LEAs and Merseyside Training and Enterprise Council, developed a programme to evaluate the effectiveness of study support. The study followed fifty-three schools over a three-year period to:

- ascertain the impact of participation in study support activities on the attainment, attitudes and attendance of a large sample of students in secondary schools serving disadvantaged areas;
- develop and disseminate models of good practice, through the support to schools of Critical Friends, and training events and publications.

Evidence, both from case studies and the authentic voice interviews, showed not only raised attendance and measurable gains in GCSEs for those who attended on a regular basis but, more significantly, a growth in confidence, self-esteem and renewed interest in learning. As the report concluded[24]:

> Engagement leads to a virtuous circle of experience of success, growth of self-confidence as a learner and so to further engagement in learning. Students become more self-regulated learners. Once a critical mass is reached this has an impact on the ethos of the school.

In May 1997, the potential for out-of-hours learning to contribute to the raising of levels of educational achievement was formally recognised. The DfEE publication '*Extending Opportunity: A National Framework for Study Support*' (DfEE, 1998) endorsed the term 'study support' as the generic descriptor for out-of-school-hours activities with a learning purpose. It reinforced the contribution to be made by youth services, public libraries, museums and galleries, arts and sports organisations, and business to supporting young people's learning. At the same time the government announced the creation of the New Opportunities Fund (NOF) as the sixth 'good cause' to disburse monies from the national lottery. Out-of-school-hours learning was designated as one of the recipients of the educational funds available, ultimately £205 million being made available across the United Kingdom.

Study support continues to thrive in many areas and in imaginative new guises, often without the financial support that had been forthcoming from

NOF or other sources. QUISS, the Quality Initiative in Study Support,[25] based at the University of Canterbury, offers:

- Consultancy and Services to support the development of programmes for learning outside the classroom.
- Access to national and regional networks that include experienced practitioners and academics.
- The QiSS Recognition Scheme including staff development programmes in support of the Scheme.
- Training Programmes for a range of professionals.
- Evaluation and Research.
- Advice and information.
- Case studies of good practice.

Study support continues to provide a laboratory for learning, not only for pupils but for teachers and other adults who have the opportunity to observe at first hand how young people learn and the conditions and relationships which promote learning. Without direct teaching, issues of control and discipline to worry about, teachers can stand back and reflect and, in their interventions, to start with where the individual learner is. For young people who made the commitment to learning 'out of school hours' they were rewarded by the pleasures of being with friends, a relaxed setting and different kind of relationships with their peers, their teachers and other adults. Self-evaluation is built integrally into Study Support as through The Code of Practice (described in more detail in Chapter 14) and requires connections to be made with the learning that transpires within the classroom.

Grasping the learning moment

Learning that matters and learning that sticks is often typified by its timing, by its receptivity and alertness to the learning moment. Spontaneous informal learning tends to be sporadic, often intense and deeply engaging. It is often 'just in time' learning to meet a felt need. By contrast schooling is impatient. It cannot afford to wait for the learning moment so it crams as much as it can into the span of the learning day. There is little prospect of the structures of schools changing in the foreseeable future as their custodial functions alleviate the burden on families, public services and the economy in general. If schools are genuinely to personalise learning, however, the rhythm and flow of learning opportunities will have to undergo some radical surgery and build some imaginative bridges with the experiential learning that children have too often in the past left at the school gate. That is an integral aspect of the New Relationship, the challenge to a broader conception of self-evaluation and inspection.

9 PLASCS, PATS, electronic PANDAS and other beastly inventions

This chapter explores the new world of data, breeding at a prodigious pace, and examines what data can and cannot tell us. It reminds us of the deeper question of purpose and warns that 'getting it off PAT' can also be inimical to good practice.

A group of visiting principals from the United States was bemused by a dinner conversation among their English hosts who were regaling one another with stories of Pandas and how they had recently become electrified. Only with some further explanation were the American guests relieved to discover that the cruel sport in question was one they were all too familiar with under another name, as they too were drowning in a sea of proliferating data. There is a new arcane language which has entered the educational discourse, a plethora of abbreviations, all of which carry deep significance to those for whom they have become a daily currency.

This is the new world of data, breeding at a prodigious pace, each new generation bringing new inventive ways of feeding the body politic. Data now travels back and forward between school and government agencies as a new form of currency. Schools supply the DfES with information on each pupil in their care in return for an expanded package of data on how these children and young people are performing relative to just about any benchmark that can be found.

So, annually in January or thereabouts, schools submit their PLASC (Pupil Annual School Census) data including date of birth, date of admission to the school, gender, ethnic group, first language, post code of the pupil's home and a unique pupil number identifier. In return they receive an 'Autumn Package' containing one PANDA, or to give its full title *Performance AND Assessment* data. With this large body of information available to DfES each aspect of a pupil identity may then be tabulated against their performance so that fine benchmarking can offer surprise or confirmation of performance, for example by a recently admitted summer born Somali girl whose first language is not English, living in an undesirable area of the city. No child is left behind in this annual harvest. Pupil Referral Units, General Hospital and Independent schools are required to complete a paper School Level Annual

School Census (SLASC) while Nursery schools have the option to complete either a PLASC return or a SLASC return.

'PLASC provides essential information needed to understand what's going on in schools and ensure that national policy is developed sensibly and appropriately', says the DfES,[1] while pupil numbers provide the basis for allocating funding to LEAs and to schools. This extensive national pupil database, and the publications which emanate from it, provide a cornucopia of data for researchers, while government departments, external agencies and all make use of this information for a variety of purposes.

From the school's point of view its purpose is to support headteachers and their governors in the process of target setting and school improvement and therefore, in response to requests from heads, distribution of PANDA reports in the autumn term allows schools to use the information as early in the school year as possible. The PANDA report is also described by DfES as 'a management tool to help school managers see how effective their school is in comparison with other schools'.

What's in a PANDA?

The Autumn Package, containing PANDA does two things. It provides national information to allow comparison and benchmarking plus individualised school data. So schools receive:

- National summary results.
- Tables of benchmark information to enable comparisons to be made with similar schools.
- Value-added information to enable comparison of pupils' relative progress.
- Optional activities designed to help teachers using comparative performance information for the first time.
- Supplementary information about your individual school together with 'easy to understand' judgements about how the school is doing in key areas.

Information in the PANDA report shows data held by the Government on schools and what becomes available to Ofsted inspectors when a school is inspected. There are three different types of PANDA report – for primary schools, secondary schools and special schools. The Ofsted website provides anonymous versions of each of these in order to familiarise a wider audience with the nature of the beast. The national summary results for a secondary school, for example, provides the following information:

- Percentage of all pupils, boys and girls entered for 5 or more GCSEs, achieving 5 or more A*-C, achieving 5 or more A*-G, achieving 5 or more A*-G including English and maths, entered for 1 or more GCSEs, achieving no passes in 2004.

- For subjects English, maths, science (any), drama, communications studies, classical studies, P.E, R.E, media studies, design and technology, information technology, business studies, home economics, geography, history, humanities, social science, music, modern foreign languages, art and design, English literature for entries, A*-C and A*-G.
- Recent trends in the percentage of all pupils, boys and girls entered for 5 or more GCSEs, achieving 5+A*-C, 5+A*-G, entered for 1 or more GCSEs, achieving no passes, any pass and average points score (capped) over the last five years.
- Divergence as a percentage from the National average for all pupils, boys and girls for English, maths and science.

The benchmark tables enable a secondary school to make more detailed comparisons of KS4 performance in any given year against national performance and as against similar schools. 'Similar' schools are banded according to the percentage of pupils known to be eligible for free school meals and prior attainment at Key Stage 2 and 3.

Accompanying the PANDA report is an annexe called the National Summary Data Report (NSDR) containing guidance and an extensive range of information collated from inspection evidence, allowing comparisons such as pupil–teacher ratios, unit costs and patterns of strengths and weaknesses in schools nationally. Each package also contains activities designed to help those looking at comparative data for the first time, providing a step-by-step approach to each analysis. The activities also provide a list of key questions designed to help governing bodies identify key areas for improvement.

While the PANDA report is confidential and Ofsted will not publish it without permission, it is available to the LEA and the DfES. Schools themselves are free to share the information with their staff and distribute their PANDA reports as they see appropriate.

From 2005 onwards PANDA reports were issued electronically via the PANDA website (ePANDA). Schools without access to the internet are able to request a paper copy. The electronic version comes on a CD ROM and schools can input their own data, allowing schools and governing bodies to undertake various 'what if' exercises and help them plan for the future.

Table 9.1 illustrates for a primary school the range of data that is held for each individual pupil at Key Stage 2.

Getting it off PAT

The introduction of the Pupil Achievement Tracker (PAT) software has allowed schools and LEAs to import and analyse pupil performance data against national performance benchmarks published in the Autumn Package. School staff can now use value-added data to compare progress of individual pupils or groups of pupils between key stages in comparison with progress nationally. The PAT also provides a tool specifically designed to assist schools

Table 9.1 Data table for primary school (Key Stage 2)

Background information	• Name, address and telephone number • School type/category • Age range • Charter mark (if applicable) • Total number of pupils on roll (all ages) • Total number and percentage of pupils with statements of SEN • Total number and percentage of pupils with SEN, without statements • Number of pupils on roll aged 11
Value-added measure	• KS1-KS2 VA measure based on progress between KS1 and KS2 • Percentage of eligible pupils included in the VA measure (coverage indicator)

Key Stage 2 Test results	• Total number of pupils eligible for assessment under the 2005 Key Stage 2 arrangements on roll at the time of the tests
	• Percentage of pupils in the school for the whole of their KS2 education (mobility indicator)
	• Number and percentage of pupils eligible for KS2 assessment with statements of SEN
	• Number and percentage of pupils eligible for KS2 assessment with SEN, without statements
	• *English*
	  – Percentage of eligible pupils achieving Level 4 or above
	  – Percentage of eligible pupils achieving Level 5
	  – Percentage of eligible pupils who were absent or
	  – unable to access the test
	• *Mathematics*
	  – Percentage of eligible pupils achieving Level 4 or above
	  – Percentage of eligible pupils achieving Level 5
	  – Percentage of eligible pupils who were absent or unable to access the test

Average point score	• *Science*
	  – Percentage of eligible pupils achieving Level 4 or above
	  – Percentage of eligible pupils achieving Level 5
	  – Percentage of eligible pupils who were absent or
	  – Unable to access the test
	Points allocated for each pupil's results using equivalences adopted in the Autumn Package
	Pupils that are absent or unable to access the tests are not included in the calculations for the average point score

Year on year comparison	• Aggregate of the three test percentages for 2002 • Aggregate of the three test percentages for 2003 • Aggregate of the three test percentages for 2004 • Aggregate of the three test percentages for 2005
Absence rates	• Total number of pupils of compulsory school age on roll for at least one session • Percentage of pupil sessions (half days) missed through authorised absence • Percentage of pupil sessions (half days) missed through unauthorised absence

in target setting for individual pupils, departments and the school as a whole. The PAT uses the following national data:

- National summary results and trends.
- KS4 benchmark information based on KS2 prior attainment or KS3 prior attainment and on free school meals.
- Value-added data for KS2 to KS4 and KS3 to KS4.

The PAT can then generate tables which provide data at whole school level in relation to raw scores and value-added scores correlated with percentage of pupils eligible for free school meals, the school's previous KS3 results, and in relation to all schools. All tables cover mainstream, maintained schools in England with GCSE results in 2004, and exclude independent schools, special schools and pupil referral units (PRUs).

Value-added Graphs allow a school to evaluate its effectiveness for the school overall and for different groups of pupils. The DfES helpfully provides this example based on a sample class of five pupils (Table 9.2).

The inclusion of a wider range of qualifications has required the adoption of a new scoring system, developed by the QCA. The QCA's new scoring system has led to significant changes to the way the average points score is calculated. In the old system for example, a GCSE at grade G was worth 1 point; in the new system it is worth 16 points. An A* in the old system was worth 8 points and in the new system is worth 58 points. The new system has also reduced the ratio between grades. Table 9.3 illustrates thee new grade points.

The data for the five pupils shown in Table 9.2 can be plotted on a line graph as in Figure 9.1. This shows a median line to represent the 'average' as in the pupil sitting halfway between highest and lowest score with the two adjacent lines representing 25 per cent (or the quartile) of scores which fall above and the 25 per cent which fall below the median. This leaves, of course a further 25 per cent in below all three lines – the bottom quartile, (e.g. Aziza) and 25 per cent of pupils above all three lines in the top quartile (e.g. Trisha).

More information is available on the Achievement and Attainment Tables website: (www.dfes.gov.uk/performancetables) and for more details on

Table 9.2 Five exemplary pupils

Pupil	Key Stage 3 Level			KS3 Average points	Capped GCSE Points score (Best 8 GCSEs)
	English	*Maths*	*Science*		
Mick Jones	6	7	7	43	218
Trisha Baines	B	A	A	21	226
Joshua De Souza	5	6	5	35	320
Natasha Clarke	7	6	7	43	460
Aziza Paris	5	N	4	30	124

Table 9.3 The revised points system

Grade	Points	
	Full GCSE	Half GCSE
A*	58	29
A	52	26
B	46	23
C	40	20
D	34	17
E	28	14
F	22	11
G	16	8
U	0	0

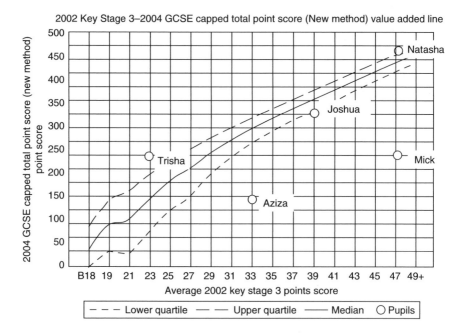

Figure 9.1 Key stage scores and the value added line.

GCSE, GNVQ and other equivalent qualifications the web link is http://www.dfes.gov.uk/performancetables/nscoringsys.shtml#sc.

The Fischer Family Trust

Many schools now complement the DfES data with information from The Fischer Family Trust. Its database which now contains performance information on over 10 million pupils in England and Wales together with a range of analytic tools to support self-evaluation and target setting. The

Trust has recently contributed a range of background materials to include in an Ofsted training CD, in due course to be made available to schools through the Ofsted website. Called 'Interpreting Data', the CD focuses upon the data analyses currently provided in the Performance and Assessment (PANDA) report, and includes reference materials for some of the different analyses that schools use, including those from Fischer Family Trust. Data, support materials and much else can be downloaded from www.fischertrust.org.

The value-added conundrum

Value-added data is somewhat of a minefield and may cover, as well as uncover, a multitude of sins. A simple measure of value-added data for an individual pupil shows the difference between where a pupil was at a given point and when he or she is at a later point, for example, between KS2 and KS3. This is simple VA based on one measure. However, Contextual Value-Added (or CVA) takes account not only of prior attainment, but also a number of other pupil and school characteristics associated with performance differences that are deemed to be outside a school's control. In other words, trying to hold all the external variables constant assumes that one can then get a purer measure of what the school is actually adding, so allowing a teacher to gauge expected performance and set targets accordingly.

At school level the complexities of VA are conflated further to render a school-level value-added score. The aggregation of pupil-related factors to add to prior attainment include gender, ethnicity, age in year, special educational needs (SEN), Free School Meals (FSM) and a postcode-based measure of affluence or deprivation, English as an additional language (EAL) status, mobility, and looked after children status. The published data will show an average figure of prior attainment plus the range or within school variation. While it may be claimed, tenuously, that a pupil level value-added score can be put to formative purposes, such is the complexity of the CVA primer, the justification for its use is as an indicator for normative comparison against other schools.

Through PANDAs and PATS, CVA data is already being made available to schools, their LAs and SIPs for SSE and improvement planning, and will continue to be refined as the model is developed. The Government's intention is to pilot secondary school CVA indicators (KS2–4 and KS3–4) so that in 2006 they can be published in the Secondary Tables while piloting primary school CVA indicators (KS1–2) in 2006 so that they can be in the published Primary Tables in 2007.

Questions of purpose

It is apparent from these quotes that the PLASC and PANDA data serve at least two masters. Schools willingly, or less willingly, provide vital personal data on each of their pupils so that they themselves can be held to account for the performance of those pupils by their political masters, and are thereby complicit in feeding performance tables and parental choice. At the same time the data supplied by DfES is used to set pupil and school-level targets and to provide a database which will inform teaching and learning. While it may be argued that these disparate aims are not in conflict, they are not easily reconcilable either. There is now a substantial body of opinion and evidence[2] that formative and accountability data are uncomfortable bedfellows and that indicators can pervert the cause of learning.

In fact, we can infer at least six different kinds of putative functions of the data:

- To provide data for research studies
- To inform policy making
- To hold schools accountable
- To provide information for parental choice
- To inform whole school planning and improvement strategies
- To provide formative data for teachers.

The least contentious of these is for research purposes, since researchers, at least good ones, problematise their data, raising and nullifying hypotheses and, as often as not arriving at inconclusive findings. More contentious is how these same data are used to inform policy-making, which eschews some of the caveats that researchers would bring to it. Policy-makers are famously intolerant of researchers' equivocation, preferring the crispness of definitive answers and 'hard' numbers. Not unrelated to this is the third use of these data – to hold schools to account. As has been repeatedly shown,[3] despite value-added measures, it is schools in the most disadvantaged of areas that are most likely to be called to account for underachievement. Using these same measures as a basis for parental choice compounds the felony as it is the most educated and motivated of parents that add value to a school, so by their opting out of low attaining schools it perpetuates a downward spiral from which schools find it almost impossible to escape.

The OECD's 2004 PISA Report[4] concludes that many of the aspects of educational disadvantage are not amenable to education policy and that it is only in the longer term with a rise in the educational achievement of parents and wider economic development that the attainment gap will be reduced. This is not, however, simply a counsel of despair as one of main messages from the 2004 report is that the closer policy and practice is to the individual learner, the greater the likelihood of impact. This means teachers having a sensitivity to students' background, knowing where students are in their learning, and schools identifying ways of supporting students in an internal school climate conducive to engagement with learning, together with external climates which sustain learning.

What schools can do is examine the wide variation in performance within their own organisations. The OECD reports that variation in performance *within* British schools is four times greater than that between schools. Even when social background factors are removed, variation is greater in British schools, than in almost any other developed nation.[5] Tackling this has been described by Richard Harrison, formerly of the DfES,[6] as 'the greatest educational challenge of our time' implying that it is within the power of schools to reduce the disparity of pupils' experience of success.

Working with a group of pilot schools NCSL is helping them investigate ways of dealing with variation and developing new approaches to both identify and reduce it. The participants are also exploring ways of sharing their findings with schools nationally and are developing a toolkit to support other school leaders in tackling variation within their schools. Being aware of the variation between the highest and lowest achieving pupils within the school is a first step. The next and most important step is to begin to explore some of the factors that may correlate, or begin to explain, the reasons for that variation. For example, in one secondary school (Dartmouth Community College) whose story is told on the NCSL website[7] KS4 Heads of Department spent considerable time analysing the previous year's results and trying to identify trends in pupil performance. Three key influences on students' GCSE grades proved to be:

- Attendance: pupils who regularly attended lessons
- Completion of coursework and homework: pupils who were conscientious about deadlines
- Curriculum content: Pupils who made the decision to reduce the number of exam courses they were following and focus on core subjects.

While such findings are perhaps not greatly surprising they do offer some evidence rather than simply guesswork and can inform both school and classroom practice. In South Dartmoor Community College this was only the beginning of a larger story leading to teachers identifying and supporting students more effectively and tailoring support strategies more appropriately.

It is also important to bear in mind that data can mislead as well as inform and that the danger is particularly acute when there is too much data or when data carries with it high stakes takes consequences. The counsel therefore is to remember that data can be seductive. It can, by weight of numbers, carry with it an apparent authority, especially given its provenance with the statistical offices of government. The advice for every member of school staff is to approach the use of data with care and discernment, taking care not to allow this plethora of data to marginalise other, equally or more important, information or divert staff from other perhaps more critical priorities.

For more information see the DfES Achievement and Attainment Tables website, www.dfes.gov.uk/performancetables, and Statistical Services website, www.dfes.gov.uk/rsgateway, for further details.

10 Every Child Matters?

The Children Act and the ensuing publication of Every Child Matters (ECM) promises to radically change the nature of inspection and self-evaluation. It extends the boundaries of the school and the task of leadership, placing an extended responsibility on schools for effective liaison and collaboration with other agencies. This chapter examines the five 'outcomes' of ECM and their implications for the work of schools and teachers.

Every Child Matters. It is, like any truism, hard to dispute. Yet the need to assert it points to something that has been deeply missing in quality assurance within the old relationship. Its publication is also curiously coincidental with the American policy *No Child Left Behind*, the policy under the Bush administration which has also apparently rediscovered education as a mission to all children. Both English and American documents stem from a similar source, that is, concern over the measured gap between the highest and lowest achievers with the tackling of that disparity represented as the responsibility of individual schools. The evidence of between school and within school variance[1] is enough evidence for politicians to convince themselves that schools can make a substantial difference and be held to account for raised standards of performance.

Like its American counterpart *Every Child Matters* is not a soft-centred liberal document but one that actually carries high stakes consequences for schools. What it does acknowledge, however, is that achievement is a more far-reaching notion than test scores and that schools are not solely responsible for pupil outcomes. It presents the kinder face of policy-making as pursuing a child-friendly agenda, its five key 'outcomes' derived from consultation with young people themselves. The subtitle of the document *Change for Children* is an explicit acknowledgement that there is an urgent need for a new relationship, one which reaches out to other services for children and families. It places an extended responsibility on schools for effective liaison and collaboration with other agencies. The following description of the key elements of ECM requires a close reading of the vocabulary and register of policy literature and critical appraisal of the potentially far-reaching implications for schools as well as other services.

The five outcomes are at the heart of the 2004 Children Act which provides the legislative underpinning for *Every Child Matters*. These are:

- staying healthy
- enjoying and achieving
- keeping safe
- contributing to the community
- social and economic well-being.

Every Child Matters: Change for Children sets out a national framework for 150 local programmes of change to be led by local authorities and their partners along with a more detailed Outcomes Framework for Inspectorates[2] and other partners 'to inform local needs analysis and the monitoring of progress towards priority targets and indicators'.

The *National Service Framework for Children, Young People and Maternity Services* (NSF) makes it the responsibility of everyone and everybody 'delivering services for children and young people' to improve outcomes whether in childcare settings, schools, health services, social care, youth services, the police and criminal justice system, the voluntary and community sector and cultural, or sports and play organisations.

In realising this Local Authorities have a responsibility to bring together local partners through Children's Trust arrangements. These have the following essential components:

- Professionals enabled and encouraged to work together in more integrated front-line services, built around the needs of children and young people. This means both high-quality universal services such as early years and childcare provision, personalised learning in schools and a wider range of opportunities and support for young people. It also implies effective targeted and specialist services such as services for children with disabilities, for those looked after by local authorities, or young people engaging in offending behaviour or substance misuse.
- Delivering more integrated services requires new ways of working. A Pay and Workforce Strategy set out the action needed nationally and locally to help shape and deliver the workforce of the future.
- Common processes designed to create and underpin joint working, supported by a Common Core of skills and knowledge, a Common Assessment Framework and improved practice in information sharing.
- A planning and commissioning framework which brings agencies and their resources together where appropriate and ensures that key priorities are identified and addressed through local needs analysis and the development of a Children and Young People's Plan.
- Strong inter-agency governance arrangements, in which shared ownership is coupled with clear accountability, including the development of Local Safeguarding Children Boards.

- Regional Change Advisers and other strategic advisers based in Government Offices with a key role in working with local authorities and their partners to support the development of Children's Trust arrangements. The Government, working with a wide range of national partners, provides leadership support and development. Progress is monitored and reviewed through an improvement cycle for children's services, including the development of Annual Performance Assessment based on the Outcomes Framework and Joint Area Review.

In addition to resources devoted to improving services to children and young people, specific resources are being made available to support the *Every Child Matters* programme, including £22.5 million in 2006–7 and £63 million in 2007–8 to help local authorities implement change.

The Government is developing further ways of communicating to ensure that everyone involved knows what ECM means for them. *Working with voluntary and community organisations to deliver change for children and young people*, published alongside *Every Child Matters* sets out how the Government intends to work with the voluntary and community sectors in delivering this agenda.

This broader encompassing agenda has implications for schools, governors, headteachers, teaching and support staff, for parents and for students.

For schools it means closer collaboration with their communities and the agencies which serve those communities. This will mean a continuing move towards extended schools which will become the hub for all children's services in each local authority, offering services such as social care, healthcare and childcare. In Scotland, known as 'new community schools', these began in 2000, inspired by the American model[3] of 'the full service school'. The notion of 'full' service signals a shift from the partial service of classroom teaching to a one-door entry that leads into the whole range of services which a family might need. The one-door entry obviates the frustrating, time-consuming and ultimately self-defeating process of shuttling between one agency and the next, each conveying a weary disinterest in issues which fall outside their bailiwick.

For governors there is a statutory duty to establish a policy and procedure for safeguarding and promoting the welfare of children, a set of responsibilities which extend beyond the immediate boundaries of the school building. Governors will have to ensure that child protection arrangements reflect guidance issued by the Secretary of State, reviewing policies, including health and safety, bullying and providing for children with medical needs, as well as children with other social and emotional needs.

For headteachers the implications reach well beyond the school precincts as heads are the first point of contact with directors of other services who need to develop collaborative strategies at the highest level. Aspects of this liaison have to be delegated, as heads do need to attend to the immediate business of leading their schools. They need however to be familiar with the statutory responsibilities, the professional values and the working protocols of other services. And it is down to them to take a lead in establishing communication channels which allow for swift and spontaneous contact as the occasion requires.

For *teaching and support staff* there are professional development implications, for example, information and training on child protection issues, sensitising staff to indicators and symptoms of special needs. Staff also need to be attuned to the work of other agencies, their professional values and working practices and be open to challenge about their own practice. There will be an increasing need for staff to share information and collaborate with childcare professionals regarding individual pupils. The Government argue that the changes should not increase teachers' workloads but should free them to teach. Where there are well-established procedures and prescient leadership this may be the case. Without skilful management, sound infrastructure and appropriate support the challenge for teachers and support staff should not be underestimated.

Local authorities are the body charged with making this work. Putting the needs of children and families first and the logic of joined up services is unarguable but there is not a lot of encouragement so far as to practices which exemplify a smooth articulation and delivery of services. In Hertfordshire, one of the first authorities to move to integrated children and family services, its then CEO Ray Shostak used the case study of Carole and her family (Figure 10.1) not only to bring home the absurdity of multiple and unco-ordinated interventions but to highlight the nature of the mountain to be climbed.

The likelihood of any family being able to manage this nexus of relationships, let alone a family or lone parent in disadvantaged circumstances, is slim. The potential benefits to children and families of a one-door access become obvious but nowhere has it yet proved quite that simple. The history of inter-agency work is one beset with problems – differences in values, traditions and working

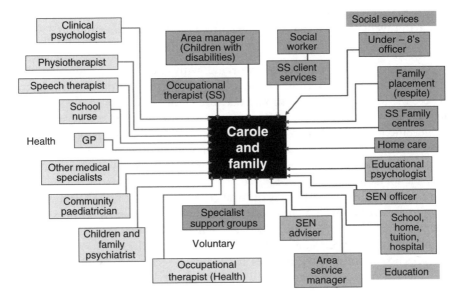

Figure 10.1 Carole, her family and social/educational agencies.

practices, territorial disputes and micropolitics[4] and, while the intention of ECM is both ambitious and right, the implications for self-evaluation and inspection are far reaching and not easily solved by rhetorical gloss.

Inspection

The grand plan is to move to an integrated inspection framework for children's services (including education) led by Ofsted, reporting on the range of local authority services. These are judged separately as well as how effectively they are working together. The Education Secretary could, in his or her wisdom, order a joint review of children's services by two or more of the following watchdogs: the Chief Inspector of Schools, the Commission for Social Care Inspection, the Commission for Healthcare Audit and Inspection, the Audit Commission, the Chief Inspector of Constabulary, the Chief Inspector of Probation.

The mechanism for judging how these services to children (including schools) are working is through Joint Area Reviews (JARs). These reviews take the place of separate inspections of councils' education and children's social care services and are intended to cover the range of services provided in the local area. Evidence from other inspections, such as in schools and residential settings, all contribute to the overall coverage. The focus of JARs is on how those services, both singly and in concert are working locally to 'improve outcomes'. So, the guidelines[5] suggest:

- Targeted inspection activity explicitly around clear outcomes for children, and focussed on the user, unconstrained by service boundaries.
- Inspection guided by assessment of all universal, targeted and specialist services in so far as they relate to children.
- Arrangements made for the effective coordination of inspection activity to prevent duplication and to reduce burdens and pressures on those inspected.

The vision is one of agencies working with such close integration and harmony, that in measuring a pupil's outcomes it will be difficult to detect where the joins are and who should take the credit. This should spell the end for league tables, the basic flaw of which is the attempt to separate out achievement as if it floated free of context and efficacy of public services. Inspection of outcomes, as detailed in Figure 10.2, illustrates graphically how problematic it is, however, to pin down both the locus of accountability and the locus of improvement.

In analysing the effectiveness of local cooperation and integration, young people are to be given a direct say in how the provision of services affect them. *The Framework for Inspection of Children's Services* sets out principles as to the purpose, coverage, conduct, reporting and quality of children's services inspections. The principles are based on recommendations, applying to inspection generally, contained in the report by the Office of Public Services Reform.

The extent to which schools enable learners to be healthy	Delete as appropriate
Learners are encouraged and enabled to eat and drink healthily	**Yes/No/NA**
Learners are encouraged and enabled to take regular exercise	**Yes/No/NA**
Learners are discouraged from smoking and substance abuse	**Yes/No/NA**
Learners are educated about sexual health	**Yes/No/NA**
The extent to which providers ensure that learners stay safe	
Procedures for safeguarding learners meet current government requirements	**Yes/No/NA**
Risk assessment procedures and related staff training are in place	**Yes/No/NA**
Action is taken to reduce anti-social behaviour, such as bullying and racism	**Yes/No/NA**
Learners are taught about key risks and how to deal with them	**Yes/No/NA**
The extent to which learners make a positive contribution	
Learners are helped to develop stable, positive relationships	**Yes/No/NA**
Learners, individually and collectively, participate in making decisions that affect them	**Yes/No/NA**
Learners are encouraged to initiate, participate in and manage activities in school and the wider community	**Yes/No/NA**
The extent to which schools enable learners to achieve economic well-being	
There is provision to promote learners' basic skills	**Yes/No/NA**
Learners have opportunities to develop enterprise skills and work in teams	**Yes/No/NA**
Careers education and guidance is provided to all learners in Key Stage 3 and 4 and the sixth form	**Yes/No/NA**
Education for all learners aged 14–19 provides an understanding of employment and the economy	**Yes/No/NA**

Figure 10.2 Inspecting for improvement (2003).

Self-evaluation

In theory, *Every Child Matters* should not make any difference to schools in which self-evaluation is well embedded in the day-to-day work of staff and students. In such schools there are monitoring and evaluation procedures for bullying and harassment, for ensuring safety and well-being, for keeping in

Outcomes	Sources of evidence	Tools of inquiry
Engage in decision-making and support the community and environment		
Engage in law-abiding behaviour in and out of school		
Develop positive relationships and choose not to bully or discriminate		
Develop self-confidence and successfully deal with significant life changes and challenges		
Develop enterprising behaviour		
Parents, carers and families promote positive behaviour		

Figure 10.3 Probing the evidence base: a starter for discussion.

touch with vulnerable and disaffected children and young people, together with outreach strategies for keeping in touch with families and other local agencies. Feedback loops allow a flow of information between home, school and community. The tools of evaluation are in the hands of children as well as staff, not reliant on once-in-a while surveys but employing ongoing vigilance, record keeping and diarying for example.

This does not preclude more formalised data collection as the occasion demands, a survey, a response form following an event, a snapshot spot check administered by pupils in classrooms, playgrounds or in the wider community. Criteria detailed in *Every Child Matters* may also be explicitly addressed by using a form such as the one illustrated in Figure 10.3 as a starter for discussion around what might constitute evidence, thinking creatively about how evidence could be found and used to the wider benefit of students, staff and parents.

A case study

The following account written by a headteacher illustrates a partnership approach.

Four years ago, Cardwell School was in special measures. The turning point came when an airgun pellet came through the window of my office during a meeting. I thought 'either I'm going to give up or I'm going to do something that makes a difference'. But how? So many things were wrong. I began a strategy that eventually formed the Cardwell wheel.

It is a way of putting all the different elements together so that, at every stage, learning within school is connected to the community. It has become 'government speak' but the reality is what you do within the school to connect with families.

Take literacy. In Early Years, the children were coming in at a level where they could not communicate, they did not have the language for survival, the language for living. I sent out questionnaires to families. They were still beating my door down but at least I was asking them what they wanted. They wanted a one-stop shop, a place they could be proud of – which was great, because that is how I felt.

I got Sure Start to come in with speech and language therapists. I won a bid from DfES for two nursery nurses to work on speaking and listening with young children. It has made a massive difference – they can manage conflict, communicate feelings and learn independently and co-operatively. It is quite a joy to go in there now.

Parents come in on courses. We buddy up parents who speak similar languages (twenty-seven at last count). We have Family Liaison workers and a family therapist. There has been a lot of hunting and gathering for money, trying to get a whole community so that children feel school is a stable and exciting place to be.

Overall, it has been a success story. SATS results have gone up, our value-added is incredibly good. I do not do exclusions. Parents and children do French together. We have a big new nursery and in January 2006 will have lots more things for the community.

Reading on and between the lines

A concern for safety, enjoyment, excellence and well-being were not recently invented. These have for long been at the very core of teachers' concerns, if at times observed in the breach. Before the invention of ECM there were schools using self-evaluation tools to gather information on such things as safety, enjoyment, life skills and well-being.

As with all such manifestos, the ECM documentation requires a careful documentary analysis, unpicking the use of terminology and phraseology, perceiving what lies beneath the overt content and what a new school-community relationship really means for practice. Such a critical analysis might begin with the framing of the four key areas as 'outcomes'. The reasons for this are not hard to find. Within a general policy thrust premised on outcomes, 'processes' would be seen as an unacceptable second best to 'hard' attainment measures. Yet, patently, being healthy, staying safe and enjoying learning are not outcomes at all but ongoing and developmental, and intrinsic to what Jerome Bruner describes as *The Process of Education*.[6]

Accordingly, the five ECM outcome status within the New Relationship carries with it the implication that these aspects of children's well-being can no longer be taken for granted but need on the one hand, to be subject to measurement both by self-evaluation and by Ofsted inspection, and on the other, to take account of the school's widening remit to collaborate with other services to children and young people.

The wider responsibility placed schools has also be contexualised within government policy on workforce remodelling and what is described as 'modern professionalism', lying at the heart of New Labour commitment to reforming public services. Mark Smith[7] writing on behalf of Infed (a watchdog organisation on informal education) writes:

> The basic concern is, on the one hand, to make those working in public services more disposed to the implementation of government policies (rather than what they might discern as being right for the individual, group and community). On the other hand, there is a desire to contain costs. The result has been an attempt to remove areas of professional discretion (through the implementation of procedures, common assessment frameworks and the like); to shift responsibility for the 'delivery' of key elements of education to those less expensive and less skilled practitioners (the use of the word 'delivery' here immediately transforms education from a process to a product); and to encourage flexible working patterns.

The concern expressed here is about the further restrictions that policies, however apparently well intentioned, affect those who work with children, including teachers. Government documents and Ministerial speeches are quick to add that the new school-community relationships will not increase teachers' workloads. This is to miss the point as well as being largely untrue. If there is to be a genuinely new relationship the implications must be radical. New ways of thinking and collaborating cannot simply bypass teachers and allow them to get on with teaching, as if teaching were some insulated activity disconnected from learning and the multiple contexts of learning. The inherent fallacy is that teachers are apparently expected to continue to simply 'deliver' the curriculum while above and around them others take care of the strategic matters and the fallout of inclusion policies.[8] If schools are to be genuinely 'full service' and integral to a child and family service, how can teachers liaise with other professionals without increasing their workload? How can inclusion policies work without some fundamental changes in teachers' conditions of work, expertise and professional development? How can government attune itself more intelligently to the needs and priorities of teachers and the massive implications of a paradigm shift in the nature of school education? Time and experience on the ground will ultimately tell if ECM is a liberating or constraining framework.

More information is available on www.everychildmatters.gov.uk, including copies of the documents, downloadable presentations and a forward look at forthcoming publications and consultations.

11 The SEF and how to use it

A school always prepared for inspection, but not always preparing for inspection, is a self-evaluating school.

(Leicestershire County Council)

The summer of 2005 saw a flurry of activity as many English headteachers spent their summer holidays hurriedly completing the school Self Evaluation Form (the SEF) in case of a drop-in visit by HMI. This chapter explores different ways in which the SEF may be used to the schools' advantage, reiterating the Chief Inspector's message that the SEF is NOT self-evaluation, and that schools can find other ways to tell their own stories.

The Self-Evaluation Form, now affectionately known as the 'SEF', is a critical document in the new inspection process. While it may be an insufficient instrument to capture the vibrant nature of a school's life, getting it wrong will be used by Ofsted as a contra-indication of good leadership and management. Its introduction in the summer of 2005 provoked something approaching mass hysteria as heads due for inspection hurried to meet the deadline for completion of the SEF. The advice that it was not compulsory was met with general disbelief. A glimpse into how schools went about the task provides a trail of clues as to a school's culture and approach to self-evaluation.

Who did it?

Mr Smith on the beach with his laptop

Mr Smith, alerted to the possibility of an Ofsted, given the last visitation four years ago, devoted his summer holidays to filling in the SEF including a few days on a Spanish beach. Although recognising that this was not the ideal way to proceeds it was a pragmatic response to a potential crisis, relieving staff of the burden immediately on their return to school, perhaps even endearing himself to them for carrying this weight by himself. It was an onerous task to find the evidence, sifting through mounds of documentation, minutes and performance management records. Although in need of a another holiday on his return to school, Mr Smith found it a useful exercise, alerting him to just how much he did not know and how much he did not have to hand by way of evidence. It prompted him to think of how to put in place a more continuous ongoing process of self-evaluation.

Ms Smyth in her office with the SLT

Ms Smyth kicked off discussion of the SEF with her senior team towards the end of June. She arranged a series of SLT meetings to pull together the various strands of the SEF, each member opting to gather evidence in one of the key areas. Over a series of five weekly meetings each member brought his or her report to be interrogated by colleagues, revised and eventually agreed as robust enough to be incorporated in the final document. Ms Smyth took responsibility for fine tuning the SEF and joining the dots. Having gone through the exercise once, Ms Smyth decided that next time round this could be devolved to departmental level, with each department going through a similar exercise to that of the SLT, with the senior leadership team performing the final editorial role.

Mrs Smiley in the staffroom with the whole staff

When she first became aware of the New Relationship, Mrs Smiley brought together the whole staff and presented them with key extracts from Ofsted and DfES documents, arranging a follow-up meeting at which they would be asked to come having read the relevant texts, prepared to share their views on how the school should approach the SEF task. At the next meeting she opened up discussion on their views of self-evaluation and its links to the SEF. They discussed how they should proceed and how responsibilities might be divided among the staff. Over the following weeks members of staff worked in pairs or three on aspects of the SEF to which they could contribute, coming together as a staff to share their findings. The senior leadership then presented the draft document to the governors for discussion, taking final responsibility for drawing up the finished SEF.

The School Improvement Team in dialogue with colleagues

The 'SIT', composed of a cross-section of six staff, with the task of keeping their colleagues up-to-date on self-evaluation, saw the opportunity presented by NRwS to review their own progress as a school with self-evaluation. Bringing the whole staff together, the SIT organised a workshop in which small cross-departmental groups worked together to review purposes, frameworks, tools and products. Groups then sub-divided, each half group meeting with another half group, this time with the role of critical friend and the task of interrogating their evidence base. Returning to plenary, discussion ensued on how their disparate bodies of practice and supporting evidence could be incorporated into a summary story for external audiences including Ofsted. Staff as a whole found it difficult to agree on whether or not to use the SEF. The SIT suggested, and it was agreed by the senior leadership team, that on this occasion they would pull their findings together in the SEF and, through what they learned from that experience, determine to be bolder in the future.

Completing the SEF proved for many heads to be a frustrating chore, especially those who laboured over an on-line version and tackled the task single handedly in the splendid isolation of their offices. Few who completed it found it a satisfying experience. However, it is intended not to be a form filling exercise but a record of the school's own ongoing self-evaluation. As Ofsted advises[1]:

> The existence of a SEF itself it will not demonstrate that a school has secure methods of review and evaluation, but the quality of completion will be a clear pointer to the effectiveness of the practices (particularly of leadership and management) within the school. . . .

Inspection with heart

In the New Relationship the SEF is 'at the heart of the new inspection arrangements'.[2] It allows inspection to be shorter, sharper and to focus on the school's evaluation of itself. The SEF asks schools to:

- evaluate their progress against an inspection schedule;
- set out the main evidence on which this evaluation is based;
- identify their own strengths and weaknesses;
- explain the action the school is taking to remedy the weaknesses and develop the strengths.

The SEF template retains much of what went before in the school S4 but now also takes into account the requirements of *Every Child Matters* (Children's Act) and its five key outcomes. Leicestershire County Council illustrates the relationship as shown in Figure 11.1

When the inspection team draw up their report they bring together the school's view of itself together with their own view, justifying where those perspectives might differ. The leadership and management section of the inspectors' report includes an evaluation of quality of the school's self-evaluation process that led it to make its judgements in the SEF. A SEF judged to be good or outstanding would reflect a school's ongoing self-evaluation, describing a process of evidence-based practice and the aspects of school and classroom life that such a process had uncovered. When there is a rich body of evidence to draw on the SEF can afford to be short, concise, evaluative and evidence-based. And, adds, the Ofsted guidelines 'honest'.

The school demonstrates that it: Ofsted uses it to:

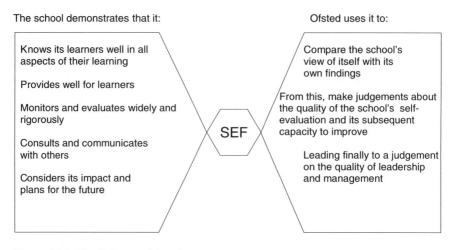

Knows its learners well in all
aspects of their learning

Provides well for learners

Monitors and evaluates widely and
rigorously

Consults and communicates
with others

Considers its impact and
plans for the future

SEF

Compare the school's
view of itself with its
own findings

From this, make judgements about
the quality of the school's self-
evaluation and its subsequent
capacity to improve

Leading finally to a judgement
on the quality of leadership
and management

Figure 11.1 The Leicestershire plan.

> If you cannot say what you need to in about **20** pages, you are probably
> *describing* what you do rather than *analysing the impact* of what you do.
> Remember you are trying to convey what parents, pupils and other
> stakeholders think of the school and give a succinct evaluation.

Providing a SEF that meets all the criteria of brevity, wit and honesty relies
not only on fine judgement but also political and presentational skills. It is
not surprising therefore to find consultants being brought in, or bought in,
by schools, and courses being offered by entrepreneurial agencies on how to
complete the SEF. It is a task difficult to achieve, however, without a genuine
retrospective story to tell.

The nature of advice provided by consultants or bespoke courses includes
the following:

Know what is expected

As might be said to an exam candidate the first rule is – answer the set question. In other words, there is a strategic or tactical element to getting down
the essential content and meaning. In order to ensure a clear understanding
of those expectations it is important to refer to the evaluation schedule in the
Framework for Inspecting Schools. Anticipation means putting yourself in the
shoes of the visiting team and considering 'If you were an inspector what
questions would your SEF lead you to ask?' From their point of view
the primary questions will be 'What does this document tell me about the
unfolding living process of self-evaluation in your school?' At least that is
what a prescient HMI would ask, and should, ask.

Identify the key messages you want to convey

There is a subtle balance to be achieved in both answering the set question and ensuring you get across the messages you want to convey. There is a danger in too slavish a conformity to the formula and formulaic language. Creativity and sincerity also need to shine through any written report. Inspectors, like exam markers, weary of stereotypical and uninspired writing, will see through obfuscation and lack of substance. Their advice is 'Be specific. Ask yourself "Have I captured what makes our school tick, what makes it special, what makes it as it is?" ' Creativity and self-confidence mean there is latitude to depart from the script and provide some value-added of your own.

Keep pupil outcomes to the fore

A school's story is bound to be larger and more varied than simply 'outcomes'. However, Ofsted guidelines make it clear that leadership, culture, out-of-school activities and other aspects of school performance have all, as far as possible, to be related to pupil outcomes. This is an unreasonable demand given decades of research which are unable to demonstrate any direct links between, for example, leadership and pupil outcomes. Like so many other things in school life effects are mediated. For example, heads may encourage and provide opportunities for peer observation and feedback, leading to greater collaboration and sharing of good practice which may increase pupil engagement and, in the long-term, pay-off in better exam performance. What *is* reasonable is to provide a rationale for innovation or shifts in policy and how this is intended to impact in the longer term on higher levels of motivation and achievement. Too simplistic a casual inference is liable to overclaiming and ultimately to prove counter-productive.

Keep in mind the ECM agenda

The five aspects of the ECM agenda are of key importance but at the same time illustrate just how difficult it is to be simplistic about outcomes. Evidence here is bound to be qualitative and may include for example, pupil work, examples of pupil progress effectively followed through over time, reports from parents and community partners, evidence from out-of-school activities such as study support in the form of pupil diaries, or drawn from the Code of Practice (see Chapter 8). These may be linked to numeric indicators such as attendance at school and at out-of-school activities. This may all too easily turn into a highly contrived exercise, however, unless there is a prior commitment to a school ethos in which enjoyment, safety and well-being are implicit in behaviour, relationships and language, made explicit in the day-to-day life of classrooms and in complementary out-of-hours learning.

Consider the audience

In all writing the prime consideration is for the readership. Writing for Ofsted inspectors is liable to be of a different tenor than writing for parents or governors. Since Ofsted advice asks schools to consider 'How you would summarise the findings for a new governor or interested parent?' the implication is that the SEF is tailored to that audience and Ofsted's assessment has to do with how well the school tells its story to those key stakeholders. This calls for a balanced judgement with an eye on two bodies of readers.

Keep it simple

There is a fine balance to be struck in the demand to keeping language simple and direct for a lay audience while dealing with some seminal educational issues. Even terms such as 'outcomes', while endearing to Ofsted, may be off-putting for parents. It is important, therefore, that the SEF is not a hurried form-filling exercise conducted by the head or senior management team, but a document that evolves over time through consultation with parents and governors so ensuring not only accuracy but also achieving a tone and register that is meaningful to parents while incisive enough to speak to an HMI.

Examine the precedents

The interactive SEF website proves advice on how to complete the SEF, with bullet point prompts to help to flesh out the response. The document *A New Relationship with Schools: Improving Performance Through Self-evaluation* gives a number of examples from schools, with accompanying commentary on Ofsted judgements as to the adequacy of the evidence base.

Validate the evidence

The SEF calls for evidence underpinned by judgements as to what constitutes evidence. It must, say the guidelines, be 'authoritative', 'convincing' and 'verifiable', by inspectors or other independent parties. Although outcomes are seen to be the gold standard, changes in structures, appointment to key positions, revised forms of communication and reporting, the nature of monitoring and systems to support newly qualified teachers are all cited by Ofsted as examples of evidence. While these are evidence of something that has taken place and may well be verifiable they are essentially 'input' evidence and say nothing about what the impact of such changes has been. As far as possible impact measures should be used, and it is vital to be specific rather than general. However, it has to be borne in mind that 'evidence' is a term with wide margins of latitude and that much of what is worthwhile is not easily verifiable. A high level of awareness and critical attitude to the nature of 'evidence' required is itself testimony to the rigour with which the school is approaching its own evaluation.

Distinguish among types of report writing

The guidelines advise schools to be evaluative rather than descriptive, evidence-based rather than impressionistic or subjective. It should therefore include the following:

Evidence: How do we know what we know?
Diagnosis: What are the key, most telling, strengths and weaknesses (or areas for development?)
Judgement: How do we attribute meaning to the evidence and diagnosis?
Action focus: What has already been put in place and what now needs to be addressed?
Targeting and planning: How ambitious and realistic are targets and the planning to achieve them?
Stewardship: How effectively have we managed resources and achieved value for money?

These can all be addressed yet still deliver an arid report. An outstanding report should also have flair. It should bring to life, through short anecdote and example, the vigour and creativity of pupils and teachers, allowing their voice to come through. There is an element of artistry in painting the portrait of a school's vital energy combined with a hard-headed attention to the data.

Revise before submission

As with good counsel to students – always revise your work before you submit it. Have you:

- Read it through?
- Made sure it is short and to the point?
- Answered all of the questions?
- Made your judgements clear?
- Reflected stakeholders' views?
- Does it give a fair and honest picture of what the school is like?
- Have you been clear about actions being taken to improve?

A global judgement, using the four Ofsted categories on overall effectiveness is then asked for as shown in Table 11.1. This summary is referred to by Ofsted as part of Advice and Inspection's monitoring.

1 = Outstanding
2 = Good
3 = Satisfactory
4 = Inadequate

Table 11.1 The SEF summary

Section		Key stage
		GRADE 1–4
3	Learners' achievement and standards in their work	
4	Learners' personal development and well-being	
5	Quality of teaching and learning	
	Quality of the curriculum and other activities	
	Quality of care, guidance and support	
6	Effectiveness and efficiency of leadership and management	
7	Overall effectiveness	
	Capacity to make further improvement	
	Improvement since the last inspection	
	Quality and standards in the foundation stage	

The parts that make the whole

Part 1 of the SEF asks for main characteristics of learners, distinctive aims and features of the school, contextual or other issues acting as barriers to raising performance, additional characteristics of the school together with main priorities that affect the context of the school's work

Part 2 of the SEF, Views of Learners, Parents/Carers and Other Stakeholders, gauges the range of stakeholder involvement in influencing the direction of the school. The term 'stakeholders' cover a multitude of sins and includes 'internal' groups such as governors, teachers, LSAs, support and caretaking staff, office staff, pupils and parents, and 'external' stakeholders such as community agencies, county councils, business partnerships and other affiliated schools.

The invitation, or requirement, to include this range of views may set off a flurry of activity, questionnaires and surveys in profusion. For a school that has no such data to hand this may seem like a necessity, but it is likely to prove counter-productive, serving short-term goals and raising expectations without the long-term groundwork needed to create the appropriate climate. A secondary head's advice is worth remembering in this context – 'Do not turn over any stone unless you are prepared to deal with what you find under it.' A school with a strong self-evaluating culture is aware of the views of its key stakeholders and, for the purposes of the SEF, is able to garner selective evidence from what is already on record. Table 11.2 shows some examples.

While the primary task of inspection teams is to evaluate the quality of the schools' self-evaluation, Ofsted also helpfully provides an audit grid for schools to do this for themselves. This begins to assume the character of Chinese boxes or wheels within wheels. It is akin to what is known as double loop learning,[3] the single loop being the process of completing the SEF, the

Table 11.2 The views of stakeholders

Teachers	Pupils	Governors	Parents	Other agencies
Peer obser-vation and impact Evaluations of in-service Teacher self-evaluations Peer evaluations Reports on teacher-led initiatives	Incidence of bullying Portfolios of work Evaluations of learning Evaluations of teaching Photo evaluations Interviews	Reports of governor meetings with action points Governor-led initiatives and impact Records from governor surgeries	Feedback from parents' evenings Record of complaints, action taken and follow-up Parent initiatives and impact Letters from parents Parent postbox comments and suggestions	Surveys of community agencies Records of case conferences and action taken Evaluative reports of school visits

double loop as the process of returning to it at with a critical eye. Under 17 key criteria the[4] audit grid allows a school to review the quality of its self-evaluation on a four-point scale from outstanding to inadequate.

Figure 11.2 suggests some of the do's and don'ts of completing the SEF. The do's emphasising the need for evidence and judgement rather than description and assertion, the don't reminding us that 'evidence' can take many and varied forms and that strategies, events, images, processes and plans are important evidence of school culture and leadership.

In summary

Figure 11.3 illustrates the relationship among the parts when the SEF is built from the ground up. The left-hand side of the diagram shows the ongoing flow of self-evaluation, feeding into and feeding off the continuing dialogue. It shapes the school profile, not as a snapshot but as a living and growing entity. The right-hand side depicts the more formal and occasional process of review. It is informed by self-evaluation, by meetings with the SIP, leading into the formulation of the Single School Plan. The Single Plan and the Profile are discrete but symbiotically related. The SEF, which sits in the middle of the diagram, is updated from time to time as new insights emerge from self-evaluation. These may be validated by sound evidence or held in suspense as important but requiring further scrutiny and exploration of sources for evidence.

During NCSL workshops on self-evaluation school leaders were asked to consider what already existed in their schools that had never been formally recognised as self-evaluation but were nonetheless important indicators *for them* of school quality. Like Molière's Monsieur Jourdain, who was surprised to discover he had been talking prose all his life, these school leaders

Do	Don't
Convey a clear picture of how well the school is doing	Assume you can only tell your story in words and bullet points
Provide evidence of how you know what you know	Be intimidated by the demand for outcome 'evidence'
Show what you are doing to build on successes and remedy weaknesses	Be defensive about what remains to be done. Show you have it in mind and plan
Demonstrate impact	Substitute quantity for quality
Interpret the evidence	Make assertions without supporting argument
Ensure contributions from a wide range of sources	Conduct hurried surveys
Match judgement to evidence	Expect numbers to speak for themselves
Try to make the links between data sources, for example, between quality of teaching and pupil achievement	Overclaim causal links
	Be too introspective
	Simply describe change
Link to your School Improvement Plan	
Develop processes for regular updating	Leave it to the head or senior leadership team

Figure 11.2 Do's and don'ts of SEF evidence.

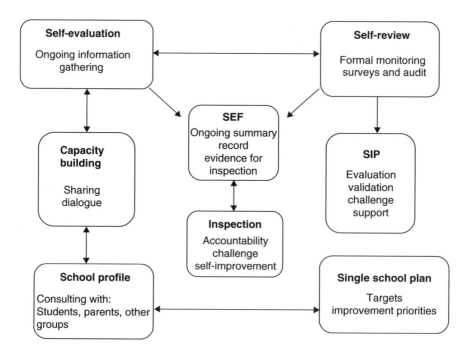

Figure 11.3 The relationship of the parts to the whole.

surprised themselves by the treasures within their own schools that they had simply taken for granted and never considered as relevant evidence for self-evaluation or for the SEF. In Gareth Morgan's phraseology[5] they had 'edited their understanding of reality to suit narrow purposes'. If staff, students and parents are encouraged to keep a note of significant events, management of critical incidents or breakthrough practices, the SEF summary document would be enriched by a reservoir of evidence on which to draw. Like the Boy Scouts the school can be ever prepared, taking inspection in its stride, framing it as a welcome validation and challenge to the school's organisational intelligence.

12 Who needs a School Improvement Partner?

Critical friend or Trojan collaborator?

Is maith an scathan suil carad
A good mirror is the eye of a friend

The school improvement partner is a key element in the NRwS jigsaw. Whether it is justifiable to describe this role as that of 'critical friend' is the focus of this chapter. Drawing on what has been written and researched about critical friendship a number of questions are addressed, most significantly for schools at risk of 'improvement notice' and possible closure.

Who needs a School Improvement Partner? All schools do, says the government, casting the SIP as an integral element of the New Relationship. Whether this stems from a desire to support schools in their improvement efforts or to keep a watchful eye on them is a moot point.

The Teacher Net (teachernet.gov.uk) offers the following reassuring words based on schools' experience of the SIP:

How would you describe the relationship with
the SIP?

> I feel that it's a very positive one. Our SIP challenges us, but he's also realistic and very supportive – I'll be able to ask him to look at my self-evaluation form when I complete it next term. I think it helps that he's a headteacher from a school in a rural area, as am I, so he understands the issues affecting the school. He's also vastly experienced.

As a government journal they would say that wouldn't they? Anecdotal evidence[1] from other heads presents a more mixed picture. It suggests that the matching of the SIP to the needs of the school is somewhat of a lottery, that the status of practising head is not without its drawbacks and, more significantly, that their ambivalent role as a 'conduit' to government is likely to inhibit a more genuinely open and reciprocal relationship.

The institution of the SIP draws from a fairly substantial body of evidence that schools are more likely to improve when they enjoy external support.

For example, Baker and associates[2] compared schools which drew on external support and those that did not, concluding that with the right kind of support, challenge could positively effect improvement. At the same time it opened to question the notion of the autonomous self-improving school. As we have learned from numerous studies,[3] schools, like human beings, need friends.

What 'support' implies is, however, open to question. Support is not some objective fact, a simple matter of input or provision. Support is in the eye of the beholder. It is a subjective phenomenon with an emotional connotation of meeting one's needs at a given period. As needs emerge, dissipate and assume different forms over time the nature and timing of support becomes a complex judgement.

What then is the nature of support offered by the SIP? What is his or her role and function? What passport does she or he bring to gain legitimate entry to the school?

SIP as critical friend[4]

The SIP is described in government documents[5] as a 'critical professional friend' to the school, helping its leadership to evaluate its performance, identifying priorities for improvement, and planning effective change. The government's aim is for three quarters of all SIPS to be fellow headteachers, tested, selected, trained (by the National College and contracted out to other private agencies), appointed (by the LA) and monitored by government through LEAs. His or her role is to 'build the school's capacity to improve the attainment of pupils and to achieve other key outcomes for pupils that bear on attainment'. The SIP acts for the school's maintaining authority and is authorised to approve – on behalf of the LA and DfES – the performance targets set by the head and governing body of the school.

The guiding principles of the SIP's work are:

- strict adherence to confidentiality;
- respect for the school's autonomy to plan its development, starting from the school's self-evaluation and the needs of the community, especially the children;
- focus on pupil achievement, and the many factors which influence it, including the importance of pupil well-being;
- professional challenge and support, so that the headteacher feels that the practice is improved by interaction with the SIP and there is evidence of impact;
- evidence-based assessment of the school's performance and its strategies for improving teaching and learning;
- intervention in inverse proportion to success;
- coherence, so that external agencies consistently support the school's normal cycles of evaluation, planning and action.

Some of these principles characterise the work of a critical friend, most obviously among these, respect for the school's autonomy. There are, however, significant differences between the SIP as described here and the essence of a critical friend relationship.

The nature of the agenda. Typically, in a genuine critical friend relationship the agenda is negotiated according to the needs of the school. The critical friend is not simply passive in her role but helps to shape the agenda. By contrast the agenda as set out above circumscribes the SIP role and explicitly gives central place to a focus on pupil achievement and school performance. These words, with which few could reasonably disagree, do, however, carry a quite specific frame of reference and denote predetermined governmental criteria. In practice, while SIPs are likely to work to a more flexible and responsive brief, they do have to constantly bear in mind that they are accountable to the LEA and Government for adherence to their prescribed remit.

The promise of confidentiality. This is either naïve or ill informed. No professional working with a school can promise confidentiality because it is something they may be required to break if they discover illegal activity, for example, evidence of abuse. In an accountability relationship such as that of the SIP it is simply an untenable proposition. What this actually means is an injunction to act with discretion and not talk out of turn with other schools or other parties.

The essential contradictions. A SIP cannot respect the autonomy of the school, establish a relationship of confidentiality while at the same time 'intervening' in inverse proportion to success. Being 'authorised to approve' performance targets together with the power of intervention is a clear message that this in no equal partnership. Your 'friend', in your own best interests of course, will report you to higher authorities if it is his or her judgement that you are not successful.

The accountability factor

The tensions and contradictions in the SIP's role are brought into sharper contrast when his/her duties and lines of accountability are spelt out.[6]

- Discuss and assess a school's self-evaluation and school improvement plan against available evidence including the Ofsted report, and comment on the effectiveness of these.
- Provide an objective review of the school's performance data by considering its most recent national test results, trends over time, other pupil achievement data and analysing the evidence for the school's improvement.
- Discuss the school's targets and priorities for the coming year, based on the analysis of the data above, to ensure that they are ambitious but realistic.

- Challenge the school where necessary, particularly on its capacity to improve and whether it is focussing on the most important priorities for improvement and development.
- Discuss a package of support and challenge for the school (provided both by the LEA and/or external sources) and ensure that this is appropriately managed to give the school maximum value (particularly in the case of complex arrangements for schools in difficulties).
- Report the outcomes of the 'Single Conversation' to the school's Governing Body, the headteacher and the school's maintaining authority.
- Provide advice and guidance to the governing body to inform the performance management of the headteacher.
- Contribute to the effective development of the SIPs programme.

To each according to their needs

Typically, it is advised, a SIP should devote five days to a school every year, not all of which have to be spent at the school 'depending on the circumstances of the school and the nature of its needs'. The word 'needs' is another of the ambiguous terms in the government lexicon. It does not refer to what might be called primary, or 'felt' needs but rather to 'learned' or 'acquired' needs. We are given something of the flavour of 'needs' in Ministerial advice[7] which lays emphasis on targets 'set against national priorities', 'satisfying all monitoring requirements with accountability for pupil outcomes', and 'not process measures'.

A five-day calendar

The five days, it should be noted, includes time for the SIP to advise the school's governing body on the performance management of the headteacher and the school's performance management arrangements. Four additional days a year are earmarked for professional development and for national, regional and local networking, and possible involvement in headship appointments as decided by the LEA. A suggested calendar for the SIP's work is shown in Figure 12.1.

The singular conversation

The 'single' conversation has a number of possible meanings. The intended meaning is of one coherent conversation rather than serving many masters or mistresses. While not necessarily limited to one annual conversation it is a singular conversation as the following suggested agenda reveals. The emboldened words loom large.

How well is the school performing?

- What does the *data* and documentation on all pupils' attainment, well-being and progress say about the ambition of the school?

Visit type	When	In school	Out of school (preparation, reading, report-writing)	Total days
Familiarisation visit*	Early autumn	½	½	1
Target setting	Autumn	½	¾	1¼
Programme of support	Autumn	½		½
Head teacher's performance management	Autumn	¼	½	¾
Termly progress evaluation visits	Spring	½	¼	¾
Termly progress evaluation visits	Summer	½	¼	¾
Totals		2¾	2¼	5

Figure 12.1 A suggested calendar for the work of the SIP.

- Are there significant *variations* and areas of underperformance within the school?
- What evidence is there that the school is addressing the range of outcomes identified in *Every Child Matters?*
- How well is the school helping pupils to *progress* to the next education stage and beyond?

For secondary specialist/leading school

- How well is the school using its specialism/leading status to improve its own and others' performance?

What are the key factors?

- How robust is the school's self-evaluation? Does the school regularly measure progress in practical ways? Are there other sources of evidence it could have used? Has the school interpreted the evidence correctly and are its judgements sound?
- How effective are the school's core systems and policies? (pupil assessment and target setting; CPD across the school; performance management; behaviour; curriculum; middle management).
- Is the school making the best use of its resources?

What are the priorities and targets for improvement?

- Is the school choosing the right priorities for the next academic year?
- Is the school setting its ambitions for the medium term high enough?
- Is the school setting priorities and targets appropriate to achieving its ambitions for pupils?
- What aspects of practice could be shared with others beyond the school so as to contribute to raising attainment and achievement more widely?

How will the school achieve them?

- Is the leadership team and are the governors choosing and effectively implementing high-impact, sustainable *strategies* for improving teaching and learning?
- Is the *development plan* deliverable? Has the school the capacity to carry out the plan successfully? Is it monitored and evaluated?
- What *support* from outside (including National Strategies; wider children's services; school-to-school networks) does the school need?

How are the school's performance management systems contributing to raising attainment and achievement?

- Has the headteacher met the previous performance management objectives set by the governing body?
- What would be suitable objectives for governors to set the headteacher for next year?
- Has the school got integrated performance management and pay policies?

What's in the SIP kitbag?

The SIP is also required to be armed with what are described as 'Core Data' which include value for money benchmarks from the DfES benchmarking website, the latest Ofsted report and action plan and *Every Child Matters* data including attendance, exclusions, local youth, crime, local drugs/alcohol abuse, obesity etc. This is complemented by a plethora of detail on staffing, budgets, curriculum planning, bids and tenders, reports from Link Adviser and local authority consultant, Local Area Children and Young People's Plan, Local LSC data/reports, Strategic issues affecting the locality and much else besides. In addition, the already bulging kitbag has a compartment for school-generated documentation such as the SEF, the school development plan, performance management policy and data.

All of this furnishes the single conversation which, says the guidance, will have a common core as depicted in Figure 12.2. Given that three quarters or

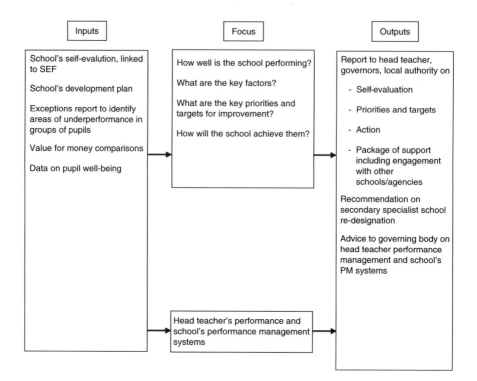

Figure 12.2 Guidance on inputs, focus and outputs.

so of SIPS are expected to be practising headteachers the allotted five days looks a meagre offering in return for the heavy duty requirement and responsibility of the role.

Outputs of the single conversation

In the 'real' world, if such a thing exists, not all 'conversations' have carefully defined outputs. This singular conversation, however, is followed by a singular report. 'In all cases', it is advised,[8] 'the School Improvement Partner should follow the local authority's standard reporting requirements and paperwork'. The SIP should report the main outcomes of the single conversation to the governing body, forwarding a copy to the local authority and the headteacher. This should include a commentary on the quality of the school's self-evaluation, priorities and targets in the school development plan, progress on achieving them and a recommendation about the action planned by the school, and any external support needed.

As the SIP is 'independent' of the school he or she may make a judgement of the school different from the headteacher's and offers independent 'advice' to the governing body on the headteacher's performance management objectives 'informed by light touch validation of the processes'.

The documentation continually emphasises the autonomy and new found freedoms of schools within the New Relationship. So, it is claimed, the school is free to draw upon whatever external support it needs to achieve its aims. This freedom comes with a major caveat. Schools assessed by the LA or Ofsted as requiring intervention will not enjoy that luxury, although this may ironically be the time when they most need trusted friends. It is when a headteacher faces 'the dark night of the soul'[9] that he or she is most need of a confidant or true friend with whom to share honest doubt.

The sting is in the tail

Where a SIP has concerns about the capacity of the school to improve and he or she cannot secure agreement on action by means of professional dialogue with the headteacher and governors, the SIP has to alert the maintaining authority so that early action can be taken. Triggers for concern include:

- the school not recognising significant underperformance
- the school lacking the leadership capacity to improve
- the school being at risk of an adverse Ofsted report
- for secondary, the school being at risk of failing to be re-designated for its specialism.

This may prompt the authority to use its statutory intervention powers, unaltered under New Relationship. Whatever form this intervention takes, the SIP may play a lead role in monitoring the support provided. If monitoring is performed by any other body the SIP should be kept informed.

Possible courses of action are set out at three levels. Level 1 may be taken by the SIP alone, reporting concerns to the governors, alerting the maintaining authority and advising on appropriate action. Level 2 follows on from the SIP alert. The maintaining authority can issue a formal warning to the school, initiate a change programme with the agreement of the school – such as partnership or federation with other schools, change to leadership structures, or intensive support and/or alert Ofsted to the need for an early inspection. Level 3 follows from a formal warning. The maintaining authority can then: withdraw the school's delegated budget (under SSFA 1998 as amended), appoint additional governors, or apply to the Secretary of State to replace the governing body with an interim executive board.

Where there is an adverse Ofsted report the Education Act of 2005 identifies two categories of school causing concern:

- a school requiring special measures, that is, one that is failing to give its pupils an acceptable standard of education, and with leadership that does not have the capacity to secure the necessary improvement;
- a school needing significant improvement, that is, one performing significantly less well than might be expected.

Where a school falls into one of these two categories the SIP is expected to initiate urgent action to address the issues identified by Ofsted whether personally or through other agencies and ensure that the relevant information is passed to National Strategy staff so that they can take the necessary supporting action, agreeing with the maintaining authority who will lead action, against clear timescales and integrated into the planning and monitoring systems of the school.

The maintaining authority can, with advice from the SIP, activate a range of statutory interventions[10] or non-statutory improvement strategies such as taking back a school's delegated budget, appointing additional governors, appointing a new Chair of Governors, replacing the whole governing body with an Independent Executive Board (IEB), directing the LA to appoint an external partner to improve the school, or directing the local authority to close a school.

From the LA's point of view there are clearly tensions. While on the surface, giving them greater responsibility in practice it is a further emasculation of the LA role. It is an intermediate agency but with further limitation of their discretionary powers. The training is done by the National College but the managing and monitoring of the SIP is the responsibility of the LA. This raises questions of how the relationship can be managed effectively, how the authority is to reconcile the role of the SIP with its advisory services and ultimately – What's in it for the authority?

When is a critical friend not a friend?

There are obviously circumstances in which the SIP can act as a critical friend because there is no conflict over the school's progress and success. There are also many occasions where that will not be the case. As the school has to accept the appointed 'friend' (with one refusal permitted) the marriage may be under strain from the outset. It is where the SIP moves from a friendly role to that of critic and then to overt policing of school compliance that the designation of 'critical friend' does not match the substantial body of writing and research on the qualities and functions of that role.

The precepts of critical friendship shown in Figure 12.3 are taken from a seven country international project[11] in which teachers and school leaders from seven countries identified the do's and don'ts of critical friendship.

A critical friend will:

- Listen/hear/observe
- Learn (about the school culture and goals)
- Demonstrate positive regard for, and sensitivity towards the school and its community
- Help to identify issues and make creative suggestions to help the school become better at what it does
- Offer sources of evidence and/or expertise
- Work collaboratively in exploring alternative approaches
- Encourage collegiality, including the sharing of ideas among teachers and schools
- Offer a thoughtful critical perspective on learning, culture or leadership as appropriate
- Be honest, accessible, flexible, discrete, friendly, patient, communicative and accountable to the school

Figure 12.3 The 'do's of critical friendship.

These qualities and working patterns do not at first sight appear in conflict with the following list of person specifications of the SIP as detailed in the guidelines, although an astute reader may pick up some differences in language and tone in the following:

- Highly motivated, enthusiastic, strategic leader
- Open minded, active listener
- Able to cope with challenge and conflict
- Creative in problem solving
- Credible; commands respect in a wide range of circumstances
- Able to ask probing, challenging questions and use influencing skills effectively
- Persuasive communicator, articulate in speech and on paper
- Able to give accurate feedback
- Able to receive and act on feedback about own performance
- Keen to keep learning.

It is when we come to the counterfoil suggested by the seven country participants of the Leadership for Learning Project that the differences become sharply defined. Asked to define what the critical friend should NOT do, the group (in fact a large group of 80) came up with the list shown in Figure 12.4.

Contrast these with the following taken from the person specification of the SIP:

- Makes reliable, independent judgements about performance and potential.

The critical friend will not:

- Assume a directive role
- Offer solutions to problems, or provide 'quick fixes'
- Rush to judgement, make assumptions or judge without substantial evidence
- Pretend to know the school better than those in the school
- Have hidden agendas
- Impose agendas of his/her own
- Undermine the authority of others
- Use school data without consent
- Compare invidiously with other schools
- Cause problems

Figure 12.4 The 'don'ts of critical friendship.

- Consistent in assessment of managers' capability to deliver improvement and evaluate impact of actions.
- Applies rigorous analysis to form soundly based judgements.
- Takes people to their limits, but not beyond, and has expectations that are aspirational, yet realistic.
- Pursues challenging questions, probes explanations of root causes and apparent inconsistencies, and identifies key issues.
- Rigorous; not satisfied until all angles are investigated.
- Explains how judgements were made and justifies them in the face of opposition.

What is immediately striking about these items is the tenor of the language. It is tough and uncompromising. It is 'rigorous', 'probing', 'pursuing', 'performance-orientated', 'taking' people to their limits. There is nothing conditional, tentative or negotiated about the SIP's judgements. They are 'reliable' and 'consistent', justifying their judgements in the face of opposition. From these descriptors they might well be Ofsted inspectors.

It might be countered that critical friends as defined within the academic literature are simply too soft-centred to achieve the cutting edge critique and serious challenge that schools need if they are to improve. Critical friendship is not, of course, the only form of support that a school can appeal to. Schools increasingly use mentors and coaches who fulfil quite different functions and there are times when a school may need a strong directive intervention. What is important to recognise is the distinction among these different roles, where they are more or less apposite and when they are actually in conflict. The flaw in the construction of the SIP is the essential dishonesty of the 'package'. The roles of adviser, friend, supporter, confidante as well as judge and executioner cannot be reconciled when actually put to the test. There will be many circumstances in which those tensions are not made apparent or tested and where there is a harmonious and productive relationship between head and SIP, but there will be other occasions in which the tensions in the role are exposed and brought unhappily to the surface. It is in these circumstances that the dark night of the soul is not simply the province of the headteacher but the SIP whose friendship is given a moral test.

An abundance of qualities

Figure 12.5 presents a list of qualities[12] that might be expected of a critical friend. It is a formidable and quite daunting list, setting standards that might be taken more as developmental aspirations than a summative checklist. These could be used by critical friends as a basis for self-evaluation and for their own personal development. School colleagues could use them to inform their awareness of the potential of critical friendship, and to help shape the particular combination of essential and desirable characteristics they should seek in a critical friend for a specific project or purpose.

As with any competences list considerable caution needs to be exercised. Words mean different things to different people. Some characteristics are easier to observe and assess than others and can therefore be given undue

Roles	Behaviours	Qualities	Skills
Facilitator	Listens	Respect	Interpersonal skills
Supporter	Questions	Empathy	Group work skills
Critic	Reflects	Genuineness	Listening
Challenger	Feeds back	Confidence	Observing
Motivator	Summarises	Optimism	Questioning
Adviser	Challenges	Sensitivity	Managing conflict
Catalyst	Motivates	Insight	Team building
Networker	Reassures	Thoughtfulness	Collaboration
Listener		Commitment	Technical skills
Participant		Self-effacement	Data analysis,
Role model		Self-sufficiency	interpretation and
Enabler		Resilience	synthesis
Disseminator		Courage	Managing change
Monitor and		Diplomacy	
evaluator		Impartiality	
		Initiative	
		Reflective	
		Self-critical	
		Flexible	
		Resourceful	
		Tolerant of	
		ambiguity	

Figure 12.5 Roles behaviours, qualities and skills of the critical friend.

prominence. Listing many discrete points can lead to an atomistic approach which is not helpful to the critical friends themselves, to those who support their development, or those who seek to work with them. It is when the focus is on the activity, the texture and testing of the relationship, the give and take, and the process of knowledge creation that we come to understand what critical friendship really means.

The NAEIAC framework

The list of qualities for Educational Improvement Officers (EIPs) provides an interesting contrast to the profile of the SIP. In autumn of 2005 the National Association of Educational Inspectors, Advisers and Consultants (NAEIAC) produced their own framework describing the skills and abilities required to undertake the role of an education inspector/adviser/consultant. Its six key dimensions are:

1   Developing self and others
2   Professional leadership to build capacity
3   Accountability – evaluating practice
4   Promoting learning
5   Working with and developing organisations
6   Developing and sustaining partnerships

The language used in all of these areas emphasises partnership, support, listening and understanding, building capacity, challenging appropriately, all of this 'underpinned by a strong belief in the ethical purpose of advancing effective learning'.[13]

The documents provide a useful contrast with SEF guidelines, and while it suffers from lists of bullet points which do not make compelling reading, it does offer a starting point for discussion among a school staff, helping to reflect on what is important to them, the kind of person they should look for as a critical friend and providing a framework of values and priorities for evaluating the work of their SIP.

A useful source on the role of the critical friends is Critical Friendship, InFORM. October 2003, Number 3, Sue Swaffield with a contribution from John Jones. (available from jg323@cam.ac.uk) This 7-page summary provides a useful introduction to the issues and provides a helpful bibliography on previous research.

13 Googling around
The connoisseur's guide

Google and other companion search engines can alone furnish a school with all it needs to know about inspection and self-evaluation. Without a discriminating set of guidelines, however, it can be a frustrating and tedious business. This chapter offers a guide to some of the most useful sources and suggests some questions that need to be addressed in the process.

To google or not to google. That is the question. It seems to be less and less of a question as Google is now the search engine of choice and has become a vocabulary word in its own right. How Google manages to find just what you are looking for in microseconds remains for most people a complete mystery. You might ask Google to disclose something of its inner secrets by entering *how Google works* into the search engine. This will give you an extended narrative of Pigeon Rank technology, from which the following is a short extract.

By collecting flocks of pigeons in dense clusters, Google is able to process search queries at speeds superior to traditional search engines, which typically rely on birds of prey, brooding hens or slow-moving waterfowl to do their relevance rankings. When a search query is submitted to Google, it is routed to a data coop where monitors flash result pages at blazing speeds. When a relevant result is observed by one of the pigeons in the cluster, it strikes a rubber-coated steel bar with its beak, which assigns the page a PigeonRank value of one. For each peck, the PigeonRank increases. Those pages receiving the most pecks are returned at the top of the user's results page with the other results displayed in pecking order.

Beneath this tongue-in-cheek description is an essential element of truth which is the PageRank system which scans or 'crawls' through an index to find the most cited document corresponding best to people's subjective idea of importance. Google assesses a page's importance by the number of 'votes' it has received from other sites but does not take this at face value. It also analyses the page that casts that vote. Votes cast by pages that are themselves important weigh more heavily than less important pages. So the results of your search are liable to find you, in 0.12 seconds, a preferred order in what you are looking for.

Finding the key word

The key of searching effectively is to find the right words and combination of words. Self-evaluation is a possible starting point. At the time of writing this generated over 14 million hits while self-evaluation (hyphenated) produced under a million. As ought to be expected with a PageRank system these become progressively less and less useful as you proceed beyond the first half a dozen pages.

Self evaluation (unhyphenated) leads you immediately to some unexpected and sometimes exotic sites. One of the first things you will find is the ADA checklist for hotels and motels. This may not be exactly what you are looking for but makes diversionary and interesting reading nonetheless.

> The self-evaluation begins by identifying barriers to effective communication within each function of your hotel; determine how the communication barriers are currently being addressed, if at all, and then identify the range of solutions available which will eliminate or minimize these barriers to communication. Is your current response adequate, or must you do more? Which solutions are effective, least expensive, or easiest to implement?

Equally fascinating is Kevin Grold's self-evaluation scale – for adults only. (http://www.1–800-therapist.com/ses_ver_2_4.htm). It offers a checklist for evaluating your current state of health and well-being Figure 13.1.

These two examples illustrate something important about the net. One, the importance of refining the research term, two, the ability to get lost in fascinating but often irrelevant sites, three, the potential for learning something which has little to do with your initial intention but may provide an unexpected insight.

Self-review and school self-review produce a similar plethora of results as do self-assessment and school self-assessment.

Self-assessment

Self-assessment is North American terminology and will direct you to a wide range of American sites, some of which may be useful but also very time consuming to peruse. Confusingly there are British examples under this heading as well. One of the most useful sources under this heading is the NAHT 2005 publication *Making Self-assessment really work*. It is intended to

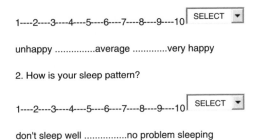

1. How has your mood been lately as compared to your normal state?

1----2----3----4----5----6----7----8----9----10 | SELECT ▼ |

unhappy ....average ....very happy

2. How is your sleep pattern?

1----2----3----4----5----6----7----8----9----10 | SELECT ▼ |

don't sleep well ....no problem sleeping

Figure 13.1 Checklist for evaluating current state of health and well-being.

ensure 'that the self-assessment process and report helps put good school leadership back in the driving seat', encouraging schools to use self-assessment to become increasingly 'self-directed', ensuring a school-based 'user friendly' approach. It is designed to inform the Ofsted SEF with guidance on how to use the self-assessment report as the basis of the 'single conversation'.

Also under self-assessment, Tameside local authority has a website which draws on the Business Excellence Model with a suggested framework for how assessment of the school's strengths and weaknesses can be implemented. It is a useful example of the confusion over what constitutes evidence. The website home page contains these words on its home page. 'Self-assessment should be based on facts not individual perceptions'.

What constitutes facts and what constitutes perceptions is not made clear but the following sentences only serve to confuse rather than enlighten:

> By inviting a group of staff to reflect on where their school has areas of strength and areas for improvement, an honest analysis of the school can be produced by the people who know the school intimately. The product of a self-assessment usually takes the form of a detailed report identifying strengths and areas for improvement.

This illustrates some of the inherent weaknesses of models such as the one advocated here. It is premised on staff judgements. It assumes a particular validity for those who know the school intimately. It appears to equate an 'honest analysis' with 'fact'.

Self-review

A search under self-review leads to a large number of New Zealand sites since self-review is the term used in that country for a well-developed system which may repay a virtual visit. Under the generic heading of school self-review you will also find a number of English LA schemata. Some, such as Norfolk's, are for access by headteachers within the LA and take the form of on-line completion of a database. Others give access to local authority guidelines such as, for example that developed by Rochdale's School Improvement Service. This framework uses self-evaluation alongside self-review, making a distinction between them – self-review referring to data collection, self-evaluation referring to judgement made on the basis of evidence. Self-evaluation is 'characterised by openness and consultation and is a regular part of the school's working life.' (http://www.rochdale.gov.uk/docs/education/sse.pdf).

This same theme is echoed in the Archdiocese of Westminster site which states:

> Self-evaluation is a continuing process of review, celebration and planning for improvement. It is not a one-off process leading to inspection but a continuous way of working to help us see more clearly and engage more deeply with the essence of the Church's mission to education. It is a whole community task.

While the reference here is specifically to a Catholic set of values, most of the statements which staff are asked to consider have much wider application and are framed not as summative or definitive measures but 'to encourage conversation and further reflection' on mission and purpose (http://www.westminsterdiocese.org.uk/redept/Secondary%20Catholic%20Life.doc). A number of sites take a specific focus on self-review. These include Portsmouth's Race Equality/Cultural Diversity performance criteria which have been developed in conjunction with headteachers and the Ethnic Minority Achievement Service in Portsmouth. These were developed in order 'to offer something which goes beyond the "tick box" format' and gives to schools a way of assessing their progress and quality of race equality provision in relation to a set of agreed criteria. (www.blss.portsmouth.sch.uk/emtag/selfR_ requ.shtm).

Another more specialist offering is Nottingham LA's website with a suite of tools for reviewing special needs and inclusion and containing sets of questionnaires which evaluate barriers to inclusion, staff attitudes to policy and SEN training, and the role of the governing body. (www.nottinghamschools.co.uk/eduweb/Department/department-template).

The Merseyside SEN Partnership brings together work from eight LEAs in the North West Group and its website gives access to two publications *Benchmarking Special Educational Needs in the North West and Merseyside* and *Self-Evaluation Materials*. These give a flavour of the range of work and interests being pursued by the Partnership. (http://www.merseysen.org.uk/pages/viewpage.asp?uniqid=727).

The Doncaster local authority site includes instruments for reviewing behaviour, harassment, bullying, attendance, punctuality, and staff development in relation to these areas. There is accompanying guidance on coping with severe behavioural difficulties. (www.doncaster.gov.uk/Images/School%20Self%20Review%20(BSP6)_tcm2–19705.pdf).

While these sites contain a mix of self-review and self-evaluation guidelines, the predominant emphasis is on rendering judgements at whole school level as to quality and effectiveness. Despite disclaimers that review is a preparation for inspection, and in spite of advocacy of ongoing self-evaluation, these sites do not illustrate tools of self-evaluation which might lend themselves to day-to-day use, nor do these guidelines suggest how a truly embedded approach would work.

School self-evaluation

A search under this title provides an array of LA sites, most of which tend to be structured around preparation of the SEF. The Hertfordshire site is a good example of one whose templates are helpful in taking you systematically through the SEF, in particular suggesting the kind of evidence that could be gathered from stakeholders. Leicestershire also offers a very comprehensive approach to the SEF, working through each of the sections, offering advice on the actions and on the actions needing to be taken prior to writing up commentaries and arriving at final grades.

Essex local authority has developed a School Self-Evaluation Tracker (SSET), a software package designed to 'help schools through the self-evaluation maze'. It uses a 'Smart Chart' to give users an instant graphical view of areas of strength and areas of improvement within the school. Statements on the planner are colour coded to allow schools to identify areas of strength and areas of improvement and to add comments to specific judgements and electronic forms of evidence to support their judgements, such as Word files, pictures and sound files. SSET also produces the 'Summary Profile', (an Essex document that allows a focussed discussion between the School Development Adviser and the School). Action Plans can then be created from the priorities for improvement and printed to be shared with staff members. (http://targettracker.org/products/SSET/).

The Becta matrix

The Becta matrix is an example of an on-line tool to support self-evaluation and action planning. Developed by NCSL and Becta it allows schools to review their current position against a set of statements arranged on a six-stage continuum from 'not yet decided' to 'embedded' and 'innovative'. As shown below the user can click on an example for a practical illustration of that criterion in action. Schools are also invited to submit their own exemplars. An action plan is generated automatically based on the responses entered, together with support and guidance.

Once registered, the matrix saves the user's work and allows them to edit it according to their individual needs. The example below is from the Learning and Skills sub-section (Figure 13.2).

Not yet decided ⊙	
Localised ○	Learner access to e-learning is limited to external Internet sites. E-learning material is not specifically linked or recommended to learners.
Co-ordinated ○	Some e-learning resources are available within the college network. Plans are in place to extend access to curriculum content and to increase delivery through e-learning.
Transformative ○	Web pages for learners, with links to both internal and web based e-learning resource areas, are set up or planned in most programme and subject areas. Flexible delivery targeting the community and workplace learners is being piloted.
Embedded ○	Subject and course based websites link to a wide range of e-learning materials and resources including external purchases. Web based curriculum materials are referenced and indexed within a formal intranet or Learning Platform / VLE structure.
Innovative ○	E-learning resources form part of a blended learning delivery strategy across the curriculum for local and distance learner target groups. Teaching staff take an active role in content management and review.

Figure 13.2 The BECTA matrix, learning and skills.

Source: The matrix can be accessed via: http://matrix.becta.org.uk

Self-evaluation and organic planning

Cambridge Education

Cambridge Education (formerly Cambridge Education Associates) has developed an on-line self-evaluation and school improvement framework which allows schools to draw together everything into a single system including school development plans, literacy/maths action plans, self-evaluation and an attached evidence base. Staff are able to access all the material from the desktop, creating 'organic' plans that grow and evolve in time. The process is also designed to encourage 'distributive leadership' because any member of staff from a support assistant to the headteacher may log on to, and make their own contribution to, self-evaluation and to the school improvement plan. With their own log-in password they can update their own personal actions and responsibilities. The 'evidence library' allows documentation to be uploaded and stored against the School Improvement Plan which can be printed out or exported to Word and PDF. Likewise, the Ofsted self-evaluation form can be printed automatically, 'perfect for the new 48-hour notice inspections'.

Accessed through Schoolcentre.net.

Transforming Learning. The Hay Group

Transforming Learning is a professional development service for teachers, team leaders and headteachers delivered through the Internet. The Hay

Group worked with schools and authorities to develop a private password-protected account through which relevant school staff could access an instrument which would help them evaluate aspects of the school and classroom environment. It provides teachers and headteachers with feedback from colleagues and pupils on:

- The motivational climate teachers create in their class
- The climate team leaders create in their teams
- The context for school improvement that headteachers create in their schools.
- The leadership styles demonstrated by headteachers and their leadership teams.

Together with feedback it offers tailored advice, development guidance and action planning.

At classroom level teachers can nominate pupils to evaluate classroom climate on nine dimensions which have been correlated by Hay-McBer research with more effective pupil learning. Using symbols as well as written text children as young as seven are able to use the on-line tool to rate their classrooms on these nine dimensions. The system analyses their answers and provides feedback to the teacher. The instrument may be used privately by teachers as an opportunity for individual development or as part of a planned, targeted approach to raising standards by collating anonymous, aggregate data on classroom climate across the school. The schema is based on research by Hay-McBer into teacher, team leader and headteacher effectiveness.

Transforming Learning www.haygroup.co.uk/Expertise/downloads Teacher effectiveness can be found on: http://www.teachernet.gov.uk/ educationoverview/briefing/strategyarchive/modelofteachereffectiveness/.

The European School Self-evaluation framework

The Standing International Conference of Inspectors brings together inspectors from all over Europe to try to agree some common approaches to inspection and self-evaluation. The European School Self-evaluation (ESSE) framework is intended to guide inspectors or external agents visiting a school in which self-evaluation has recently been implemented. The main purpose of the ESSE framework is to enable the collection of evidence and the formation of judgements about the effectiveness of the process of self-evaluation within schools and of the effectiveness of the external support provided by countries/regions to school self-evaluation. Although the framework focuses on the effectiveness of self-evaluation, rather than self-evaluation itself, the documentation is used by schools in Europe in conducting self-evaluation, in particular with reference to Part 2 which sets out the quality indicators. The framework can be accessed at http://sici.org.uk/ESSE/.

School self-review: emotional needs, achieving, behaving and learning in education

An example of a model specifically for special schools or special needs is offered by the organisation ENABLE (standing for Emotional Needs, Achieving, Behaving and Learning in Education). It provides guidance on review of school life against a check list of good practice. Seven aspects of good practice are identified with accompanying indicators.

The forms provided can be used to carry out an audit of current provision, generate discussion, and begin the process of self-evaluation and/or record progress in school improvement. They can be used to support managers and staff to identify areas for development. As such, they can support schools to focus on improving the provision for emotional and social development within their development planning process.
(http://www.enable-online.com/program/school_self-review.htm)

Self evaluation for extended schools

ContinYou is a charitable organisation established in 2003 bringing together Education Extra and the Community Education Development Council (CEDC). Its focus is on learning opportunities complementary to school as in study support and community programmes. Its primary aims are to tackle inequality and build social inclusion and offering opportunities to people who have gained the least from formal education and training.

ContinYou has developed an audit toolkit titled 'How are we doing? A self-evaluation toolkit for extended schools'. It is designed to encourage the involvement of headteachers, governors, parents, students, and partner agencies, in self-evaluation. Alongside the audit toolkit, an action plan has been developed to enable each school to move to the next point on the continuum, offering to schools a structured way to collect into a portfolio all their practice and how to demonstrate evidence of their progress towards becoming extended schools. The portfolio is intended to complement the new Ofsted self-assessment framework (www.continyou.org.uk).

The Scottish model: how good is our school? self-evaluation using performance indicators

Scotland moved to self-evaluation in 1991 and since then has been progressively refining and slimming down the approach in response to feedback from teachers. How Good is Our School?, revised for the third time in 2005, describes how HMI evaluate the quality of provision in schools and provides a framework for schools to evaluate themselves. Seven Key Areas are outlined with a cluster of indicators under each of these themes.

HGIOS, as it is widely referred to in Scotland, has been used widely in schools in England and been translated into a number of other languages, in German for example, *Wie gut is unsere Schule?* The pdf version can be accessed at: (www.scotland.gov.uk/deleted/hmie/schoolsfolder/SchoolsFolder/ HGIOS.pdf).

Investors in People

The Investors in People Standard is a business improvement tool 'designed to advance an organisation's performance through its people'. It has been both applied and adapted for use in schools and many of them have been evaluated and hallmarked with the IIP award. Step by step, it is designed as a flexible framework, which a school can adapt for its own requirements, mirroring the business planning cycle of plan, do, review.

The website at iip.co.uk gives access to The Standard Overview.pdf.

Other similar models widely used in business, and now in some schools, are as follows.

Charter Mark

The Charter Mark is the Government's national standard for excellence in customer service. Like Investors in People it gives a registered certification hallmark. It differs in orientation from IIP by being directed to external, rather than internal, quality of care. The Charter Mark Team, part of the Prime Minister's Office for Public Services Reform, describes itself as both a self-evaluation tool as well as external validation of the quality of public service. Organisations that undertake the formal assessment process are independently evaluated and assessed by one of four accredited Assessment Bodies.

ISO 9000

ISO 9000 is the generic name given to the family of standards for Quality Management Systems or QMS. As with Charter Mark and IIP its focus is on customers. The current set of standards, revised in 2000, suggest a core set of eight quality management principles around which the quality of an organisation, or a school, may be evaluated. While relatively uncommon in the school sector they suggest criteria which apply specifically to leadership and management.

The European Business Excellence model

The European Foundation for Quality Management's (EFQM) 'Business Excellence' model, sometimes known as the European Quality Award was developed in the early 1990s and adopted for use in the United Kingdom in 1992. Its three central planks are leadership, processes and key performance outcomes. The model while broadly applicable to a school context is heavily biased to customer satisfaction.

Other Commercial models include:

Cocentra, with 'a distinctive focus on evaluating the school's organisational culture', 'in-depth evaluation' of teaching and learning and includes a teacher self-review protocol. It promises 'the transformation of organisational values and systems'.

Tricostar offers 'an interactive, on-line self-evaluation package designed specifically for education' is based directly on OFSTED criteria.

Serco learning offers a school self-review tool designed to help measure the effectiveness of the organisation through Ofsted or self-defined frameworks.

Angel Solutions' self-assessment portal can be used to help a school gain insight into the probable outcome of their next inspection.

Mentus has a 'Verifier' tool which takes users through the process and produces an on-line SEF, emphasising this as a journey of enquiry and discovery rather than simply as an end point.

Spending time and money wisely

There is possibly little to choose among commercial websites but all cost money and promise a saving in time. A distinguishing feature would be whether they simply offer a quick and dirty way to complete the SEF to the satisfaction of inspectors or whether what they offer is really a developmental tool to help staff and students to explore their practice more critically and creatively. Overemphasis on the SEF and Ofsted should be a disincentive.

In judging the value and appropriateness of the various frameworks and tools on offer it is important to:

- look at the date on the website – if there is one – to determine how current the framework is;
- consider who is seen as the potential user(s) and the underlying premise as to who is involved in self-evaluation;
- evaluate how user-friendly and easily navigable it is;
- consider whether it has formative rather than simply summative potential;
- consider its relevance to the New Relationship in its wider aspects including ECM;
- assess its fitness for purpose – how adaptable is it to the need and stage of development of the school?
- examine the costs and possibly hidden costs;
- consult other satisfied or dissatisfied users.

And as a final postscript Google search will also find you this: 'You utterly useless piece of yak dung. You bungling, clueless, incompetent fool. You absolutely pathetic, hopelessly inept apology for a human being.' 'You...'

Oops! Sorry about that, but I have just been standing in front of a mirror practising once more my latest techniques of self-evaluation or, as I intend to call it in future, 'autocritology', a new science I have just copyrighted (patent, jargonisation and accompanying bullshit pending). Ted Wragg Inspection is on critical list. TES 05 March 2004.

(www.tes.co.uk/section/story/?section=Archive&sub_section=News+%26+opinion&story_id=391857&Type=0).

14 The tools of self-evaluation

If you want people to change how people think give them a tool, the use of which will lead them to think differently.

(Buckminster Fuller[1])

This chapter categories the tools of self-evaluation under context and fitness for purpose, potential advantages and potential disadvantages. It illustrates these with a number of tools at classroom, school and community levels.

Giving people tools to use changes their behaviour and shapes their thinking. The SEF and its predecessors have powerfully influenced the behaviour of school leaders. In some cases it has been a dutiful and strategic response to the demands of Ofsted, unaccompanied by a deeper change of heart. In other cases the SEF has been instrumental in helping school leaders think about issues of quality, effectiveness and the nature of evidence but, in the process, embracing this as self-evaluation. It is timely for heads and teachers to be reminded that the SEF is not self-evaluation and that there exist different kinds of tools which, in the hands of teachers and students, offer different lenses through which to view the world, and focus thinking in new directions.

Self-evaluation, the prevalent and recurring theme of this book, is what happens in the day-to-day work of schools and classrooms. It happens most of the time spontaneously and intuitively. It is embedded in the teacher–pupil relationship and in the daily discourse of the staffroom. It takes place at the photocopier and in the administration and management offices. It is implicit in the work that teachers take home with them and in the planning and preparation for the next lesson. The informal and unrecorded nature of this should not diminish its importance because self-evaluation is the process of making meaning of everyday experience with a view to maintenance and improvement.

Tools come into their own when they help to focus attention and lend a sharper edge to what is seen and heard. The right tools can help to spot the learning moment or the leadership moment. The right tools can help to make thinking visible and transferable. The right tools can help to perceive leadership in the mundane and see the extraordinary in the ordinary. The day-to-day tools of self-evaluation must, however, meet a number of criteria if teachers, pupils or other people are going to use them. They have to be:

- Economical – simple and easy to use
- Informative – telling you something new
- Formative – offering options as to where to go next
- Adaptable – able to be used flexibly and accommodated to pupil, class or school needs
- Convivial – creating a sense of enjoyment, purpose and challenge.

The tools of self-evaluation have multiple contexts of use and multiple users. This may be portrayed diagrammatically as a rippling out in concentric circles from the central focus on the pupil both as subject and user of self-evaluation tools, to the next circle of the classroom where users may be pupils and teachers or other invited visitors, to the middle management or departmental level and then the whole school. Moving beyond the school walls, parents, communities and other agencies may all be the subject and users of self-evaluation tools and with the advent of *Every Child Matters* this has now assumed a higher and more urgent profile (Figure 14.1).

The inner circle

At the centre of the concentric circles is the individual pupil. He or she is the primary locus of evaluation and is the source of a growing amount of data. As discussed in Chapter 9, PLASCS, PANDAS and PATs track and document every aspect of a pupil's behaviour that is in any way measurable. While this mountain of data may be justified as in the interest of the individual it

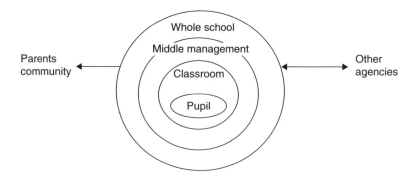

Figure 14.1 Circle of influence.

also treats the pupil as a proxy indicator of school effectiveness and as such may neither have a formative value nor focus on those things which are about learning and growth. Although it is possible for this form of data to be generated and used by the pupil himself or herself, in practice, the data collected tends to be *about*, not for, the pupil and collected on his or her behalf by adults and by the faceless demands of the 'system'.

Convivial tools are those which help children and young people think about their learning, to reflect on where, how and with whom they learn best and to extend their repertoire of learning habits and skills. Convivial tools help pupils to identify the factors which help and hinder progress and equip them to assume responsibility for their own learning. They enable children and young people not only to be knowledgeable about their own learning preferences but also equip them to extend their learning repertoire. They help learners to critically appraise the conditions which support effective learning including the quality of teaching.

Jones[2] and colleagues' description of student engagement provide a set of criteria by which to evaluate the process and progress of learning.

> In engaged learning settings, students are *responsible for their own learning*; they take charge and are self-regulated. They define learning goals and problems that are meaningful to them; have a big picture of how specific activities relate to those goals; develop standards of excellence; and evaluate how well they have achieved their goals. They have alternative routes or strategies for attaining goals and some strategies for correcting errors and redirecting themselves when their plans do not work. They know their own strengths and weaknesses and know how to deal with them productively and constructively. Engaged learners are also able to shape and manage change.

Learners do not achieve that level of engagement, however, without the requisite tools or ways of scaffolding their approach to an issue or problem. Tools may take a very simple form such as a set of guiding questions which come to be used routinely and eventually internalised, for example:

* What do I do when I do not understand something?
* What have I done successfully in the past when faced with a problem?
* How could I think differently about this?
* Do I look for help or persist in trying to solve the problem?
* Who do I look to for help?
* How much do I help other people when they are stuck?
* What have I noticed about my learning?

These are essentially learning how to learn questions. Because they probe not *what* has been learned but the longer term, more deeply embedded process of learning itself. Other examples which meet the five criteria suggested above are:

Traffic lights

Traffic lights is perhaps the most economical and simple to use of all tools. It invites pupils to reflect on the current state of their learning in relation to a particular task or activity. If they feel confident that they understand a given piece of work, they use a green indicator. If they are not quite sure of their understanding they use amber. If they are uncertain or confused they use a red indicator. These could take the form of a coloured circle on card held up at a given moment during a teaching sequence, a coloured sticker on the corner of the desk as a less public signal to the teacher or to one's peers. The traffic lights are used not as a summative assessment tool but as self-reflection on one's own learning, perhaps as an expression of a learner's confidence in their learning. Their formative purpose is for the pupil to think through what they need to do to move from red or amber to green, perhaps with the help of their green light peers. An even simpler version of the traffic light is the thumbs up, thumbs down or thumbs sideways.

The basic concept of the traffic lights can be extended to other contexts and uses. It may be used to feed back to the teachers on the high and low points of lessons. It has been used to good effect in classroom where at given points in the lesson pupils are asked to agree, disagree or signal 'undecided' in response to a statement, proposition or hypothesis. Similar techniques may be used in school council meetings, in Circle Time or in teacher meetings or workshops, for example.

A graph of engagement

A simple tool which requires nothing more than the occasional jotted note is the graph of engagement over the course of a lesson. At regular intervals, every 10 minutes say, the pupil notes what is happening and scores his or her own level of engagement on a four-point scale. This tool was designed by young people themselves[3] as a way of portraying an individual view of classroom life over the course of a day or, as in the example shown here (Figure 14.2), of one specific lesson. It illustrates the kinds of activity that are most and least engaging and is a tin opener for a learning/teaching conversation.

The second circle

The second circle is about the nature of the classroom as an arena for learning and teaching. There is an accumulating wealth of data about a class grouping, providing aggregations and disaggregations of thirty or so

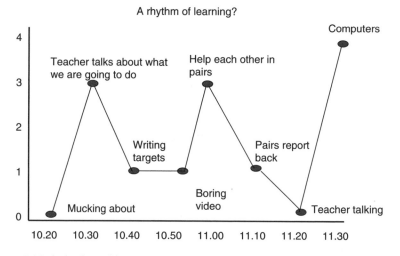

Figure 14.2 A rhythm of learning.

individuals, data which are of limited formative value but have a powerful use as a proxy for teacher effectiveness and accountability. Essential to a convivial self-evaluation, however, is that it provides insights into the classroom as a physical and social context for learning and that it affords teachers and pupils a more sophisticated understanding of what happens in the complex interplay of learning and teaching.

It is important that self-evaluation tools are able to throw light on the social group, the peer group influence and the nature of collective learning. In a context where assessment is highly individualised, self-evaluation needs to cast the net wider so that it is able to understand the way in which group processes affect the acquisition of knowledge and the impact of classroom dynamics on this.

In an Amsterdam school a teacher starts the school year in this way. For the first period of the first day he invites the class to explore the classroom, to rummage around the books, to open drawers, to examine desks and chairs, to consider lighting and heating and then to render a judgement on this space as an environment for learning. While not a tool in any strict sense of the term it is an approach which carries a powerfully symbolic message not only about context and climate of learning and teaching but the role of pupils as more than passive consumers.

One of the primary and most visible 'conditions' in the classroom is the teacher. While teachers can get feedback on their teaching from the most valuable of sources – their pupils, they need also to be self-reflective, aided by tools which help them retrospectively to evaluate their teaching and prospectively to shape their future behaviour. A very useful illustration of this is to evaluate styles of questioning, using the following set of criteria.

Questioning

Do I:

- ask too many questions at once?
- ask a question and answer it myself?
- ask questions only to the brightest or most likeable?
- ask a difficult question too early?
- ask irrelevant questions?
- always ask the same type of question?
- ask questions in a non-threatening way?
- indicate a change in the type of question?
- use probing answers?
- give pupils time to think?
- see the implications of answers?
- build on pupils' answers?

These questions may be shared with pupils so that the criteria become visible and built into classroom routine. With these in mind pupils can more insightfully evaluate the quality of teaching while also applying these criteria to their own questioning of their peers and of the questions they ask themselves.

Questions such as these also provide an agenda for inspection and appraisal. Teachers are now accustomed to being observed, by local or national inspectorates, by HMI, Ofsted, EFSTYN or, in more recent years, by senior leaders as a routine aspect of performance management. Observation by a third party is one of the foremost tools for exploring the learning/teaching relationship but also one of the most fallible. Much depends on the context, the purpose and the preparation. Both inspection and performance management are essentially summative and assume the function of review rather than self-evaluation. When observation is planned, negotiated and collegial observation assumes an exploratory and dialogic character.

An observation tools meets the criterion of economy when it is chosen by the teacher because it is not an intrusion or time-consuming extra. It is seen as having a potential pay-off, whether in better pupil behaviour, greater levels of pupil engagement, or more satisfaction and enjoyment for the teacher herself. If it is to meet the conviviality criterion, self-evaluation has to begin with the teacher's own reflection on what has happened. This can be an honest and critical appraisal because there are no high stakes consequences or categorical judgements and because it is formed in the presence of a trusted colleague or critical friend and may be part of a mutual exchange which takes place over time.

The key to the success of this is being clear about the focus of the observation, planning and agreeing beforehand, setting aside time for discussion following the observation. Whatever protocol is used, seeing and describing is inevitably a subjective process. The observer is never a neutral figure in the classroom and the nature of their role or involvement needs to be thought through and agreed.

There are many different guidelines for classroom observation. The one shown in Figure 14.3 was developed in the University of Washington and offers a useful guide for both observer and observed.

The NUT offers advice[4] which applies to all observations whether collegial or statutory, for performance management purposes or as applied to Ofsted.

- Has the purpose of the observation been made clear?
- What is the focus of the observation?
- Which lesson(s) or part of the lesson(s) is going to be observed?
- Has there been an opportunity to discuss the context of the lesson?
- What level of involvement will the observer have in the lesson?
- When and how will feedback be given?
- What use will be made of any information arising from the lesson?

The third circle

The quality of teaching relies in turn on support from middle management. In secondary schools effectiveness research[5] has identified the extent to which improvement effects may lie at departmental level and there is now much greater transparency in exploring the differential among secondary school departments. How a school may take a closer look at differential performance at departmental level is illustrated by a University of Staffordshire Project which examined variation in examination entries at 16 by subject department. While this project was across schools the kind of results obtained could be found within any single school using data provided by PANDAs. While these data are not formative they do raise very important questions for reflection and discussion among a staff at departmental level. The Staffordshire study found the following:

- Significant variation in proportion of a student cohort entered for examination in different schools. The range was History (16–46%), Geography (23–57%), French (26–73%), German (2–42%), Spanish (6–20%), Business studies (2–35%), Home economics (2–20%). Only a small proportion of these variations could be accounted for by size or type of school attended. In other words these were in-school variations.
- Social class background showed substantial variation in the likelihood of students being entered for certain subjects, notably French, German and History.

If you are being **Observed:**	If you are the **Observer:**
Before	**Before**
Be prepared to discuss with the observer: • Goals for the class • What you plan to do in class that day • What you want the observer to pay attention to Tell the observer • Where you would like the observer to sit • If you would like the observer to take part in class • Where the class meets, and when	Clarify the purpose of the observation: • For individual teaching development? • For a specific purpose (e.g. behaviour)? Meet with your colleague to discuss: • What will happen in class that day. • What to pay attention to • Describe what you will be doing during the observation Schedule a meeting to discuss the observation.
During	**During**
Introduce the observer to the class Explain the purpose of the observation Explain the observer's role to the students Soon after class, write down your reflections on the class so that you will be prepared to discuss it with the observer	Record observations: • What is the teacher doing/saying? • What are students doing/saying? Record your impressions and questions; for example: • 'Is there another way to present that Concept?' • 'Seems clear, but students look confused. Why?' Note time intervals of what you observe in your notes Participate in the class only if invited to do so.
After	**After**
With the observer, reconstruct what happened in class Think about goals for the class and the specific class session that was observed. Be prepared to describe: • What you felt went well • What you would change • What was typical or atypical about the class Ask for specific descriptions and constructive suggestions.	With the teacher, reconstruct what happened in class. Ask your colleague to describe: • What he/she felt went well • What he/she would change • What was typical or atypical about the class Listen to your colleague Describe rather than evaluated what you saw Finally, offer constructive suggestions.

Figure 14.3 Observing and being observed.

- A pupil's sex also had a significant effect on the probability of being entered for examination, the only exception to this being Home Economics. Females are much more likely to be entered for Home Economics.

- Absolute departmental performance as measured by the percentage of students achieving GCSE grades A* – C was negatively associated with the probability of a student being entered for examination in French, German, Geography and History but not in Business Studies and Home Economics, perhaps reflecting 'cream skimming' in subjects that attract a relatively higher proportion of students from higher SES backgrounds.

The above is simply a sample of a much wider-reaching analysis of results which may be a source of endless delight for the avid researcher but are of much greater immediate value to a school staff in forward planning. In the spirit of self-evaluation, findings of such an inquiry should also be transparent and discussable, not only by teachers and support staff but by students too who are, it is repeatedly claimed, the 'clients' of the school.

Whether in secondary or primary schools, middle management is recognised as highly significant as the mediating tier between senior leadership and the classroom, and is the rationale for the National College programme *Leading from the Middle*. A qualitative tool for discussion at departmental level is shown in Table 14.1. This tool is most suited to a large secondary

Table 14.1 Evaluating the learning culture

Indicators of a learning culture	My view group view	Small group view	Whole group view
Pupils are clear about the purposes of what they are learning Pupils are helped to become independent learners In this department people research, inquire and reflect critically on practice Teachers are open to change but critical as to what is most important in terms of learning Teachers in this department learn together, exchanging ideas and practice There is a strong ethos of mutual support among staff People talk about and value learning, not just grades, marks and test scores Our departmental work is characterised by people deciding and acting together There is a strong congruence between departmental priorities and those of the school as a whole All staff have opportunities for continuing professional development			

department, one of at least six members, but it may be adapted for use in a smaller department or in a primary school. The idea is that each person goes through the statements on their own, giving a rating such as 1 to 4 grade or any other device of their choosing. After about 5 minutes or so they go into pairs and compare grades, probing one another's source of evidence. After 10 minutes or so of this paired discussion they resume as a whole group to consider the implications of their 'findings' and to consider what evidence they may wish to focus on to confirm or refute their judgements and where this might take them in the future.

The fourth circle

At whole school level tools of review and audit are of two kinds – quantitative and qualitative. The quantitative data portray the school in terms of grades, scores or value-added. The qualitative measures are judgements, essentially subjective, formed on the basis of evidence and rendered quantifiable by a 1 to 4 descriptor such as 'outstanding' or 'good'. While taken together the quantitative and qualitative measures may say quite a lot about the quality of a school, they are essentially summative in character and limited by the attempt to arrive at a relatively crude shorthand digest. This does not preclude, of course, a rich formative dialogic process through which these summary judgements are arrived at, and it is in this respect that a 1 to 4 grading may serve to focus and stimulate dialogue.

Painting the school

An approach that stands at the opposite end from the statistical representation of a school's quality is portraiture. This is the term used by the Sarah Lawrence Lightfoot[6] to denote an art form that is also in a sense a science because it is scrupulous in its regard for evidence. The process is likened to the weaving of a tapestry, 'designed to capture the richness, complexity and dimensionality of human experience in social and cultural context, conveying the perspectives of the people who are negotiating those experiences'.[7] Lawrence Lightfoot's portraiture is primarily in the form of written texts, as rich in description as a novelist but without a fictional content, while her colleague and co-author Hoffman-Davis uses visual forms to convey the potential richness of a non-linear medium.

The potential of visual representation is described by Eliot Eisner[8] in these terms: 'Visual forms – maps, pictures, bar charts, for example – are synchronic in character and afford us an 'all-at-onceness' in our perception that reveals what would be hard to grasp in diachronic forms such as language and number'.

Lawrence Lightfoot makes a distinction between listening to people's stories and listening *for* people's stories. The distinction is an important one as it implies a deep form of listening to what lies beneath the words.

Those who work with young children or children with special needs have to employ this kind of listening and look for alternative forms of expression. Visual forms such as drawing and painting can be a more accessible medium than the written or spoken word. For example, drawing of what they like and dislike about their school can be highly revealing as in Figure 14.4,[9] especially when probed sensitively with a teacher or trusted adult.

The advent of digital cameras has opened up opportunities for photo evaluation or photo inquiry, offering another powerful and flexible visual medium. In one version of photo evaluation children are given a camera and invited to take photographs of places in the school where learning is enjoyable or tedious for example. A simple protocol is outlined by the Austrian educators Michael Schratz and Ulrike Steiner-Loffler.[10]

Video offers a further medium which, with easy-to-use and creative digital editing can tell a school's story with greater texture and human impact than any set of statistics. The creative use of video is nowhere better exemplified than one made by a group of secondary students in a Perth school in Scotland, telling the school's story through a pastiche of the X Files, the opening shot showing the two intrepid investigators approaching the school through a murky mist, entering the school office and leafing through school files to discover the truth about the school, eventually turning on the television to reveal members of staff talking about how they measure the school's success.

A DVD made by a young teacher and pupils in Birley Spa school in Sheffield[11] is further illustration of the creativity and impact that the visual medium allows. The 25-minute video is constructed in the form of a news broadcast with two presenters, male and female, acting as anchor and introducing the reporting team, all of them children from Birley Spa itself, all aged between 6 and 11. The pupils conduct short interviews with teachers, headteacher and fellow pupils and take the viewer on a guided tour through playground, classrooms, school council meetings and other sites where learning takes place, and in which relationships are tested and forged.

Figure 14.4 A 7-year-old's eye view of school life.

   Skilfully edited the video captures in a space of 25 minutes the ethos and character of the school, illuminating its many strengths, providing graphic evidence through words and images that go to the very heart of what the school is about. While the video does not claim to tell the whole story or provide a stand-alone evaluation of the school, what it does is to provide a summary 'document' which lays the foundations for the dialogue and invites critique. It illustrates that self-evaluation need not be a dutiful chore and that pictures can sometimes say more than a thousand words.

Building social capital

Capacity is built through the kind of sharing that pupils can do but equally, or more significantly, through the too often hidden expertise and craft knowledge of teachers. Figure 14.5 shows a matrix which could be used by

Deepening (high)

Strong on human capital. Teachers reflect on and research their own practice, some through further qualifications and sponsored research. Professional time is used for personal development. There is a high level of critical self-evaluation and many teachers show enthusiasm for a broader repertoire of evaluation and development tools. There is a variety of practice and values across the school.	Strong on social capital. Teachers routinely reflect critically on their practice, sharing their findings with others, triumphs as well as disasters. Evidence is sought and critically evaluated. People listen sensitively to one another but are not afraid to challenge. They routinely and informally visit one another's classrooms, exchanging ideas and resources. Values are discussed but differences are acknowledged and learned from. Ideas are evaluated on their merits without regard for status or hierarchy. There is shared responsibility for the induction of newly qualified teachers and classroom assistants.

Broadening   Broadening
(low)   (high)

There is a strong sense of individual autonomy. Teachers privatise their practice and jealously guard expertise and resources, investing their energies in their own class and their relationships with their own pupils. They disengage themselves from school-wide development if it is not seen as in the interest of their class or of direct relevance to teaching and learning.	There is a strong collegial spirit in the school. Staff have pride in their school and see it is a good school whatever the outsiders' view. Teachers share ideas and practices and learn from one another. Staff have a strong sense of solidarity in evaluating and resisting change which is not widely agreed. They place a high premium on consensus and have low level of tolerance for idiosyncrasy and deviance.

Deepening (high)

Figure 14.5 Assessing social capital.

an individual, a group or a whole staff to consider how they would epitomise the school as a place in which knowledge is shared, on the one hand broadening the knowledge base, on the other deepening it. The lower left-hand corner characterises a school high on individual autonomy and privatisation of practice. The lower right-hand characterises a school where knowledge is more broadly shared but without the challenge that problematises and deepens informed practice. The top left is the deepening quadrant but still individualised while the top right portrays a situation where knowledge and practice are not only deepened but also shared.

Using this matrix as a basis for discussion is likely to reveal that categorising a school is not quite that simple, that it is often a matter of time, task and context. That is, a school may be highly collaborative, exploiting its hidden capital to the full, for example on a whole school project, a concert, fund raising, or a parents' evening, but then that energy being put back into its separate compartments when revising for tests or exams.

The fifth dimension: beyond the school walls

The term school self-evaluation is now so well established that it tends to ignore the learning that goes on beyond the school walls, learning which is more pervasive and influential on attitudes and life chances than what takes place within classrooms. Little has been published on self-evaluation as applied to community or home learning although there is a considerable body of research on home and community effects.[12]

Table 14.2 Construction sites

I learn best:				
Place	*Purpose*	*People*	*Time*	*Strategy*
In my room	To get it done and over with	By myself	Early morning	Memorising and testing
In the sitting room	To please the teacher	With friends	Just after school	Self-questioning for understanding
In front of the television	To avoid trouble	With parents(s)	Early evening	Visualisation techniques
Walking the dog	To get better grades	With brothers or sisters	Late evening	Teaching others
In the library	To help me master the subject	With pets	Saturdays	Making summary notes
In an internet cafe	To increase my enjoyment in learning	With dolls, teddy bears	Sundays	Mind mapping

Table 14.3 The toolbox

Tools of evaluation	Context and fitness for purpose	Potential advantages	Potential disadvantages
Analysis of quantitative data	Quantitative data covers a range of indicators of school effectiveness, including attendance and attainment and numerous dissagregations, for example by sex, social indicators and prior attainment. Value-added analysis is providing a further source of data to be considered	Data on attainment can offer a summative, diagnostic and formative purpose and give teachers information previously unavailable to them. These data need to be used and selectively, accompanied by expert advice on their potential and limitations	Expertise and confidence in dealing with quantitative data and multiple, and sometimes contradictory sources. Can be very time consuming and overwhelm other sources of evidence
Questionnaires	A versatile tool which can serve a range of purposes, generally used in whole school context but may refer specifically to classroom, out-of-hours learning or other contexts for learning	Provide quantitative data Are quick to use Easy to analyse Offer a broad overview Are anonymous Can also be used to gather qualitative data	Can limit responses Are usually open to a variety of interpretations May encourage random answers rather than considered reflection Are context sensitive and not hugely reliable.
Individual interviews	May be used for a variety of purposes and be conducted by external critical friends, teachers or by pupils interviewing one another, often older pupils interviewing younger peers. Training is an important prerequisite	Can provide in depth insights in a context where there is anonymity and no need to conform to classmates or teacher expectations	On the part of the interviewee requires verbal skills, a willingness to open up and trust the interviewer. Can be uncomfortable and exposing for pupils Relies on high-level interviewer's skills. Is time consuming and not very cost effective

Table 14.3 Continued

Tools of evaluation	Context and fitness for purpose	Potential advantages	Potential disadvantages
Group interviews	Used to cover greater ground and in a less time than individual interviews. Well-handled, allows for rich dialogue, consensus and challenge	Pupils, teachers and parents may be more relaxed in group setting. Ideas are sparked and insights gained which might not emerge from an individual interview. More cost effective than individual interview	Dangers of peer pressure and conformity to mainstream views. Difficult to quantify unless voting or other recording systems are used
Focus groups	Used, and often confused, as group interviews but with a more structured protocol, usually led by someone with trained expertise	Is able to extract the maximum information by virtue of its tight structure	Requires expertise in managing a group and relies on training
Observation	One of the most commonly used methods for evaluating quality. May be open or highly structured. May be used by senior and middle leaders, by peers, or in some cases by pupils	Gives direct access to what teachers and pupils are actually doing rather than what they say they do. Can be used for a variety of purposes with differing foci	Reliability is low as people see different things Observation schedules are hard to follow and can become so detailed they miss the whole picture
Group card sorts	Card sorts come in many forms but usually involve a group choosing or prioritizing items that they agree on as representing their view of practice	Its hands-on format benefits people who are more reserved or less articulate. Stimulates dialogue	May allow stronger members of the group to dominate. The end result may be meaning less without a record of the dialogue leading up it
Q sort	The Q sort is an individual card sort in which a pupil, or teacher,	Is particularly useful with children and young people	Is hugely time consuming in collation and analysis of data

(Table 14.3 continued)

Table 14.3 Continued

Tools of evaluation	Context and fitness for purpose	Potential advantages	Potential disadvantages
	goes through a set of cards, placing them in one of three or four piles which might be similar to the categories found on a questionnaire	because of its hands-on nature Is less intimidating than a questionnaire	
Sentence completion	Providing a prompt such as 'I learn best when...' can be a helpful starter for pupils but also for a range of other users, teachers or parents for example	Provides the stimulus for an open-ended response and can tap into feelings	Low in reliability as it depends a lot on context, recent events and feelings at the time
Drawing and paintings	Very useful with young children but can also be powerful when used used with adults to portray their school, their job, or their relationships, for example	Is creative. No right and wrong answers Generates insights less easily accessible through paper and pencil or conversation Pupils are more likely to talk about things they have created themselves	May be highly ambiguous, difficult to analyse and requiring high inference, unless used as a basis for a more extended individual or group interview
Photo evaluation	May take a number of forms. Is particularly revealing when pupils work in groups with a camera to lens record places or people that are most rewarding and those that a re least rewarding	Allows a school to see itself through a different and graphic ness of those with the camera Is an enjoyable activity for pupils Can be empowering	Is limited by the medium to what can be seen and by the perceptive- May be threatening and reveal things some people would rather not have exposed

Table 14.3 Continued

Tools of evaluation	Context and fitness for purpose	Potential advantages	Potential disadvantages
Spot checks	An instrument which gives immediate feedback on what is happening at a given moment in the classroom or elsewhere, such as in study support or homework, for example	Gives an instant snapshot of pupil engagement and feelings and provides the basis for a rich conversation about teaching and learning	Can expose practice and accentuate differences in teachers' and pupils' perceptions which may be discomforting
Force field analysis	A tool with a wide application in business and education, the force field examines the conditions which either inhibit or facilitate development – applied to a school or classroom culture or any other learning setting	Is simple, easy to use and economic. A simple tool which pupils or teachers can complete in a fewminutes it can reveal the 'toxins' and 'nutrients' in a school culture, leading to consider how these may be addressed	May be threatening in what it reveals and by virtue of its selectivity may leave a lot unsaid
Pupil work	The actual work produced by pupils in its various written, visual, musical and dramatic forms provides one of the most tangible sources of evidence on the quality of learning Critical discussion of selected exemplars among a group of staff also serves a larger formative purpose than self-evaluation	The product of pupils' work is one of the ultimate tests of quality and provides a range of artefacts that are not revealed by most forms of standardised assessment	Involves subjective judgement Is time consuming and is best served when there is longitudinal evidence of progression

(*Table 14.3 continued*)

Table 14.3 Continued

Tools of evaluation	Context and fitness for purpose	Potential advantages	Potential disadvantages
Shadowing	Shadowing usually takes place over a day or longer. It may take the form of shadowing a pupil, a teacher or headteacher. It is a way of getting a broad cross sectional view of their experience	Allows the observer to see classroom and school life 'from the inside' as it were Rather than more extended moving picture	Is time intensive Requires an ability to know what to focus on and how to make the most of reflective conversation with pupils or teachers When shadowing a pupil over a day it can become tedious and it is easy to lose concentration
Critical incident analysis	Used to replay an event and 'unpack' it in detail to reveal what went wrong or what could have been done differently	Potentially very powerful in analysing key moments or sequences of events in school and classroom life	Requires skills in critical critical analysis, openness and suspension of blame
Role play	An extension of critical incident analysis, used to recreate a situation, replaying it through drama to illustrate a pupil's perception, or to examine some detail or aspect of the event	Enjoyable. A break from pencil and paper routines. Can be very revealing in holding up a mirror to a teacher or to the school	Requires skills and confidence on the part of the players and can meet with resistance Is limited to what can be represented in this medium
Diaries and logs	Keeping a record of events, successes, problems raised, solutions found, can be used by pupils, teachers, middle or senior leaders, governors or parents	Provides an ongoing record for self-evaluation Can be rich in detail and insight	Diaries/logs are necessarily subjective and portray things through a single lens

Homework is one area in which self-evaluation is highly relevant. It puts to the test the ability of pupils to be self-managing, self-assessing and self-evaluating when there is no longer a dependency on teacher direction. Homework often takes the form of a piece of work to be duly completed and returned to the teacher for comment rather than being subjected to critical appraisal in terms of its content (self-assessment) and in terms of the learning style and context in which it was undertaken (self-evaluation).

Learning out of school is an ideal context for self-evaluation because there is time and space for reflection and self-evaluation, testing the quality of learning without teaching. A set of questions such as those illustrated in Table 14.2 is a good starting point.

Learning out of school

Out-of-school hours learning (sometimes referred to as OHSL) has expanded rapidly in the last decade, generally known as study support but encompassing a whole range of activities to which the term 'study' sits uneasily, for example sports and other outdoor activities. Ironically it is in many of these that self-evaluation has the longest history and is most critical to success. Goals, target setting and performance review are integral to most sporting activities. Likewise in music, dance, drama and the visual arts qualitative evaluation is often at its most rigorous and demanding.

The Code of Practice for out-of-hours learning, first developed by The Prince's Trust and now distributed by the DfES, provides models for study support centres, libraries, community and resource centres to use to evaluate their own provision, inviting pupils, students or other participating adults to ask questions and seek evidence for their judgements. Under each of the three headings – emerging, established and advanced – it poses questions for pupils, teachers, volunteers and other involved parties to use to validate their stage of development. Examples of practice are provided in each of the three categories to illustrate what an 'emergent' or 'established' or 'advanced' centre would look like.

Self-evaluation may extend its compass beyond the school as the unit of inquiry, locating itself as an agency within a wider community and attempting to view itself through the eyes of others. As extended schools and full-service schools come into their own, the nature of their improvement and accountability inevitably broadens its focus in tune with its extended aims. As the effectiveness of a school's work with other agencies assumes greater significance so the need for collaborative self-evaluation strategies increases. The *Every Child Matters* framework of indicators is at first sight a daunting prospect for schools. Yet, when they recognise that they *contribute*, rather than take sole responsibility for, safety, health and well-being, for example it opens up new possibilities for extending the notion of 'self' and encourages a sense of inter-dependence and learning exchange rather than an embattled competitive outlook on the world.

15 The leadership equation

Inspection has progressively focused its attention on school leadership, usually a reference to the headteacher or senior management team. Leadership is, however, a more complex equation. This chapter considers the role of leadership within the New Relationship and questions the place of the four C's – consultation, consensus command and control.

In the end all roads lead to leadership. It is through leadership that new relationships are built and come to have meaning for those without any formal leadership status. However, we need to dig deep to apprehend what leadership means in the complex equation of school and government agencies. A new relationship with schools may be presented in simple terms of government and schools in partnership but in reality 'government' is a somewhat nebulous concept and 'school' is not simply the governing body, the headteacher or senior management but a range of staff all with a vested interest in educating children. To this task they bring differing attitudes, values and political views.

Leadership at government level is equally complex, dispersed and far from transparent. The leadership and governance of schools which shapes the vision and frames policy is worked out in the interplay of agencies – the Qualifications and Curriculum Authority, the Teacher Development Agency, the DfES and Ofsted, none of which is able to exert its authority without the influence of the Cabinet Office, the Cabinet itself, the leadership of the Prime Minister and the informal 'kitchen cabinet' whose influence on educational policy is powerful but almost impossible to penetrate. Within this continually shifting scene, concealing a perpetual struggle for power, leadership is distributed and negotiated among and within the offices of government, only directly touching a teacher's life through the visitation of an Ofsted inspector. For headteachers their most immediate point of contact with government policy will in future be through the SIP.

The SIP is the new face of the LA whose leadership has been progressively neutered over the decade and half since Margaret Thatcher declared war on them. The autonomous, self-improving, self-evaluating school, independent of the LA is however increasingly dependent on the vagaries of national

Innovate		Avoid mistakes
Think long term		Deliver results now
Be flexible	**BUT**	Follow the rules
Collaborate		Compete
Delegate		Retain control
Encourage teamwork		Assess individuals
Promote generic approaches		Specialise

Figure 15.1 The paradoxes of leadership.

decision-making. For senior, middle and classroom leaders it is the very invisibility of policy leadership at national level that demands a sharpened awareness of policy leadership at school level.

In this policy environment headteachers find themselves caught in a force field of countervailing pressures. One is pushing them towards more heroic charismatic leadership, the other to a more distributed and democratic leadership. One holds them accountable for narrow performance outcomes while another advocates a broad welfarist approach through the five priorities of ECM. One impels schools to intense competition while another urges collaboration, sharing and networking. One measures success of the school as an autonomous institution, while a counter force extends the boundaries of school to greater community and inter-agency collaboration. Figure 15.1 illustrates some of the paradoxes that need to be addressed and managed within the New Relationship.

Jethro's advice to Moses some centuries ago has a contemporary relevance. 'the thing that thou doest is not good. Thou wilt surely wear away, both thou, and this people that is with thee: for this thing is too heavy for thee; thou art not able to perform it thyself alone' (Exodus 18: 17 –18).

The heroic fallacy

There is an evangelical tone to this counsel from the National College of School Leadership – 'Recognise that the answers lie within ourselves'.[1] Such statements which locate the issues within the inner self, whether the individual or the organisation, do however, offer a seductive half-truth. Self-belief is an essential precondition of leadership but without the wisdom to know what can and cannot be changed, a vision may prove to be cruelly deceptive in the face of overwhelming social, economic and political odds. Governments like to cite cases of schools improving with the arrival of a new head but these are matched by less publicised examples of heroic head-teachers unable to implement or sustain any long-term change.[2] Contesting the assumption that things can be fixed by strong leadership and a cascade of best practice, Sharon Gewirtz[3] writes:

> One of the assumptions underpinning current government thinking on education in the UK is that so-called failing schools are largely the product of poor leadership and teaching and that, through the 'cascading of best practice', all schools can be a success. A contrasting view is that good leadership and teaching can only ever have a fairly minimal effect on school performance and that in trying to locate the source of underperformance, there is a need to focus on factors which are beyond the control of schools, namely social inequality and poverty.

In the business world the failure of much heralded saviour leaders is well documented.[4] Many of those who have succeeded have been a consequence of happenstance, the right person at the right time in the right place, their success not transferable to a different context and a different set of circumstances.

There is something about change

Leadership is virtually by definition concerned with change. Where there is no change there is no need to lead since there is no challenge, no vision, no disruption to the natural order. This is, of course on the assumption that there is a static natural order, whereas we know something about 'entropy', the continuous dispersion of energy so that stability is merely an illusion. Change tends to be seen as an occasional disruptive event, 'a punctuated equilibrium' as opposed to a view of change as the inevitable state of things. Adopting the second of these two views a school may be seen as perpetually in an unsteady state, constantly 'importing chaos'.[5] Where there is a constant flux, unpredictability and a turbulent external world, organisational growth is premised on the ability to live with paradox and thrive on discontinuity. Leadership is then concerned with understanding, and helping others to understand, the nature of change. With a broader and deeper awareness people are in a better position to adapt critically and creatively to new ideas.

> I cannot help fearing that men may reach a point where they look on every new theory as a danger, every innovation as a toilsome trouble, every social advance as a first step toward revolution, and that they may absolutely refuse to move at all.
>
> (Alexis de Toqueville)

The capacity for adaptation within an organisation is illustrated by a now well-known metaphor of how different people respond to change. It derives from the work of Everett Rogers[6] who characterised organisational behaviour as shown in Figure 15.2.

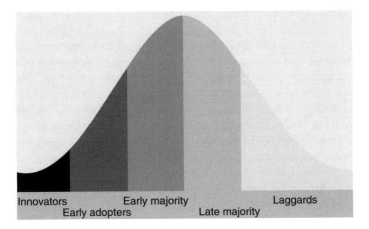

Figure 15.2 Adapting to the flow of change.

Each of these members or groups may play a leadership role in some form. The innovators are the venturesome and visionaries who welcome change and risk-taking. They may be leaders in a heroic sense but fail to take other people with them. The early adopters are the more studied and thoughtful opinion leaders and may bring along some of the early majority. The early majority are more cautious but willing to go along with what they see as a safe investment. They may exercise a more tentative form of leadership with their peers. The late majority is more likely to adopt a follower role, to take their time, to approach innovation with scepticism, their leadership being expressed as a backlash against change. The laggards are deeply suspicious of change and tend to make their point of reference what happened in the past. They may exert a subtle or subversive leadership role.

These caricatures may sound a familiar note with headteachers but need to be treated with some caution. By putting people into such definitive categories it blinds us to the versatility and unpredictability of human beings who respond differently in different relationships and contexts and who may, in one sphere of activity, be an early adopter but be a late majority in another.

A wave of change passes through an organisation because there are 'agents' or leaders who influence others. They do so often indirectly rather than directly, by example, by modelling, by demonstrating the value of doing things differently. They:

- develop in others a need for the change
- establish information-exchange relationships
- help to diagnose problems
- create a desire or intent for change
- translate intent into action

- stabilise adoption of new ways of doing things and prevent discontinuity
- shift others from reliance on the change agent to self-reliance.

In Rogers' schema 'adoption' comes from exposure to new knowledge and, with the help of colleagues, people are eventually persuaded of the value of change, making a decision to try it out. If there is some evidence of success it is seen to work and he or she may then implement the change, finally becoming confirmed by tangible benefit from its use. He or she may then take the initiative in leading others to adopt the practice in question.

Rogers' description of the process may perhaps strike a simplistic note but as he himself points out, when we look at what comes before and what follows any communication event we realise it is only a part of a much larger process. The Rogers' model does point to something important in the adoption of procedures such as target setting, peer observation and self-evaluation frameworks. Conceptual frameworks or protocols do not make sense simply on paper or in the abstract. They are made sense of inside people's heads, through dialogue between people and within a change-friendly or change-adverse culture. No matter how elegant a self-evaluation framework may be, it will almost always be modified and de- or re-constructed when people understand it and adapt it to their own context. Like any piece of knowledge, it is made meaningful by being remade. Any conceptual model, any framework or attempt at improvement, must respect those fundamental tenets. It must:

- Start from teachers' own experiences and understanding
- Have some purpose which makes sense within the culture of the school
- Respect and relate to the context of teachers' work
- Have a structure which helps to make sense of the experience.

The task of leadership is to make visible the *how* of learning. It achieves this by conversations and demonstrations around pupil learning, professional learning, organisational and systems learning. Leadership nurtures the dialogue, extends the practice and helps makes transparent ways in which these three levels interconnect. It promotes a continuing restless inquiry into what works best, when, where, for whom and with what outcome. Its vision is of the intelligent school and its practice intersects with the wider world of learning.

Leadership as distributed

What hinders headteachers from letting go of their heroic leadership? In a recent study on distributed leadership[7], headteachers were shadowed in order to identify how distribution worked in practice. Many of these heads admitted to a need to be in control, to be ready to intervene, to meet the expectation that they would exert their authority, solve problems and make life easier for their staff as well as for other stakeholders. Heads admitted to the anxiety of not being in charge and they worried about too much surprise.

> There is however a dilemma. If you give somebody a role and responsibility and that's important to them and they do the job well, when or how far do you step back and not intervene and let them get on with the job so that in the end, the head becomes so removed from the school because you're not intervening?
>
> (Secondary school headteacher)

Being 'removed from the school' suggests a concern about becoming surplus to requirement. Some heads admitted that the dependency of others on them was reassuring and reinforced a sense of being in control. They confessed to enjoying an authority and identity that was respected. The exercise of too much independence on the part of others may undermine that human need to be needed.

Consultation, command and consensus

Distribution clearly implies an ability to relinquish one's role as ultimate decision-maker, trusting others to make the right decisions. A belief in the potential and authority of others, listening, negotiation and persuasion are the levers that allow trust to gain a foothold and leadership to be shared. Trust is more likely to be in evidence when people understand and experience the difference between consultation, command and consensus. For senior leaders it implies making informed judgements as to when each of these strategies is appropriate, while also ensuring that there is a shared understanding among staff as to the relevance and transparency of these three leadership strategies.

Consultation is the process by which heads listen to others but hold on to the right to decide. Decision-making by consensus distributes that right to others but can, in some situations, be paralysing of leadership. Leadership by command may come easily to some but for the headteachers in the NCSL study it was seen as troublesome, appearing to imply something undemocratic, running at cross grain to the ethic of distribution. In the following primary head's description of 'benevolent dictatorship' we can detect something of the struggle to reconcile consultation and consensus with command and control.

> I try to talk things through in a longer term. I try to motivate people to take decisions but in the end I'm the one who is accountable, the one whose neck is on the line as it were. So I delegate much leadership but my intuitive style is somehow benevolent dictatorship.
>
> (Primary Headteacher)

In a high stakes policy environment the buck stops with the head and to trust too much to others is to risk too much. While alive to the dangers of mistrust, heads were also acutely aware of ways in which trust could be misplaced or betrayed, so while working on the one hand to share leadership and generate trust, heads also hold staff to account through performance monitoring, comparative benchmarking and scrutiny of attainment data. They acknowledged that these measures tell a partial and misleading story, holding teachers to account for things they do not believe in. But it was said, in an oppressive policy climate, there is little room for deviation or dissent. With the promise of a new covenant between government and schools trust may perhaps come with a less cautious caveat. A new relationship relies on a sharing or distribution of leadership, an implied mutual acceptance by staff of one another's leadership potential.

An infant school head commented that 'people must have high self-esteem because people need confidence to engage in distributed leadership'. She argued that a climate of trust was a necessary but not a sufficient condition for teachers to believe they could truly lead others because trust is a multi-faceted and a multi-level concept. It operates at four levels – the individual level which may be characterised as trustworthiness, the interpersonal level (reciprocal trust), at whole school level (organisational trust) and at the wider community and public level which may be defined as social trust. It is when there is alignment across these levels that new relationships can be forged. Recognising the inherent tensions and having confidence to lead staff through the attendant minefields demands considerable acuity in reading and interpreting the situation.

Heads who have worked most successfully through this dilemma are finding the means to creating more lateral learning and exchange among equals, more peer mentoring and evaluation, a fostering of mutual critique and challenge modelled by those in senior and middle leadership positions. While difficult to achieve within a hierarchical structure, the intent, as described by one secondary head, is to embed a sense of reciprocity, what an Van Leeuw[8] has called the 'me-you-too' principle. This distributive ethic is different from distribution as delegation, described by Rogers[9] as symbiosis.

> Symbiosis is a term used to describe a form of reciprocal relationship in which there exists an implicit give and take and a level of mutual respect. This is by definition different from the concept of 'delegation', which underpins much of thinking about distributed leadership. While delegation is expressed in 'giving' responsibility to others or allowing responsibility by structural default, symbiosis has a more organic quality.

Holding on and letting go

In workshops with headteachers and teachers we explored the 'force field' of factors that pushed heads back to more coercive styles, especially when trust was betrayed, when risk-taking became too risky and accountability rose to the top of the agenda. The volatility of school life, the continually shifting balance in relationships, the ebb and flow of confidence and trust featured prominently in headteachers' discourse. Such discomforts were not exclusive to heads. Teachers, whether in formal leadership positions or 'without port-folio', could readily identify with those same issues. They experienced the similar push and pull in relation to fellow staff, between pupils and teachers, between teachers and support staff and in relation to the parent body.

Elmore and colleagues[10] describes this as internal accountability, which exists in 'powerful normative cultures' built on four types of reciprocal relationship:

- *respect*, listening to and valuing the views of others
- *personal regard*, intimate and sustained personal relationships that undergird professional relationships
- *competence*, the capacity to produce desired results in relationships with others
- *personal integrity*, truthfulness and honesty in relationships.

These hallmarks of a normative culture are what provide the sense of agency, the willingness to take risks, to both offer and accept leadership arising from a discerned reciprocity. It is in this context that we can begin to make sense of teacher leadership, not as tied to status and position but as exercised individually and in concert within a culture which authorises and confirms a shared sense of agency.

Reflecting on the seven key components of self-evaluation, the policy context in which they are set, and the repertoire of sources and tools available, a number of challenges for leadership emerge.

Be clear about the distinction between self-inspection and self-evaluation

A clear danger to be avoided is for a leadership team to become resident inspectors in their own schools. The distinction made in Chapter 6 is an important one to bear in mind. Staff need to be helped to understand self-evaluation as what they do every day intuitively, as an integral aspect of their professionalism. Making it systematic, open to critical appraisal and sound evidence means that the larger, episodic process of review is no longer onerous and inspection loses its threat.

Encourage diversity and honest dissent

Self-evaluation is a dialogic process, one of constant challenge and insight, bringing within it a vitality and constant discovery. 'Organizations require a minimal degree of consensus but not so much as to stifle the discussion that is the lifeblood of innovation' write Evans and Genady.[11] Pupils, teachers and headteachers experience things differently. They see things differently and bring differing perspectives to bear. Schools that play safe, driven by external mandates and limiting conceptions of improvement set tight parameters around what can be said and what can be heard. They are antithetical to the notion of a learning organisation which, by definition, is always challenging its own premises and ways of being.

Encourage creative approaches

The more self-evaluation is associated with standardised and formulaic protocols the less adventurous teachers are liable to be. It should be a leadership priority to encourage teachers to experiment with different approaches, to extend their repertoire of tools, to involve pupils, to facilitate risk-taking and to convince sceptical or anxious staff that self-evaluation is not antithetical to Ofsted review formats but in fact can feed purposively into external school review.

Build from the bottom-up

If inspection and review are essentially a top-down process, self-evaluation works from the other end, from what teachers and pupils do. It starts with the individual, the group and the class. It extends from classroom to classroom through peer observation, informal conversations, sharing ideas and strategies, examining and displaying pupils' work. The task of leadership is to identify and distribute practice through mechanisms and tools which encourage sharing and trust and instil confidence among staff to offer one another collegial and supportive critique.

Put learning at the centre

Learning lies at the heart of self-evaluation. It is the DNA of the school and applies to pupil, teacher and organisational (and system) learning (see the wedding cake in Chapter 6). Staff may be encouraged to build their own criteria, or 'indicators' of a learning culture and use this as their guide to monitoring, however informally, what happens not only in classrooms but in staffrooms, lunch rooms and extra-curricular activities and classrooms.

Pupils learn a lot from the classroom cultures around them, cultures which carry the 'hidden curriculum' of conventions and expectations. Because these are hidden, inside people's heads, learning and thinking tend to be invisible. The Harvard psychologist David Perkins asks what would happen if we tried to learn to dance when the dancers around us were invisible or playing a sport in which the players could not be seen. He argues that, something close to this can happens in schools and classrooms when learning is not articulated, shared, made explicit and made open to systematic formative evaluation.

Support for self-evaluation means having processes and structures which help the silent repertoires of cognitive processes to be played out through the social interaction of teachers and pupils, pupils and pupils, staff with staff. It relies on a quality of leadership, both individual and shared, which casts these processes not simply as self-evaluation but as the very nature of what it means to be a school that learns.

Identify and celebrate breakthrough practice

One way in which change occurs and takes hold is through an infectious spread of good ideas or innovative practice. One or two people doing something exceptional may be where change takes roots. But its spread relies on two conditions – the 'stickiness factor', that is the endorsement and championing by prescient leadership, and the opportunity to be infectious because a growth promoting culture allows it to thrive. This is what is referred to as the epidemiology of change.[12]

Remind staff of what matters

It is important to acknowledge the pressures which staff work under, the difficulties faced in achieving a work/life balance, and the demoralisation which can spread like a virus through a staff. Self-evaluation can be seen as simply one more pressure, one more duty, unless it is seen as concerned with what deeply matters. When staff see it as integral to what they care about, 'self-evaluation' is no longer something alien or onerous.

Make self-evaluation an attitude of mind

How many evaluations do teachers make in the course of a day? The answer is hundreds. Teaching involves a constant ongoing series of value-judgements, instant decisions, intuitive evidence as well as seeking out more formal sources of data. Leadership means finding and experimenting with strategies, not simply to make these informal processes more explicit but to give teachers confidence in their judgement and make self-evaluation a habit and a way of thinking.

Demystify data

Data is a word that tends to strike terror into the breast of many staff because it is equated with statistics, hard maths and arcane procedures such as value-added and standard deviations. The apprehension stems in part because data is equated with numbers rather than the many other forms in which it is most typically encountered in the classroom – in conversations, pictures, video and children's writing. These data are the essence of self-evaluation and when collected systematically and selectively contribute to a portfolio of evidence.

Seeing data in this way does not come automatically. It relies on support and professional development and modelling of practice. Clarification of terminology and its underpinning concepts is also critical for teachers, not for academic reasons but because it helps to refine their thinking. When staff understand concepts such as criteria, indicators, standards, benchmarks or targets, they are less likely to respond with knee-jerk resistance to top-down initiatives. They are in a better position to offer their own view and to relate these ideas to their own situated practice.

Create opportunities for governors to share ownership

Governors are key players in self-evaluation, their role having achieved a higher profile within the New Relationship. Rather than being simply informed or ritually consulted, when included integrally in the process, governors can be both an important source of intelligence as well as a vital source of support. One starting point can be with governors' evaluation of their own work and impact. Approached with a pre-determined set of criteria self-evaluation is likely to be seen as threatening. On the other hand, a question such as 'How could we know how well we are doing?' is likely to generate lots of ideas which can then be turned into criteria or indicators which prove to be both owned and useful. The same process applied to the school as a whole has been found to be an enjoyable and invigorating activity for a Governing Body[13] or School Board.

When these principles are observed, self-evaluation can rediscover the vitality and creativity that was diminished by the heavy hand of Ofsted prescription. It does rely, however, on a visionary, creative and determined leadership.

16 What can we learn from other countries?

In a globalised world, inspection, self-evaluation and their interrelationship do not develop in splendid isolation. Policy-makers watch carefully to see what other countries are doing. The examples from other countries described in this chapter challenge some of our taken-for granted procedures and may inform future directions for the New Relationship.

School self-evaluation is now seen as a matter of priority in most economically advanced countries of the world. It flows from a shared concern for quality assurance and effectiveness, fuelled by international comparisons which rank countries on a range of common indicators. It is a logical extension of an international move to devolve decision-making to local school level, as much a political and economic motive as an educational one.

In European countries such as Norway, Denmark and Sweden where central government has in recent years begun to play a leading role in quality assurance, self-evaluation has acquired a sense of urgency. It is largely in response to pressures from international comparison and is integrally related to other reforms in school structures and leadership. In more decentralised administrations, such as Italy, Germany or Switzerland self-evaluation is a more localised issue. Individual states, provinces or cantons are developing their own approaches, tending to draw on models from elsewhere, often supported by a higher education project. This is also true of 'new accession' countries. In Poland for example, the University of Warsaw supports a network of fifty schools drawing on the Socrates European model. In the Balkan countries self-evaluation has been given impetus by a UNESCO project in which seven states have worked together to devise a self-evaluation toolbox, aimed at introducing the concept and the practice to schools where there had been no previous experience of evaluation from the inside.

The United States, Canada and Australia all reveal a patchwork of different initiatives, not only according to the state or province but often to even more local initiatives. In Rhode Island, for example, the School *Accountability for Learning and Teaching* (SALT) scheme takes as its focus teachers' practice, evaluated by teachers. The review team is composed of practising Rhode Island teachers together with a parent, an administrator and a member of university staff. The team spends four to five days in the school, writes a report which is negotiated with the school, the process of which can be lengthy but is highly valued in teasing out evidence and the basis for judgements made. The team then draws up 'a compact for learning', the purposes of which are to ensure that school staff have the capacity to implement improvement.

An example of an approach at school district level is in Trenton, New Jersey where *Strategic Inquiry* is the name given to a co-operative process in which the external team act as critical friends, spending an intensive week in the school, suspending judgement, getting to know the school by shadowing students, taking lunch with them and staff, observing in classrooms and participating in professional development sessions. They report back to the school with a set of questions to stimulate further dialogue and planning for improvement.

Schools speaking to stakeholders

In Quebec province in Canada, a project at McGill University, *Schools Speaking to Stakeholders* took as its starting point the key concerns of the stakeholders – teachers, students and parents and built a self-evaluation model from the bottom-up.[1] The pilot schools involved in the process benefited from their sense of ownership in the project and the authenticity of the focus on what mattered. This initiative was overtaken by a more top-down model from the Quebec Ministry, an impatient intervention that is repeated over and over in many areas where a state or province in the search for uniformity compels schools along a more compliant path.

Such local initiatives often find it hard to survive in a more directive climate but where no such central direction exists, there is space for other models to be developed. So in the United States, for example, the National Central Educational Laboratory (NCREL) publishes an approach and a self-evaluation tool offering six key areas[2] for consideration by schools, each accompanied by key questions:

Quality: How good is...(something) and/or How well is...(something) done?

Equity: How fair and impartial is...(something) and/or How fairly and impartially is...(something) done?

Alignment: How well do...(things) fit together?

Integration: How well is...(a key practice) embedded in the broader context and purpose?

Support: To what extent are individuals in favour rather than neutral or against self-evaluation?

Engagement: To what extent is there individual commitment to, and ownership of, the process?

KEYS to excellence in your schools

KEYS is an American example of a self-evaluation programme which schools can buy into. Its aims are to help schools improve their effectiveness by offering a *tool* and a *process* rather than a *package*. School staffs are given thirty five research-supported indicators of school effectiveness to help them review their progress in five core areas:

- Shared understanding and commitment to high goals
- Open communication and collaborative problem solving
- Personal and professional learning
- Continuous assessment for teaching and learning
- Resources to support teaching and learning.

KEYS aims for honest appraisal through a 'self-reflective renewal activity'.[3] The process includes a wide variety of stakeholders and vested interests – teachers unions, the school district, the community as well as school leadership and encompasses the individual interests of staff members. The inherent conflict among these differing interests is taken into account, bringing the micro-politics of the school to the fore in ways that differ markedly across settings.

The framework holds a mirror to the school, opens up issues of pre-existing beliefs and patterned behaviour and invites staff to reconsider the assumptions on which they rest. A strength of the approach is its factoring in of the changing context and dynamic of school – leadership turnover, community conflict, previously engaged projects, trying to create conditions that pave the way for new ways of working. Participants' capacity to carry out renewal plans reflects, in part, what staff know and are able to do, or are able to learn to do. Members of staff who take on leadership roles are also likely to be significant factors in the success of KEYS as it depends heavily on individuals willing to take on the responsibilities of a *design team* carrying out action steps based on the survey results.

Setting this process within national policies means helping staff to see KEYS as enhancing improvement efforts rather than as an extra burden. Across the nine states engaged in KEYS, accountability measures and high stakes testing have the potential to divert energy for self-reflection. In some cases the initiative has been drowned by external pressures, workloads and other priorities. Where KEYS succeeded it was because staff were able to see ways in which to build on and enhance ongoing initiatives and there was support to help them deal with the myriad challenges they were facing.

The evaluation of the KEYS initiative has shown that participation in a self-reflective process can provide a school with extra impetus to support what staff were already doing or to help get incipient efforts off the ground. However, without critical friends or partners from outside the school, and fuel for ongoing development, it has proved virtually impossible to sustain.

There is a salutary postscript.

A renewal process that relies on the internal will of the staff and that starts with measures of school functioning – which are likely to both look bad and convey a sense of the school's failure – has little chance of engaging staff energy and opening doors to new ways of serving young people. Add to that schools in which leadership is exercised in a non-participatory way by principals or others who have authority to guide their colleagues' work. Leaders who are not at home with participatory processes will not be comfortable with KEYS or similar approaches to school renewal, and are likely to reject the process before it can get very far.[4]

Principles from Canadian teachers

At national level the Canadian Teachers' Federation (CTF) sets criteria for a professional model of self-evaluation and accountability:

- Teachers are responsible for possessing a current subject and pedagogical knowledge base, using this knowledge base to make decisions in the best interest of students, explaining these decisions about student learning to parents and the public and working to improve their practice.
- Quality classroom-based assessment must be the central feature of educational accountability.
- Accountability must reflect the multiple goals of public education and the diverse nature of students, schools and communities.
- Accountability should be focussed on supporting and enhancing student learning.
- Parents have a right to clear, comprehensive and timely information about their child's progress.
- The public has a right to know how well the system is achieving its goals.

Australia and New Zealand

As in North America, Australia has no national system but individual states develop their own self-evaluation models in accordance with state policies. For example, *Quality Assurance in Victorian Schools* is described as a 'low stakes' approach because it is undertaken by school personnel together with external review and there is no public reporting of failure. School self-evaluation is conducted within guidelines developed by the Office of Review within whose overarching framework school councils made up of parent, community and staff representatives have significant control over school policy. The triennial school review is a verification process, conducted by a panel including members of the school's community and the external reviewer. Typically, members of the school panel include the school council president, the principal and several senior teaching staff. Using 'like with like' benchmarks schools are encouraged to set reasonable and achievable improvement standards.

Unlike Australia, New Zealand has a consistent country-wide approach to school self-evaluation and external review. State schools are required to undertake a process of self-evaluation which feeds into the Schools Charter, described as a 'living' document, since it is kept under constant review. The Ministry of Education, for its part, has responsibility to support schools by providing tools and information to support teaching and learning. By examining copies of each school's planning and reporting documentation, it determines what kinds of support or advice may be most useful and necessary – and where further support may be needed. The Education Review Office's (ERO) external evaluation role is complementary to the self-evaluation that schools carry out. Through an in-depth look inside the school every few years, ERO is able to provide assurance that the issues identified and prioritised by schools have been the right ones. Schools then are expected to make use of ERO findings in refining their goals and in identifying future planning.

Self-evaluation: a practice for 'smart schools'

The purpose of school self-evaluation in Tasmania is described as developmental, helping the school community discuss and debate where it is going.[5]

> School self-evaluation is not a magic solution, nor does it produce a blueprint for action. It really has no beginning and no end. It builds on what is already there and does not seek to impose something entirely new.

The premise is that if schools are to become effective learning organisations, then they must have 'intelligence' and act intelligently. This implies that a school has the means to 'see itself' more clearly. Because school communities consist of multiple stakeholders with diverse values and perspectives they need evaluation tools which not only help people look for evidence but also recognise their local micro-politics and take into account the following:

- a range of different points of view
- the interconnections between issues
- challenges to existing beliefs, values and knowledge
- avenues to transform random information into patterns, flows and processes
- the means to order debates
- the parameters for decision and further investigation.

A key aspect of the self-evaluation process is the relationship between home and school. One of the tasks of the evaluation team (the catalyst for whole school evaluation) is to select a random sample of families from the school roll. A member of the team then rings to speak to a parent/caregiver. He or she introduces themselves, asks if it is convenient to speak for a few minutes, explains the purpose of the survey and outlines what will happen to the information given. Five open-ended key questions are then asked and noted on a check sheet. The check sheet does not have the name of the family on it. There are five key areas for discussion with the family member:

1   Are newsletters arriving home?
2   What does the family member think of the style/content?
3   Is the school report OK? How could it be improved?
4   What is the communication with the class teacher? Is the family happy with it? How could it be improved?
5   What could the school do to improve general communication?

No information on specific classes or teachers is recorded. Names of callers with specific problems are referred to the appropriate person in the school. Results are aggregated and made public via the newsletter or school website. A date for further discussion is also advertised. Families want to know what will happen as a result of their participation so it is important at the outset to tell them:

- the purpose of the survey
- how they can find out the results
- what will happen as a result of the survey
- how they can be involved in analysis
- how they can be involved in post-survey discussion and decision-making.

Involvement in self-evaluation carries with it a right to know, the implication that outcomes will be shared and that decisions made on the basis of self-disclosure will exemplify respect for persons, however small.

The bridges across boundaries project

Between 1998 and 2000, 101 schools took part in a European project[6] on self-evaluation. At the end, 98 of the 101 opted to continue because the project contained all the elements described above, a clear sense of purpose, a framework for evaluation, relevant criteria and a process which schools found engaging, challenging and productive. The key features of that project were:

- The central involvement of key stakeholders (teachers, pupils and parents) in the process.
- The identification of what matters most to stakeholders.
- The support and challenge of critical friends chosen by, or in consultation with the schools.

- The dialogue which flowed from the differing viewpoints and the press for supporting evidence.
- The repertoire of tools for use by teachers.
- The simplicity and accessibility of the framework.
- The focus on learning and support for teaching.

When it came to tell the story of the project the team decided to relate it through the eyes of the key participants – a student, a parent, a teacher, the school principal, the critical friend working with the school. The story, although authentic in its representation of the process, was fictionalised, with the nature of self-evaluation coming to life through the central character, Serena, a 15-year-old girl. In the German translation of the book it is simply entitled *Serena*. Serena's journey from passivity and boredom is accounted for by her recognition, under the guidance of an inspired teacher, that with the right tools and conditions you can take charge of your own learning. The Serena story sparked a translation into a number of European languages, all working together in a project entitled *Bridges across Boundaries*.

The seven countries involved in the Project (Greece, the Czech Republic, Slovakia, Hungary, Portugal, Poland, Switzerland) became involved through a mutual concern to embed self-evaluation in school practice. In some cases it was a recognition that if schools did not do it governments would do it for them and not always to their liking. Each country worked with a cluster of schools, with Francesca Brotto[7] as super critical friend, as well as each country being partnered with a critical friend from one of the other project countries. The mission statements with which each country framed the project reveal something of the intent to build from the ground up, to demystify self-evaluation, to embed self-evaluation as a habit, and to take ownership of the process rather than working to a government formula. The mission statements from the participating countries give something of the flavour of the issues:

- To build on and further elaborate existing experiences of school self-evaluation of the late 1990s in Greece.
- To help Czech schools try to overcome the fear and uncertainty from self-evaluation process and to help them to understand its day to day application in schools.
- To foster the ongoing development process in Hungary in the field of quality improvement of education by providing our own framework and tools for self-evaluation.
- To establish self-evaluation as a habit in our schools in Switzerland.
- To learn (with and from others) how to deal with self-evaluation in Slovak schools.
- To empower schools in Portugal to take care of a quality development policy, in an autonomous way (to have something to contrast to the mandated and formatted self-evaluation).

- To establish the idea that self-evaluation is a process of growing collaboration, and not a product (Poland).

In Switzerland the principles on which their project rest were:

- Credibility: the procedure of self-evaluation earns the trust of school staff.
- Flexibility: the methodology can adjust itself to different situations.
- Ease of use: everybody can employ the procedure without the use of special skills.
- Accessibility: the results are available to the entire school.
- Significance: the procedure of self-evaluation is focused on shared and meaningful factors.
- Reliability: the procedure can be employed in different contexts without changing its basic principles.
- Learning: the methodology allows stakeholders to develop a critical and constructive thinking about learning.

Self-evaluation and school review in Hong Kong

The newly developed Hong Kong model is worth examining as it lies closest to the New Relationship in England and offers some pointers to both the strengths and potential pitfalls of shorter, sharper inspection centred on the school's own internal evaluation.

The development of inspection in Hong Kong has a similar history to that of UK countries, perhaps unsurprisingly given its close ties to Britain and a longstanding tradition of looking beyond it own boundaries to learn from practice elsewhere. In 2004 the Education and Manpower Bureau began a pilot project to test a system to be known by its abbreviation SSE/ESR – school self-evaluation and external review. Over 300 schools participated with an external evaluation conducted by a Cambridge team[8].

For some Hong Kong schools self-evaluation had been in place for a number of years, stimulated by initiatives from higher education. For others self-evaluation was something new, while in others again there were practices implemented by individual teachers or departments (e.g., getting student feedback on teaching) but without endorsement from senior leaders or even wider awareness that such practices existed. Implementing a system of review therefore had to be accompanied by support and guidance for schools on SSE. This did not prevent teachers experiencing a high degree of anxiety prior to review as it tended to be viewed as inspection and the purpose of self-evaluation seen as a prelude to inspection rather than of value in its own right.

Each school has a school improvement team of six to eight members representing a cross-section of staff. This group has the task of supporting their colleagues in carrying out self-evaluation, using tools offered by the

Education and Manpower Bureau (EMB) and participating in preparatory training. Over a period of three months there are briefings by EMB staff and school wide development sessions conducted by the principal and/or the school improvement team. Much of this is devoted to alleviating anxiety and helping staff move from an inspection, or quality assurance, model to one in which the focus is on their own internal self-evaluation.

A whole school staff then undertake the exercise of grading fourteen aspects of school quality on a four-point scale, trying to reach agreement. Inevitably there are differing opinions and in some cases the final grade is decided by a vote among the staff, in other cases, the final decision rests with the principal. These gradings are then presented to the review team who negotiate with the senior leadership team on the basis of evidence, but the ultimate decision rests with the ESR team. Downgrading generally causes disappointment and often resentment but in most cases tends to be combined with an acceptance of the ESR team's professional judgement. This may reflect a cultural acceptance of, and deference to, authority but it raises an issue which lies at the heart of any sequential or co-operative system. In other words, who knows best? And whose views count?

The EMB accepted the recommendations of the evaluation and abandoned the one- to four-point scale as offering a too simplistic and distracting view of school quality. The evaluation also pinpointed some of the potential, as well as the potential pitfalls, of the New Relationship.

- The purpose of external evaluation has to be clearly communicated, clearly understood and clearly reflected in practice.
- Self-evaluation should be driven by a widely shared commitment to improvement and not as preparation for inspection.
- The move from inspection to review requires a different set of skills on the part of the review/inspection team and system of professional development and feedback from schools need to be an integral part of a paradigm shift in thinking and practice.
- The principle of reciprocity implies that inspection teams listen and learn and are as open to criticism as they expect school staff to be.
- Inspection teams need to be open to creative surprise and alternative approaches used by schools.

What can we learn?

All of these examples are helpful in informing practice in English schools and local authorities and their relationship with inspection. All schemes have their frameworks, striving to find the balance, neither be so loose as to cause confusion and anxiety nor so tight that people feel hemmed in and disempowered. There is a continuum in models of self-evaluation from open to closed, from the invention of the wheel at one end to the detailed step-by-step cookbook at the other. Where there is too great a degree of openness it is very difficult for schools to initiate and sustain self-evaluation. While this is possible in highly self-confident and resilient schools the greater the pressure from the outside the less will be the time and energy invested in invention. Where there is top-down pressure and time is a scarce commodity, off-the-shelf products have considerable appeal. This is likely, however, to lead both to a mechanistic approach and a disempowering of teachers. It is significant that when the Scottish model HGIOS was adopted by an enthusiastic Minister in Norway and translated into Norwegian it was disliked and resisted by teachers. This is not surprising as they had no part in its development, no engagement in the process but were simply presented with a ready-made product. A fundamental principle of self-evaluation, as noted by the European body of inspectors, (SICI) is 'steering oneself in order not to be steered'[9], that is, schools taking the initiative rather than being reactive to decisions taken elsewhere. As the Hong Kong example shows, it is helpful for the process of self-evaluation to be undertaken by a self-evaluation group drawn from a range of volunteers within the school, strengthened when there is pupil representation.

Common to many self-evaluation systems is the four-point scale for self-rating against specific indicators or criteria. These are often derived from inspection models and often come with labels attached such as 'satisfactory' or 'good'. In England the term 'satisfactory' has provoked a heated debate within the profession and been a distraction from other aspect of the process. The original Scottish terminology of *major weaknesses, major strengths, more strengths than weaknesses* and *more weaknesses than strengths* carried a different kind of message about the balance of evidence, and allowed greater scope for seeing and negotiating judgements.

As has been found in numerous self-evaluation projects it is into this large middle ground of ambiguity, a rating of 2 and 3, that most self-evaluation judgements fall. The nature of those middle ground judgements do depend to a great extent on 'where you sit', what and how much you see, the preconceptions you bring to that judgement and the context in which you place it. An inspector's judgement of a lesson made in half an hour in a classroom is often likely to differ from that of a pupil, the classroom teacher or the headteacher. While such variance is obvious and well documented, top-down evaluation schema often fail to recognise this, and by bypassing differences miss the very heart of the process, that is, the discourse in which such mismatches or varying perceptions bring to light. This is what was so powerful in the European Self-evaluation Project where teachers, pupils and parents together brought their own perspectives to bear and, through the critical friend, were encouraged to listen to alternative ways of seeing and new ways of understanding. This was a strength of McGill's *Schools Speaking to Stakeholders* and the teacher–teacher dialogue in the Rhode Island SALT programme. It is at the very centre of the KEYS programme, recognising, rather than turning a blind eye to, the multi-faceted perspectives and conflicts that exist. It sensitivity to context and micro-politics is a salient strength.

The tools that are available to schools play a crucial role in the process. The more economical and user-friendly they are the more they are likely to be used. Their primary purpose is not however to reach a summative judgment or grade, but rather to stimulate dialogue, because it is through dialogue that teachers and school leaders deepen their understanding, leading in turn to more informed planning and target setting. The support and challenge of a critical friend is often essential to steer the process, reminding people of the ground rules. This needs to be a person who is trusted, so that people can be open and self-critical without keeping a weather eye on that person's accountability or line management role. The notion of the critical friend, appointed and accountable to government, has proved problematic.

In conclusion

We have come a long way in the last few years in our understanding of learning conditions for learning, and the leadership which creates and nurtures those conditions. With that richer store of knowledge schools clearly need a self-evaluation process that keeps pace with and informs the quality of learning and teaching, helping schools to grow through the sharing of information and insight. It has been said that organisations are often less intelligent than their individual members. This is because they are not in possession of the tools to excavate the hidden treasure of students, teacher and parent knowledge. But with a shared sense of purpose, a framework, criteria and the relevant tools for the job, schools can be empowered to tell their own story.

Notes

1 New relationships for old

1 Gershon, P. (2004) *Releasing Resources to the Front Line; A Review of Public Sector Efficiency*. Norwich: HMSO.
2 Le Grand, J. (2003) The case for the internal market in J. Dixon (ed). *Can Market Forces be Used for Good?* London: Kings Fund.
3 Davies, D. and Rudd, P. E. (2001) *Evaluating School Self-evaluation*. Slough: National Foundation for Educational Research.
4 Department for Education and Skills (2003) *Every Child Matters*. London: HMSO.
5 Ofsted (2004) The *Common Inspection Framework for Inspecting Education and Training*. London: Ofsted.
6 See for example Kluger, A. V. and DeNisi, A. (1996) The effects of feedback interventions on performance: a historical review, a meta-analysis, and a preliminary feedback intervention theory. *Psychological Bulletin*. 119 (2): 252–84. and Dweck, C. S. (1986) Motivational processes affecting learning. *American Psychologist*, 41: 1040–8.
7 Office for Standards in Education (2004) *The Common Inspection Framework for Inspecting Education and Training*. London: Ofsted.
8 Department for Education and Skills (2004) *A New Relationship with Schools: School Improvement Partners' Brief*. London: DfES.
9 Ibid.
10 DfES/Ofsted (2005) *A New Relationship with Schools: Next steps*. London: DfES.
11 Department for Education and Skills (2004b) *A New Relationship with Schools*. London: DfES.
12 David Miliband, Personalised Learning, North of England Education Conference, Belfast, 8 January 2004.
13 Miliband, Personalised Learning.
14 Ibid.
15 Ibid.
16 Department for Education and Skills (2004b) *A New Relationship with Schools*. London: DfES.
17 Miliband, Personalised Learning.
18 DfES (2004) *Every Child Matters: Next Steps*. London: HMSO.
19 Bottery, M. (2003) The management and mismanagement of trust. *Educational Leadership and Management*, 31(3): 245–61.
20 Elmore, R. (2003) *Agency, Reciprocity, and Accountability in Democratic Education*. Cambridge, MA: Consortium for Policy Research in Education. p. 17.
21 Miliband, Personalised Learning.

22 O'Neill, N. (2002) *A Question of Trust*. Cambridge, MA: Cambridge University Press.
23 Elmore, R. (2005) *Agency, Reciprocity, and Accountability in Democratic Education*, Boston, MA: Consortium for Policy Research in Education.

2 A view from the schools

1 MacBeath, J. and Oduro, G. (2005) *Self Evaluation and Inspection: A New Relationship?* London: National Union of Teachers.
2 Ibid.
3 MacBeath, J. (2004) *Self Evaluation: A Guide for School Leaders*. National College of School Leadership. London.
4 Halsey, K., Judkins, M., Atkinson, M. and Rudd, P. (2005) *New Relationship with Schools: Evaluation of Trial Local Authorities and Schools* (DfES Research Report 689). London: DfES.
5 Halsey, K., Judkins, M., Atkinson, M. and Rudd, P. (2005) *New Relationship with Schools: Evaluation of Trial LEAs and Schools*, National Foundation for Educational Research.

3 A view from the Bell tower

1 The Standing International Conference of Inspectorates.

4 Inspection and self-evaluation: a brief history

1 Lawton, D. and Gordon, P. (1987) *HMI*. London: Routledge and Kegan Paul.
2 Grubb, W. N. (1999) Improvement or control? A US view of English inspection in C. Cullingford (ed). *An Inspector Calls* (70–96). London: Kogan Page Limited. Haldeman, W. K. and Hamlett, B. D. (1987) Changes in California State Oversight of Private Postsecondary Education Institutions. A Staff Report to the California Postsecondary Education Commission. Commission Report, 87 (16), 1–17.
3 Quoted in Learmonth, J. (2001) *Inspection: What's In It For Schools?* London: Routledge.
4 Levacic and Glover (1994) *Local Management of Schools: Analysis and Practice*. Buckingham: Open University Press.
5 Rosenthal, L. (2001) *The Cost of Regulation in Education: Do School Inspections Improve School Quality?* Department of Economics, University of Keele, Stoke-on-Trent p. 16.
6 Jeffrey, B. and Woods, P. (1996) Feeling deprofessionalised: the social construction of emotions during an Ofsted Inspection. *Cambridge Journal of Education*, 26 (3): 325–44.
7 Cullingford, C. and Daniels, S. (1998) *The Effects of Ofsted Inspection On School Performance*. Huddersfield: University of Huddersfield.
8 Woodhead, C. (1999) An Inspector responds, Guardian Education, 5th October edition p. 5.
9 Rosenthal, L. (2001) *The Cost of Regulation In Education: Do School Inspections Improve School Quality?* Department of Economics, University of Keele, Stoke-on-Trent.
10 Dannawy, Y. (2001) 'Should we sugar coat the truth then miss?', Unpublished M.Ed paper, Faculty of Education, University of Cambridge.
11 MacBeath, J. (1999) *Schools Must Speak for Themselves*. London: Routledge, p. 1.
12 Parliamentary Select Committee on the work of Ofsted, 1999.
13 Ouston, J. and Davies, J. (1998) OfSTED and afterwards: schools responses to inspection in Earley, P. (ed.) *School Improvement After OfSTED Inspection: School and LEA Responses*. London: Sage Publications.

14   GRIDS was a popular approach to self-evaluation in the 1970s. Commenting on GRIDS Fidler (1997 p. 63) says that teachers were 'better at identifying improvement rather than bringing about improvement'.
15   This was the brunt of the Woodhead argument at a meeting with John Bangs of the NUT and the author of *Schools Must Speak for Themselves* in 1995 and in conversation with Scottish HMCI in 1996.
16   Davies, D. and Rudd, P. E. (2001) *Evaluating school self-evaluation.* Slough: National Foundation for Educational Research.
17   MacBeath, J., Boyd, B. Rand, J. and Bell, S. (1995) *Schools Speak for Themselves.* London: National Union of Teachers.
18   Quoted from his contribution to the book Schools Must Speak for Themselves, p. 1.
19   A conversation between Woodhead and then HMCI Archie McGlynn.
20   Alvik, T (1996) *Self Evaluation: What, Why, How, by Whom, for Whom.* Collaborative Project Self-evaluation in School Development, Dundee CIDREE.
21   Leeuw, F. (2001) Reciprocity and the Evaluation of Educational Quality; Assumptions and Reality Checks. Keynote paper for the European Union Congress, Karlstat, Sweden, April 2–4.
22   Office for Standards in Education, (1999) Revised Framework for the Inspection of Schools, London, Ofsted, p. 14.
23   Office for Standards in Education, (1999) Revised Framework for the Inspection of Schools, London, Ofsted, p. 110.
24   European Consultative Body of Inspectorates (2003) *The Effective School Self-Evaluation project,* Standing International Conference of Central and General Inspectorates of Europe, Brussels European Commission.
25   Black, P. and Wiliam, D. (1998) *Inside the Black Box: Raising Standards Through Classroom Assessment.* London: School of Education, King's College.
26   British Educational Research Association, Scottish Educational Research Association, European Congress on Educational Research, American Educational Research Association, International Congress on School Effectiveness and Improvement.
27   National Association of Headteachers (NAHT) (2005) *Making Self-assessment Really Work.* London.
28   1999 Select Committee on Education and Employment, Examination of Witnesses (Questions 424–439).
29   MacBeath, J. (forthcoming 2007) Stories of compliance and subversion in an oppressive policy climate. *Journal of Educational Management, Administration and Leadership,* 35(1).
30   Interview conducted in NCSL, June 2005.
31   Senge, P. (2000) *Schools that learn.* London: Nicholas Brealey, p. 86–7a.

5 Lies, damned lies and statistics

1   Sion Simon M. P. quoted in Oborne, P. (2005) *The Rise of Political Lying.* London: Free Press p. 59.
2   Levitt, S. D. and Dubner, S. J. (2004) *Freakonomics.* London: Allen Lane.
3   Eric Alterman When Presidents Lie *The Nation, October 25, 2004.*
4   Oborne, P. (2005) *The Rise of Political Lying.* London: Free Press.
5   Ibid., p. 66.
6   Haney, W. (2000) The myth of the Texas miracle in education. *Education Policy Analysis Archives,* 8 (41).
7   Tymms, P. (1999) *Analysing Your School's Data and Setting Targets For Primary Schools OR Baseline Assessment and Monitoring in Primary Schools.* Durham: University of Durham.

8 Organisation for Economic Cooperation and Development (2004) Programme for International Student Assessment (PISA), OECD, Paris. p. 208.
9 Berliner, D. C. and Biddle, B. J. (1995) *The Manufactured Crisis: Myths, Fraud and Attack on America's Public Schools*. Reading, MA: Perseus Books.
10 Wolf, A. (2002) *Does Education Matter?: Myths About Education and Economic Growth*. London: Penguin. p. 254.
11 Andy Hargreaves quoted in keynote lecture to the International Congress of School Effectiveness and School Improvement, Rotterdam, 5th January 2004.
12 quoted in MacBeath, J. (2006) Stories of compliance and subversion in a prescriptive policy context.
13 Giroux, H. (1992) *Border Crossings*. London: Routledge, p. 120.
14 Bramall, S. and White, J. (eds) (2000) *Why Learn Maths?* London: Institute of Education.
15 Interview conducted in the NCSL, June 2005. These ideas are developed in Starrat, R. J. (2005) Cultivating the moral character. *School Leadership and Management*, 25 (4).
16 Postman, N. and Weingartner, G. (1971) *Teaching as a Subversive Activity*. Harmondsworth: Penguin Books.
17 Giroux, H. (1992) *Border Crossings*. London: Routledge, p. 120.

6 Self-evaluation, review, audit, self-assessment and self-inspection

1 GRIDS was a popular approach to self-evaluation in the 1970s. Commenting on GRIDS, Fidler (1997 p. 63) says that teachers were 'better at identifying improvement rather than bringing about improvement'.
2 Discussions between members of the NUT, the author and Chris Woodhead, continuously ran up against his fierce opposition to self-evaluation.
3 Davies, D. and Rudd, P. E. (2001) *Evaluating School Self-Evaluation*. Slough: National Foundation for Educational Research.
4 Entwistle, N. (1987) *Understanding Classroom Learning*. London: Hodder and Stoughton.
5 Eisner, E. (1993) *What Artistically Crafted Research Can Help Us Understand about Schools*. San Francisco: Presidential address to the American Educational Research Association, April.
6 Source The Xerox Corporation.
7 Quoted in Senge, P., Scharmer, C. O., Jaworski, J. and Flowers B. S. (2005) *Presence: Exploring Profound Change in People, Organizations and Society*. London: Nicholas Brealey.
8 Limerick, D., Passfield, R. and Cunnington, B. (1994) Transformational change: towards an action learning organization. *The Learning Organization*, 1(2): 29–40.
9 See, for example, MacBeath, J. and Oduro, G. (2005) *Inspection and Self-evaluation: A New Relationship?* London: National Union of Teachers.
10 Sergiovanni, T. (2005) *Strengthening the Heartbeat: Leading and Learning Together in Schools*. San Francisco: Jossey-Bass
11 Mitchell, C. and Sackney, L. (2000) *Profound Improvement*. Lisse: Swets and Zeitlinger.
12 Senge, P., Scharmer, C. O., Jaworski, J. and Flowers B. S. (2005) *Presence: Exploring Profound Change in People, Organizations and Society*. London: Nicholas Brealey.
13 Eraut, M. (1992) *Developing the Profession: Training, Quality and Accountability*. Brighton: University of Sussex.

7 Hearing voices

1 Covey, S. (2000) *The Seven Habits of Highly Effective People*. New York, Simon and Schuster.
2 Office for Standards in Education (2005) *Pupils' Satisfaction With Their Schools*. London, Ofsted.
3 Levin, B. (2000) Putting students at the centre in education reform. *Journal of Educational Change* 1: 155–172.
4 Nias, J. Southworth, G. and Yeomans, R. (1989) *Staff Relationships in the Primary School: A Study of Organisational Cultures*. London: Cassell.
5 Willis P., (1977) *Learning to Labour: How Working-Class Kids Get Working-Class Jobs*. London: Gower.
6 Mead, G. H. (1934) *Mind, Self and Society*. Chicago, IL: Chicago University Press.
7 Berne, E. (1964) *Games People Play: The Basic Handbook of Transactional Analysis*. New York: Random House.
8 Alexander, R. (2004) *Towards Dialogic Teaching: Rethinking Classroom Talk*. Cambridge: University of Cambridge.
9 The dialogic school and implications for leadership are the focus of a dialogue among head teachers together with Cambridge Professors Alexander and MacBeath (Talking to Learn, NCSL 2004).
10 Evans, P. and Genady, M. (1999) A diversity-based perspective for strategic human resource management. *Research in Personnel and Human Resource Management*, Supplement 4. p. 368.
11 MacBeath, J. (2005) La qualita non e un punto da vista? Keynote presentation and discussion, Forum Europeu d'Adminstradores de l'Educacio de Catalunya, Barcelona, November 10th.
12 Fielding, M. (2001) Beyond the rhetoric of student voice: new departures or new constraints in the transformation of 21st century schooling? in *Forum*, 43(2): 100–110.
13 Coleman, P. (1998) *Parent, Student and Teacher Collaboration; the Power of Three*. London: Paul Chapman.
14 Frost, D. (2005) Resisting the juggernaut: building capacity through teacher leadership in spite of it all. *Leading and managing*, 10(2): 83.
15 Argyris, C. (1993) *Knowledge for action: A Guide to Overcoming Barriers to organizational change*. San Franciso, CA: Jossey-Bass.
16 Mendel, M. (2003) The space that speaks in Castelli, S. Mendel, M. and Ravn, B. (eds) *School, Family and Community Partnerships in a World of Differences and Changes*. Gdansk: Wydawnicto Uniwersytetu Gdanskiego.
17 Lawrence Lightfoot, S. (2004) *The Essential Conversation*. New York: Ballantine Books.
18 Ibid.
19 Harris, J. R. (1998) *The Nurture Assumption*. London: Bloomsbury.
20 The GTC calls for a 'new relationship' between schools and parents, Mon, 29 Nov 2004. www.gtce.org.uk/Newsfeatures/press99/104282/?view = TextOnly
21 This is anecdotal evidence based on workshops with school staff, mainly head-teachers, in which they are given five alternative possibilities to choose from. More than half generally choose pupils, with teachers a close second.
22 SooHoo, S. (1993) Students as partners in research and restructuring schools. *The Educational Forum*, 57: 386–92.
23 see for example, a Special Issue of *Forum* (2001) Vol. 43, No. 2.
24 MacBeath, J., Demetriou, H., Rudduck, J. and Myers, K. (2003) *Consulting Pupils: A toolkit for teachers*. Cambridge, MA: Pearson.
25 Rudduck, J. and Flutter, J. (2004). *How to Improve Your School: Giving pupils a voice*. London. Continuum.

8 Learning in and out of school

1 Brookover W., Beady, C., Flood, P., Schweitzer, J. and Wisenbaker, J. (1979) *School Social Systems and Student Achievement: Schools Can Make a Difference.* New York: Praeger.
Mortimore, P., Sammons, P., Stoll, L., Lewis, D. and Ecob, R. (1988) *School Matters: The Junior Years.* Wells: Open Books.
2 Jencks, C. S., Smith, M., Ackland, H., Bane, M. J., Cohen, D., Gintis, H., Heyns, B. and Micholson, S. (1972) *Inequality: A Reassessment of the Effect of Family and Schooling in America.* New York: Basic Books.
3 Coleman, J. S., Campbell, E. Q., Hobson, C. J., McPartland, J., Mood, A. M., Wienfeld, F. D., and York, R. L. (1966) *Equality of Educational Opportunity.* Washington DC: Office of Education.
4 See for example, the meta study by Sammons, P., Hillman, J. and Mortimore, P. (1994) *Key Characteristics of Effective Schools: A Review of school effectiveness research.* London: Office of Standards in Education.
5 National Statistics 2005.
6 Putnam, R. (1999) *Bowling Alone: The Collapse and Revival of American Community.* New York: Touchstone.
7 Wylie, T. (2004) *Address to the Leadership for Learning Cambridge Network,* Cambridge.
8 Bernstein, B. (1970) Education cannot compensate for society. *New Society,* 387: 344–7.
9 see for example Labaree, D. F. (1997) *How to Succeed in School Without Really Learning: The Credentials Race in American Education.* New Haven: Yale University Press.
10 Bentley, T. (1998) Learning beyond the classroom, London: Routledge.
11 A National Conversation about Personalised Learning at http://www.standards. dfes.gov.uk/personalisedlearning/
12 Ibid.
13 Weiss, L. and Fine, M. (2000) *Construction Sites: Excavating Race, Class and Gender among Urban Youth.* New York: Teachers' College Press.
14 Ward, J. V. (2000) Raising resisters: the role of truth telling in the psychological development of Afro-American girls in Weis, L. and Fine, M. (eds). *Construction Sites: Excavating Race, Class and Gender among Urban Youth.* New York: Teachers' College Press.
15 Bem in *Construction Sites: Excavating Race, Class and Gender among Urban Youth.* New York: Teachers' College Press, p. 266.
16 MacBeath, J. and Sugimine, H. (2002) *Self-evaluation in the Global Classroom.* London: Routledge.
17 Ibid., p. 38.
18 In Nishimura, M. Interview in Malmö, January 2003, p. 30.
19 Talk given in Cambridge University, June 2003.
20 Sophie (Experience Report) in Nishimura p. 59.
21 Sutherland, G. (2003) Stories of change? An exploratory study of the impact of pupils' research on teachers and teaching, M.Ed thesis, University of Cambridge.
22 Winkley, D. (2002) *The Handsworth Revolution.* London: Giles de la Mare.
23 Mitra, S. and Rana, V. (2001) Children and the internet: experiments with minimally invasive education in India. *The British Journal of Educational Technology,* 32(2): 221–32.
24 MacBeath, J., Kirwan, T., Myers, K., Smith, I., McCall, J., Mackay, E., Sharp, B., Bahbra, S., Pocklington, K., and Weindling, D. (2000) *The Impact of study*

support. London: DfES. p. 48. The summary can be found at:www.
standards.dfes.gov.uk/studysupport/816987/817959/ impactrsearchword
25 www.qiss.org.uk

9 PLASCS, PATS, electronic PANDAS and other beastly inventions

1 PLASC can be accessed at www.teachernet.gov.uk/s2s/
2 For example, Goldstein, H and Thomas, S. (1996) Using examination results as indicators of school and college performance. *Journal of the Royal Statistical Society A*, 159(1): 149–163.
3 Levacic, R. and Woods, P. A. (2002) Raising school performance in the league tables (Part 1): disentangling the effects of social disadvantage. *British Educational Research Journal*, 28(2): 207–26.
4 Organisation for Economic Cooperation and Development (2004) Programme for International Student Assessment (PISA), OECD, Paris.
5 PISA p. 208.
6 Richard Harrison made his comments at an NCSL Leading Practice seminar, 'Tackling Within-School Variation' on 9 July 2004. More detail on this seminar is available at http://www.ncsl.org.uk/mediastore/image2/randd-ln-wsv.pdf
7 South Dartmoor Community College.

10 Every Child Matters?

1 http://newportal.ncsl.org.uk/the_college/press_office/college-pr-05072004.cfm?jHighlights=variation
2 Department for Education and Skills (2004) *Every Child Matters; Change for Children*, Outcomes framework. London: DfES.
3 Dryfoos, J. (1994) *Full-Service Schools. A Revolution in Health and Social Services for Children, Youth and Families*. San Francisco, CA: Jossey-Bass.
4 Macmichael, P. (1984) *Interprofessional Perceptions of Social Workers and Teachers*. Edinburgh: University of Edinburgh.
5 see Outcomes framework above
6 Bruner, J. S. (1960) *The Process of Education*. Cambridge, MA: Harvard University Press.
7 Smith, M. K. (2005) 'Background to the Green Paper for Youth 2005', *The Encyclopaedia of Informal Education*, www.infed.org/youth work/green_paper.htm. First published; March.
8 See for example MacBeath, J. and Galton, M. with Steward, S. and MacBeath, A. (2005) *The Costs of Inclusion*. London: National Union of Teachers.

11 The SEF and how to use it

1 Department for Education and Skills (2004b) *A New Relationship with Schools*. London: DfES.
2 Ibid.
3 Argyris, C. (1993) *Knowledge for Action: A Guide to Overcoming Barriers to Organizational Change*. San Francisco, CA: Jossey-Bass.

4 Ibid.

5 Morgan, G. (1997) *Images of Organizations*. Thousand Oaks, CA: Sage, p. 98.

12 Who needs a School Improvement Partner?: critical friend or Trojan collaborator

1 Conversations with and feedback from headteachers at conferences and workshops.

2 Baker, P., Curtis, D. and Berenson, W. (1991) *Collaborative Opportunities to Build Better Schools*. Bloomington, IL: Illinois Association for Supervision and Curriculum Development.

3 For example, MacBeath, J. and Mortimore, P. (2001) *Improving School Effectiveness*. Buckingham: Open University Press.

4 Department for Education and Skills (2004) *Strategies for Improving Schools: A Handbook for School Improvement Partners*. London: DfES.

5 David Miliband, 8 January 2004, North of England Education Conference, Belfast.

6 Department for Education and Skills (2004) *A New Relationship with Schools: School Improvement Partners' Brief*. London: DfES.

7 Ibid.

8 Formal Intervention Powers (SSFA 1998 as amended).

9 The quote comes from Henry V. who, prior to the battle of Agincourt is overwhelmed by doubt and needs a trusted friend to confide in. In their presentations to schools and corporations Olivier Mythodrama uses this scene from the play to highlight the dilemmas of leadership and issues of trust.

10 Leadership for Learning: Carpe Vitam Conference held in Cambridge, May 2002.

11 National Association of Education Inspectors, Adviser and Consultants, (2005) *National Standards for Educational Improvement Processionals*, NAEIAC, p. 10.

12 Sue Swaffield (2002) InForm, October 2003, Number 3. See also Swaffield, S. and MacBeath, J. (2005) Self-evaluation and the role of the critical friend. *Cambridge Journal of Education*, 35(2): 239–252.

13 National Association of Educational Inspectors, Advisors and consultants (2005). National Standards for Educational Improvement Professionals, London, NAEIAC.

14 The tools of self-evaluation

1 Fuller, B. (1976) *Synergetics: The geometry of thinking*. New York: Macmillan.

2 Jones, B. F., Valdez, G., Nowakowski, J., and Rasmussen, C. (1995). *Plugging in: Choosing and Using Educational Technology*. Washington, DC: Council for Educational Development and Research, and North Central Regional Educational Laboratory. p. 8. Available online: http://www.ncrel.org/sdrs/edtalk/toc.htm

3 MacBeath, J. and Sugimine, H. with Sutherland, G. and Nishimura, M. (2002) *Self-Evaluation in the Global Classroom*. London: Routledge Falmer.

4 Sammons, P., Thomas, S. and Mortimore, P. (1997b) *Forging Links: Effective Schools and Effective Departments*. London: Paul Chapman.

5 Lawrence Lightfoot, S. and Hoffman Davis, J. (1997) *The Art and Science of Portraiture*. Hoboken, NJ: Jossey Bass.

6 Ibid.

7 Ibid., p. 3.

8 Eisner, E. (1991) *The Enlightened Eye*. New York: Macmillan, p. 3.

9   From a four-country study of leadership: MacBeath, J. (ed.) *Effective School Leaders*. London: Paul Chapman.
10 Schratz, M. and Steiner-Löffler, U. (1998) Pupils using photographs in school self-evaluation in Prosser, J. (ed.) *Image-based Research – A Sourcebook for Qualitative Researchers*. London: Falmer, 235–251.
11 Read, I. (2005) *Making Inclusion Work*. Sheffield: Birley Spa Primary Community School.
12 See for example Bastiani, J. and Wolfendale, S. 1987, *Parents and School Effectiveness*. Routledge: London. MacBeath J., Mearns, D. and Smith, M. (1996) *Home from School*. Glasgow: Jordanhill College.

15 The leadership equation

1   National College of School Leadership (2005) *Making a Difference: Successful Leadership in Challenging Circumstances*. Nottingham: NCSL.
2   Fink, D. (1999) The attrition of change. *International Journal of School Effectiveness and School Improvement*, 10(3), 359–70.
3   Gewirtz, S. (1998) Can all Schools be Successful? an exploration of the determinants of school 'success'. *Oxford Review of Education*, 24(4): 439–57, p. 439.
4   Berliner, D. (2001) The John Dewey Lecture, Paper delivered at the American Educational Research Association, Seattle, April. and Bevan, J. (2002) *The Rise and Fall of Marks and Spencer*. London: Profile Books.
5   Limerick, D., Passfield, R. and Cunnington, B. (2004) *Towards an Action Learning Organization*. St. Leonard's New South Wales: The Learning Organization.
6   Rogers, E. (1995) *A Theory of Diffusion of Innovations*. New York: Free Press.
7   MacBeath, J., Oduro, G. and Waterhouse, J. (2004) *Distributed Leadership in Schools*. Nottingham: National College of School Leadership.
8   Leeuw, F. (2001) Reciprocity and the Evaluation of Educational Quality; Assumptions and Reality Checks. Keynote paper for the European Union Congress, Karlstat, Sweden, April 2–4.
9   Rogers, E. (1995) *A Theory of Diffusion of Innovations*. New York: Free Press. P. 6.
10 Carnoy, M., Elmore, R. and Santee S. (2003) *The New Accountability – High-Schools and High Stakes Testing*. Willmor, Vermont: Teachers College Press.
11 Evans, P. and Genady, M. (1999) A diversity-based perspective for strategic human resource management. *Research in Personnel and Human Resource Management*, Supplement 4, p. 368.
12 Gladwell, M. (2000) *The Tipping Point*. London: Abacus.
13 In the NUT research published as *Schools Must Speak for Themselves* governors were keen to be involved and embraced with enthusiasm the opportunity to define their own self-evaluation criteria.

16 What can we learn from other countries?

1   North Central Educational Laboratory (NCREL) http://www.ncrel.org/info/pd/
2   Smith, W. (1998) *Schools Speaking to Stakeholders*. Montreal: McGill University.
3   Portin, B., Beck, L., Knapp, M. and Murphy, J. (2003) *Self Reflective Renewal: Local Lessons for a National Initiative*, New York: Praeger.
4   Ibid., p. 22.
5   www.education.tas.gov.au/ooe/ppp/families/pack12.htm

6 MacBeath, J., Jakobsen, L., Meuret, D. and Schratz, M. (2000) *Self-Evaluation in European Schools: A Story of Change*. London: Routledge.
7 Francesca Brotto works for the Italian Ministry and was so inspired by the Italian translations she conceived of the Bridges idea.
8 MacBeath, J. and Clark, B. (2005) *The Impact of External School Review in Hong Kong*. Cambridge, MA: Cambridge Education.
9 http://sici.org.uk/ESSE

Index

Note: Numbers in italic indicates figures and tables.

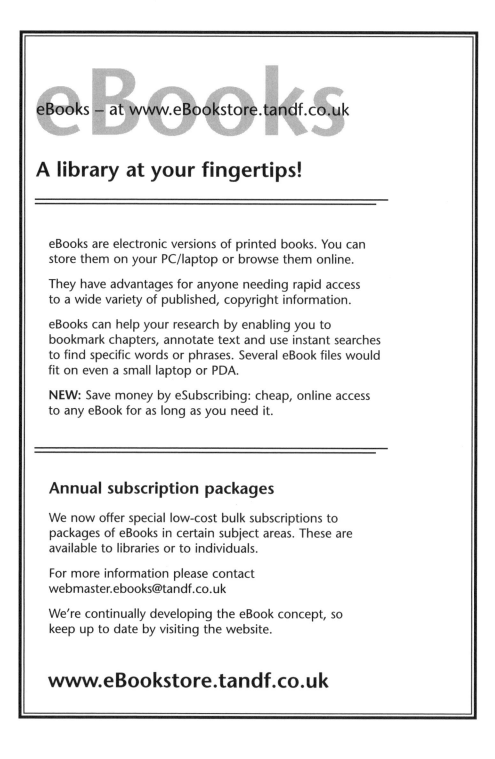

191710